THE CONSERVATIVE GOVERNMENT 1979-84

An Interim Report

Edited by DAVID S. BELL

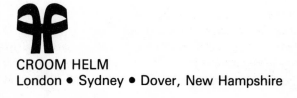

CROOM HELM
London • Sydney • Dover, New Hampshire

© 1985 David S. Bell
Croom Helm Ltd, Provident House, Burrell Row,
Beckenham, Kent BR3 1AT
Croom Helm Australia Pty Ltd, First Floor, 139 King Street,
Sydney, NSW 2001, Australia

British Library Cataloguing in Publication Data

The Conservative government 1979-84: an interim report
   1. Great Britain——Politics and government——1979-
  I. Bell, David Scott
  354.4107′02′09   JN231

  ISBN 0-7099-3258-8

Croom Helm, 51 Washington Street, Dover,
New Hampshire 03820, USA

Library of Congress Cataloging in Publication Data
applied for.

Printed and bound in Great Britain by
Biddles Ltd, Guildford and King's Lynn

CONTENTS

PREFACE

It is the Thatcher government's policies which form the subject matter of this book. Policy outcomes have been set against original intentions (where these are discernible) and the range of subjects tackled should enable an overall assessment of the Conservative governments from 1979–84. This, although not the direct aim of the book, emerges from the sector-by-sector approach: the sense in which this is 'interim' is that it is always open to a government to change direction and hence to falsify predictions and change the 'bottom line' on the balance sheet.

This is a book of policy analysis. The authors of the separate chapters review the Conservative Party's intentions and set these against the results. An endeavour of this sort is bound to have policy and political implications but this book is not a partisan work. Judgements of the Thatcher governments have not been disguised, but the authors are experts in different social science fields and no attempt has been made to coordinate a 'partisan line'. Any political relevance comes indirectly from the analysis of policy.

The book is designed as follows. The various policy areas are reviewed in Chapter 1 (the Introduction) and, although it has not been possible to cover the entire range of government policy the key areas are examined in turn. The first section deals with economic matters where decisions taken since 1979 have had far reaching ramifications in other fields and it discusses these in general terms (Peter Holmes in Chapter 2), in the labour market (Chapter 3 by David Deaton) and on low wages (Chapter 4 by Steve Winyard). Section two deals with the welfare state in broad terms: Chapter 5 is an overall view of social security policy by Doreen Collins, Chapter 6 by Bob Elmore deals with the National Health Service and Chapter 7 by Professor Gosden covers education policy. There then follows section three covering law and order (Chapter 8 by John Alderson) and local government (Chapter 9 by Professor Mike Goldsmith). The fourth and last section looks at foreign and defence policy with Chapter 10 by Ali El-Agraa on the European Community and Chapter 11 by Nigel Bowles on defence.

Each of the chapters is self-contained (although there are references back and forth) and the book is written to be read by people interested in the Thatcher governments in a general way as well as by students of particular policy areas.

D.S. Bell
Leeds University

1 INTRODUCTION: CONVICTION POLITICS

D.S. Bell

In his writings on sociology Max Weber distinguishes between two political ethics: the morality of responsibility and the morality of conviction.[1] The former is the utilitarian morality of those politicians who judiciously weigh up ends and means in a search for effectiveness (even though this is a somewhat messy process) and it is supposedly the morality of governments, 'realists' and statesmen. In its way it is pragmatic (though without the undertones of that word) and is characterised by 'political touch': it is the ability to find suitable means to the attaining of particular goals.[2] Adaptability and second best solutions are an integral part of this political morality because the political milieu necessarily involves trimming, adapting to changing circumstances and the much maligned 'compromise' — as Sydney Smith said: 'all great alterations in human affairs are produced by compromise'.

By contrast, the morality of conviction does not take into account the consequences of actions; it is not concerned with the opinions of others and, although it may attract elaborate justifications, it is sealed off from the real world. Weber states that the conviction politician only feels responsible for seeing to it that the flame of pure intention is not lowered; its practitioners have a heroic vision and they are not compromisers. Aron and others who have made use of Weber's distinction have usually cited examples of politicians from the Left (the syndicalist or the pacifist being two examples) as conviction moralists who take an 'unconditional view and ineffective action'.[3] But conviction politics is not confined to the left wing: the concepts of 'obstinacy', toughness, and unrelenting assertion of aims are as much the hallmarks of 'conviction politics' as is revolutionary intransigence. Clear-cut solutions to difficult and complex problems are one sign of conviction politics, just as 'splendid moderation' is a sign of the ethic of responsibility.

Weber's antinomies are, of course, extremes, but they represent two poles of a continuum along which various politicians can be ranged. One image of British politics is that it is essentially pragmatic and that the system leaves little place for conviction politics in what has always been an essentially 'moderate' political environment.

1

Whether this is true or not it is tempting to see a shift in British politics between the 1960s and the 1980s[4] (the 1980s may be a delayed reaction against certain aspects of 1960s politics) from consensus pragmatism to ideological politics: the 1960s ended with visionless pragmatism and the 1980s began with visionary conviction. Against this view it might be said that the Heath Government of 1970–4 started out in the 'conviction' mode, but then it soon turned turtle: this transition from 'conviction morality' to 'responsibility', the 'U-turn', has not taken place during the Thatcher years (during which policies have been tested to destruction).

In the area where this matters most, in economic policy, the government's policies achieved their principal 'success' in the reduction of inflation. But between 1979 and 1984 unemployment went up to over three million, a huge non-oil trade deficit appeared, and both manufacturing investment and manufacturing production fell to below 1979 levels. Unwillingness to change or to try alternatives indicates conviction politics; if ineffectiveness does not constitute a need to change commitments it is difficult to see what does: conviction politicians have *plus de valeur que de sens*.

Paradoxically, non-intervention and retreat from direct political involvement have become the guiding principles for political action:[5] the government has stuck to the view that it cannot do anything about unemployment, that the 'conquest of inflation' is the proper — almost sole — government responsibility and that economic recovery is up to the 'free market'. In social welfare and industrial policy this means a curious form of indirect rule in which neutral non-government institutions such as the police, the courts, or the nationalised industries are pushed into the front line to fight political battles, something which has put serious strains on social organisation and politicised much which is traditionally apolitical. Maybe, as Galbraith famously remarked, Britain is the best place for any 'monetarist' experiment because its old stable institutions and long history of democratic politics make it more resistant to social upheaval than most other societies.[6] However, before looking at specific policy areas, it might be useful to recall the main lines of the new 'convictions' put into practice by the 1979–84 governments.

Farewell the middle way

It has never been easy to distinguish hustings rhetoric from political principle and the Conservative opposition's attacks on the Labour governments during 1974-9, to most people, probably did not sound that different from the rhetoric of previous Conservative oppositions. Yet the new Conservatism — Thatcherism, the New Right, or whatever it is called — is more akin to Powellism than to old-style Butler-Macmillan Conservatism and it flatly repudiates the Keynesian interventionist politics of the post-war years.[7] However, it also departs from the 'Butskellite' consensus in another way; that is in its espousal of 'monetarism'. The conversion of the Conservative Party to 'monetarism', through the agency of Sir Keith Joseph and others, was a break with the past and with the Heath government of which he was a member.[8]

'Monetarism' has many meanings so it is not possible to hand out a monetarist *brevet* to the government of 1979-84. However, the first objective of the 1979 Conservative government was to control the money in circulation more tightly and the second was to cut public spending. The control of money supply was the main thrust of government policy: changes in the measure of the money supply became the yardsticks for judging policy; fixed cash limits replaced incomes policy as a means of dealing with excessive pay demands and the importance of those wage demands in causing inflation was downgraded, if not neglected. As it happened, 'money' in all its protean forms proved both undefinable and uncontrollable so that the use of the various measures (M1, M2, M3, M0) fell into disuse (although the deflationary aspects of policy continued).[9]

If control of the money supply failed to hold the centre stage, the government's hostility to public spending remained. This hostility had several justifications, not all of them economic: the 'road to serfdom' was supposed to pass through high public spending, the Welfare State was supposed to sap initiative and a large public sector was supposed to be inflationary in itself. Nevertheless the pattern of cuts in public spending is more haphazard than the clear-cut ideological position would seem to indicate and, although the Welfare State has been cut back, the brunt of these cuts has fallen on housing. In the United Kingdom, unlike the rest of the OECD area, there has been both real retrenchment and an attempt to undermine the legitimacy of public services.[10]

Denationalisation fits into this perspective, but also, through peculiar 'creative' accounting, has emerged as a positive gain to central government. The assumption being made by the government is that the private sector is always more efficient and less bureaucratic than the public sector, something which, for natural monopolies like the telephones, is by no means proven.[11] (Nationalised industries have also been attacked for drawing the wealth away from the 'productive' private sector.) Great emphasis has also been given to the 'cultural malaise' caused by the Welfare State: the *fer de lance* for attack on public service has been 'liberty'. To the idea that welfare services should be free at the point of service has been counterposed the notion of 'liberty' and (by assimilation) private provision. Private social services were said to offer more choice and to be more efficient, but even within these objectives some of the more adventurous schemes such as education vouchers and NHS 'hotel' charges have been abandoned as costly and cumbersome. Nevertheless the long-term aim of transferring charges(from taxation to the 'consumer')remains.

The 'liberty' which is being defended in all of this government action is a very narrow conception which includes exchange and enterprise but which excludes other positive liberties so that the all important trade-off between various values is more or less overridden.[12] This conviction approach ignores the fact that social choices are very complicated and that restrictions of liberties for some can nonetheless mean an extension of liberty for others: the taxes to pay for health and welfare no doubt prevent some people from disposing of income as they wish but then the same taxes increase the freedom for other sections of society. No moral Occam's razor can get round the problem that, in the political world, values have to be played off against each other and that this choice is not simple.

In downgrading the role of government intervention Thatcherism has emphasised the role of the market. This policy is conceived of in libertarian terms — fewer restrictions, more choice — but it is also instrumental: conditions are being created for private enterprise to do the essential economic work. Ideology and efficiency are not always consistent, but on the rhetorical level Thatcherism has always emphasised that governments should not invest directly or interfere in markets because markets express peoples' real choices. Hence the Thatcher government has talked about the need to end market 'rigidities', but has denied any connection between its policies and unemployment.[13]

It is worth recalling at this point that the non-intervention, market liberalism side of Thatcherism was foreshadowed by the Heath government of 1970 which came to power committed to running down subsidies to 'lame ducks', cutting public expenditure, selling off state assets, scrapping the National Board for Prices and Incomes, and ending the 'welfare culture'. However increasing unemployment led to a U-turn and the use of the standard instruments of anti-recession policy: increased government spending and budget deficits. The Heath government left office after a managed economic boom and a mismanaged incomes policy which culminated in the miners' strike and rejection at the polls in February 1974.

Edward Heath's experience of incomes policy and the 'winter of discontent' during Callaghan's operation of incomes policy probably led to a feeling that such policies were inoperable. But there is a further problem here: declarations that people must cooperate to stop pricing themselves out of jobs and that people must stop out-doing each other is demanding 'unrealistic' wages imply government intervention in the market. This is another version of the public goods problem which New Right theorists have attempted to argue away: if everybody moderates wage demands then everybody gains, but at the same time there is an incentive for people to overtake the more restrained with high pay rises and hence benefit from the self-discipline of others. This is a position which individuals acting in competition in the market find impossible to resolve because they cannot take collective action. With the collapse of cash limits as the Thatcherite solution to wage pressure, the next step (except for conviction) would be intervention.[14] In any case the way that conviction politics has altered and shaped policy is best seen in a sector by sector examination; this is done in the next section.

Policy and Implementation

This book has more than one theme: one is the ideological wellsprings of Conservative government action, another is the results of Conservative policies and a third is the execution of policies. The issue of the Conservative government's administrative competence — the 'banana skins' as the press puts it — is not new but was put on the political agenda by Dr Owen at the 1984 Buxton Conference. Once the decision to reduce public expenditure had been taken it was a case of 'cut now think later', as Doreen Collins says, and the wider aspect is that the government has used its huge parliamentary majority as an 'elective dictatorship' to push through policies which are ill thought out and which do not have general support. (These latter have included abolition of the Greater London Council and metropolitan counties, rate capping, and the banning of unions at GCHQ.)

Continuing this theme, Peter Holmes, in Chapter 2 of this book, draws attention to the failure of the monetarist interlude to control the money supply although the Government almost accidentally controlled inflation by means of the recession caused by the high exchange rate. The Government stood by while the exchange rate moved up to $2.40, a movement which had ruinous effects on British industry. In fact the responsibility for the malign neglect of the exchange rate and the unprecedented depression have been fixed on the government by comentators even though the general public may attribute these more to the world slump than to Thatcherism. Moreover, concerning the specific boast that inflation has been brought under control, Peter Holmes asks whether there is anything remarkable in having 5% inflation with 13% unemployed.

There is another dimension to managerial competence in the economy and that is denationalisation: the 'sale of the century'. The conviction that denationalisation is sufficient cure for the difficulties of public sector monopolies has allowed state assets to slip away at an 'unrealistically large discount'.[15] From the possession of a large portfolio, the government has, by chance, made a few sales to the benefit of the taxpayer, but the timing has, for the most part, been bad. In most cases the government sold at the bottom of the market and then saw prices rise along with the slight economic recovery. Perhaps selling assets off cheaply and failing to provide a proper framework for real competition are not of pressing concern to most people, but the loss of the North Sea Oil windfall and the consequent failure to modernise industry are not and will have long-term effects.

With the failure of monetarist prescriptions the government began to turn its attention to supply-side solutions: in particular there was the monopoly power of trade unions reckoned to be one cause of unemployment through their distortions of the labour market. In Chapter 3 David Deaton discusses the Conservative government's attempts to reform industrial relations through a series of legislative measures. (John Alderson in Chapter 8 also discusses the effect of these laws.) Unlike the governments on the continent of Europe, the Thatcher experiment has been prepared to abandon consensus and to ride out social upheaval in order to remodel the labour market. As David Deaton argues, this market reshaping has been partly achieved, but the reduction in power of the trade unions has been a result of the slump rather than the government's measures — there has not been a shift in power from unions to their members to any appreciable extent.

There is another shaft to the government's attack on labour-market 'rigidities' and that is the rate of pay settlements. One of the intentions of government policy was to introduce a new 'realism' into industrial pay bargaining by creating consciousness of the costs of pay rises to businesses. However, one of the paradoxes of the Thatcher years is that real wages have not adjusted to the rise in unemployment (with all the implications that has for competitiveness).[16] The government believes that lower wages will create employment and, although the attempt to push wages down to Korean or Brazilian levels would be impossible, the policy has effectively produced a 'low-wage' sector of the economy — as Steve Winyard shows in Chapter 4. This is, of course, another facet of the 'two nations' problem but one which has not received much public attention. At this point the possibility of incomes policy enters again because collective wage restraint has been mentioned by the Chancellor, despite the difficulty of fitting this into the *sauve qui peut* philosophy of Thatcherism.

Although the Thatcher government shied away from a head-on attack on the Welfare State consensus, in the general area of social welfare there have been heavier cuts and more privatisation than on the continent; at the same time, and during a period of falling GNP, the UK government reallocated away from welfare and to the armed forces. (The cuts were 'without precedent'.)[17] As Nigel Bowles shows in Chapter 11, spending on defence increased by 27% between 1979 and 1984 although, as he notes, the commitment to NATO to increase defence spending by 3% per year in real terms after 1985 has been abandoned.[18] Despite the evidence that, in 1981, Britain's public spending was lower than that of other EEC countries (except Greece) and that Britain is not particularly highly taxed (taxes in Britain are becoming more regressive), the Government has persisted in trying to cut public spending even in those areas where, as Doreen Collins says, the deep cuts have already been made (in housing for example). Doreen Collins, in Chapter 5, draws attention to the piecemeal and incoherent nature of social policy in the recession and to the lack of planning.

The leak to the *Economist* of the Think Tank report which suggested dismantling the National Health Service and the subsequent uproar led to the claim by Mrs Thatcher that the NHS was 'safe' with the government. Despite this reassurance there were manpower cuts in the NHS in the summer after the 1983 elections and a comprehensive review of social services was launched. There is no necessary contradiction here: inefficiencies and waste can be reduced and resources are never unlimited (two points which do not seem to be perceived by many of the government's critics). But the position is complex: health expenditure has increased but constraints in the NHS caused by demographic changes, pay, prices and increasingly costly technology have meant a tight squeeze on hospitals (where there have been real expenditure cuts). In Chapter 6 Bob Elmore discusses the problems that the Conservatives' initial radicalism enountered and the problems which the entry of the NHS into the political arena has caused. Yet the NHS, as Bob Elmore says, remains popular and there is public resistance to a two-tier service. It might also be noted that Britain, although it spends a low proportion of its GNP on health in international terms gets value for money (although these comparisons are notoriously difficult).[19] Hence, although the government has been speeding up privatisation of the Health Service, public sector health services expenditure is still higher in Britain than in most OECD countries.

Education, which is the subject of Chapter 7 by Peter Gosden, is also part of the social welfare services and it is the one in which Mrs Thatcher has most experience. Some of the wilder ideas, such as education vouchers, have been abandoned but the Thatcher governments have nevertheless had a radical effect on education through both cuts and administrative change. As Peter Gosden points out, the pincers of reduced public spending and the need to raise standards have produced contradictory policies. Even within these constraints the cuts in the universities did not achieve the savings they were meant to (and may have cost money). Other schemes which the Education Secretary floats from time to time have met with resistance and have often been rejected as impractical, but the moralistic conviction approach favoured by Sir Keith — the 'habitual convert'[20] – does not go well in education.

Another field where the Conservative government appears to have been at cross-purposes with itself (and with Conservative tradition) is local government. Because of the drive to cut public spending and reduce borrowing, the government has increasingly come into conflict with local authorities which, as Mike Goldsmith states in Chapter 9, were once regarded as administrative backwaters. The government's failures to cut expenditure in other places led it to try to squeeze local government spending and to introduce a rate-capping bill which is an unprecedental extension of central government power and hardly consistent with 'non-intervention'. The Thatcher government also decided to abolish the GLC and the five Metropolitan Councils and to replace them with non-elected joint boards — hardly consistent with 'rolling back the state' and which mean a loss of electoral accountability. These policies have brought the government into conflict not just with labour local authorities but also with Conservative ones, with Conservative back-benchers and with the House of Lords. But centralisation was already underway before rate-capping through the control of London Transport, council house sales and of education and it could well be continued through the reserve powers given to the Secretary of State in the bill to abolish the GLC and Metropolitan Counties.

Spending on law and order increased between 1979 and 1983 by 33%, something which was one of the government's stated objectives. However, without going into the details of the evil-tempered miners' strike, the same period has seen widespread rioting and an increase in crime, although, as John Alderson points out in Chapter 8, the prospect continues to be one of disorder on an even wider scale. Moreover, during the same period a national police force has emerged, more or less by default, and this could be regarded as a considerable constitutional innovation which, like changes in the Welfare State, has happened without consultation or debate.[21] Traditionally a decentralised police force was one of the 'guarantees' of liberty in the United Kingdom but the new paramilitary use of the police raises questions about control and accountability which are not being answered.

On foreign and defence issues Mrs Thatcher's style and dislike for the traditional approach is clear cut and, as Nigel Bowles points out, they form the background to the 1983 election campaign — the 'Falklands factor'.[22] However, the record of prescription and practice is more complicated, as is pointed out by Ali El-Agraa in Chapter 10 on the European Community, and chapter 11 on defence policy by Nigel Bowles. The Conservative government's objectives were, as Ali El-Agraa shows, quite clearly set out but the political difficulties of the budget ('Mrs Thatcher's billion') and the various problems connected with that have tended to overshadow more fundamental objectives. While the issue may have disappeared from day-to-day politics with the 1984 'package', the nature of the government's European policy success is qualified. As Chapter 10 explains, the reforms of the budget are not, as the government wanted, based on ability to pay, and the reform of the Common Agricultural Policy is a long way from achievement. These EEC reforms require a political skill and diplomatic touch which Mrs Thatcher's 'can't pay, won't pay' approach and her demands to the EEC for 'my money' seem unlikely to achieve.

Defence policy has a special place in the government's priorities. Here, however, the anti-nuclear movement and the Government's response to it have created a political problem of some magnitude. In addition, as Nigel Bowles makes clear, the government will be faced with budgetary constraints before the end of the decade. Britain's retreat from imperial power has been a historically rapid one, but the extended commitments which still exist have encouraged the belief in some quarters that a world role should still be possible. As Nigel Bowles notes, Trident's price and opportunity cost is excessive and there is a feeling, even in the Conservative ranks, that this attempt to keep up with the leading powers is debilitating. The review and reappraisal of Britain's defence policy cannot be long shelved despite the nationalist rhetoric.

In all of the policy areas under review the government has carried its convictions through into policy with very little opposition from the House of Commons. But its use of the Tory majority to railroad through measures which do not have widespread support have smacked of insenstivitiy. It is too much to talk of a 'lack of legitimacy' or of an 'institutional failure' but the Government's assertion that it is the business of government to withdraw from decision-making and evade the responsibility for the wider costs to society of its own policies is a paradox to put it no higher. Conviction is all very well but the political craft usually expected from governments is to engineer consent through give-and-take; this traditional skill has been replaced by an abrasive 'no-nonsense' style which generates the impression that the government is arrogant and indifferent to the plight of society. What caused the outspoken reaction from Bishops and Churches during the miners' strike was the way that the strikers' desperation was fuelled by the government's uncaring attitude and its political blundering. The discontent and disaffection revealed by the 1981 riots and the miners' strike were fuelled by the way Mrs Thatcher's 'elective dictatorship' has behaved; they were partly a result of conviction politics, insensitivity, and the destruction of jobs.[23] The practice of consensus government in post-war Britain has meant a good deal more than merely presenting bills for the approval of the majority in Parliament, it has been a general process of consultation and compromise. This system of cooperation and bargaining may have become too inward-looking and immobile (though that is doubtful), but it was a subtle way of dealing with political pressures and, with interest groups and the candle-end economies which are going to be imposed in the future, will need this type of sensitive handling.

Notes

1. Max Weber in *Economy and Society*, quoted in Frank Parkin, *Max Weber* (Tavistock, London, 1982).

2. See Parkin, *Max Weber*, pp. 106–8.

3. Raymond Aron, *Main Currents in Sociological Thought* (Weidenfeld, London, 1966), p. 210.

4. H. Berrington, 'Change in British Politics', *Western European Politics*, vol. 6, no. 4 (October 1983), Special Issue, pp. 1–25. The end of the post-war consensus is often regarded as the most important of recent political developments.

5. Trevor Russel, *The Tory Party* (Penguin, Harmondsworth, 1978). This prophetic book outlines the new Conservatism with great clarity — see especially pp. 47–55. The electorate's uncertainty about party positions on incomes policies was a feature of the 1979 election.

6. See W. Keegan, *Mrs Thatcher's Economic Experiment* (Allen Lane, London, 1984), p. 11.

7. Trevor Russel, 'Virtus in Media', in *The Tory Party*.

8. See Sir Ian Gilmour, *Britain Can Work* (M. Robertson, Oxford, 1983).

9. W. Keegan, *Mrs Thatcher's Economic Experiment*, p. 208 and V. Keegan, *Observer*, 1 April 1984.

10. See Heidenheimer *et al.*, *Comparative Public Policy* (Macmillan, London, 1983), pp. 311–32.

11. See David Heald, *Public Expenditure* (M. Robertson, Oxford, 1983), Chapter 13 'Privatisation'.

12. A full discussion of this issue can be found in ibid., Part II.

13. See Jock Bruce-Gardyne, *Mrs Thatcher's First Administration* (Macmillan, London, 1984) for a defence of the government, but also W. Keegan, *Mrs Thatcher's Economic Experiment* and Sir Ian Gilmour, *Britain Can Work*, p. 144, for opposite views.

14. Chris Huhne, *Guardian*, 1 November 1984.

15. Chris Huhne, *Guardian*, 12 January 1984.

16. David Lipsey, *Sunday Times*, 4 November 1984.

17. C. Hood and M. Wright (eds.), *Big Government in Hard Times* (M. Robertson, Oxford, 1981), p. 24.

18. *Financial Times*, 14 November 1984.

19. *Financial Times*, 15 November 1984.

20. I. Aitken, *Guardian*, 6 April 1984.

21. *Guardian*, 2 October 1984 (see Peter Jenkins' column).

22. Peter Riddell, *The Thatcher Government* (M. Robertson, Oxford, 1983), p. 207ff.

23. Michael Stewart, 'The Miners' Strike', *London Review of Books*, 6–19 September 1984: 'It is not surprising that Lord Hailsham's ominous phrase "elective dictatorship" is being so frequently used'. This article draws attention to the reciprocal effect of extremisms of the Right and the Left.

SECTION ONE: ECONOMICS

2 THE THATCHER GOVERNMENT'S OVERALL ECONOMIC PERFORMANCE

Peter Holmes

By mid-1984 several different interpretations of the Thatcher government's economic record were possible. Mrs Thatcher saw inflation under control and a spontaneous recovery in progress. William Keegan noted the most savage deflation ever seen and an inevitably gargantuan recession.[1] Right-wing critics said the money-supply and public spending had not been properly controlled. Alec Chrystal[2] however, attributed the recession to the 'petro-pound' and remarked a certain continuity with the policies of the previous Labour government, as did Peter Riddell, who nevertheless felt the Thatcher approach had been unnecessarily costly.[3] In order to see how all these conflicting points of view may co-exist, we need to examine the different ways one can envisage the economy working and the correspondingly different notions of cause and effect underlying them.

The present government's rejection of much of the post-war economic orthodoxy makes much debate completely sterile. In the 1960s and early 1970s, there was general agreement about which way causation ran among economic factors, and argument was about orders of magnitudes of effects and about priorities. Professor Frank Paish in the 1960s was castigated as deplorably reactionary for wanting to let the unemployment rate go as high as 2.5% in order to get inflation close to zero! This would be regarded as recklessly expansionist today, when many analysts claim there is no 'trade-off' between unemployment and inflation. Mrs Thatcher's government has rejected much of the consensus on which post-war economic policy as been based. It is necessary to examine the economic principles underlying Thatcherism in a little more detail before we look at the record. Two recent books by economic journalists make it clear that monetarist ideology had not swept the Conservative Party in 1979.[4] Mrs Thatcher seems to have formulated her own somewhat more homespun ideas and latched on to monetarism as a useful legitimating device. We must therefore distinguish the underlying philosophy and objectives of the government from the intellectual clothes it wears.

We can identify several immediate objectives of the Thatcher government, goals which were themselves 'proxy' targets for certain underlying aims:

1. Holding down the rate of increase of the money supply.
2. Reducing the amount of government borrowing.
3. Cutting the overall level of, first, public spending, and secondly, taxation.

The first policy is supposed to help keep down inflation; the second and third are intended to make the economy more efficient by replacing public by private spending.

These policies were linked but logically distinct. Reagan's policies in the United States show that the budget deficit can be increased while monetary growth is restrained and while taxes are cut but public spending is raised. Monetarism as such really only relates to the first of these targets. Mrs Thatcher's acolytes (though not so much the rest of the Conservative Party, as Keegan and Riddell show) became converted to the belief that the growth of the money supply was the main determinant of the inflation rate. Monetarist theory holds that movements in the price level are proportionate to changes in the growth of the money supply. This belief is not *a priori* unreasonable, but it depends on a chain of reasoning which makes many economists sceptical about the automatic link. In its modern version monetarism depends on the hypothesis that there is for the economy, at any moment in time, a 'natural rate of unemployment' which is essentially fixed. Any attempt to raise demand to reduce unemployment below this level may be temporarily effective, it is argued, but will then lead to accelerating inflation and any gains caused by government expansionary action will be quickly eliminated. The underlying view is that total employment is determined by workers' willingness to work at the prevailing real wage, a factor considered to be totally exogenously given. At the heart of modern monetarism is the belief that whatever the government does will set off an equal and opposite reaction restoring the economy to its natural equilibrium. If you devalue the currency, the temporary increase in competitiveness may bring an expansion in output and employment, but that will then spark off inflation which will totally eliminate the initial gain. The Thatcher government was initially very much affected by the strong views of rational expectations monetarists who believe in the capacity of market forces to anticipate and offset anything the state does: on this reasoning any cuts in taxes will lead people to anticipate later tax increases as debt interest is paid off.

Rational expectations theory has various forms: all of it has it common the doctrine that market actors, i.e. firms and workers, can predict the future at least as well as the government and so apparent instability in the market is the result of calculated forethought. The version of the rational expectations thesis taken up by the Thatcher government incorporated the additional belief that monetarist theory as espoused by the government was the basis of correct thinking. This argument led ministers to believe that inflation would fall very quickly as soon as Thatcher's monetarist policies were announced, with no intervening recession. People would know that monetarism was bound to work and hence would instantly scale down their wage and price expectations and hence their wage claims and price rises. As the record shows, the immediate result of the government's policy announcements in 1979 was actually a sharp rise in the inflation rate.

In the purest monetarist doctrine government policy can only affect inflation, not the level of unemployment. Therefore the government has some intellectual grounds for its claims that it could do nothing about the level of unemployment and that one cannot get lower unemployment by being less strict about the attack on inflation. To say that there are some premises that would lead to the government's conclusions is not to say that those premises accord with the facts, however. The supposedly definitive monetarist intepretation of the British inflation experience by Milton Friedman and Nancy Schwartz has recently been effectively demolished in two studies commissioned by the Bank of England.[5] These studies conclude that movements of prices and money-supply figures just are not very close in the short run. Everyone expects that over the long sweep of history there will be correlations between prices and money supply rising over time. What one wants to know is if this correlation is close enough for short-run manipulations of the money supply to determine the immediate inflation rate. In fact, Friedman and Schwartz average all their data over 'trade cycle' periods, so that they completely wipe out all short-run deviations between movements of prices and money. It is a widespread misconception that recent experience, monetarist theorising and intensive analysis of the statistical data invalidate the alternative Keynesian view of the world. A.J. Brown argues strongly that Friedman's own data support the simple Keynesian proposition that when the economy is working at full capacity additional spending causes inflation, but that otherwise it will raise output and employment. He also stresses that the historical record as well as recent experience show just how hard it is actually to control the money supply.

Indeed the government has itself ceased to express its arguments in terms of monetarist logic. For example, if the country has a 'natural' rate of unemployment the 'world recession' should make no difference to it. If one believes that employment is totally determined by supply considerations one cannot logically argue that foreign demand can affect employment. In Mrs Thatcher's logic a world economic recovery could only have created jobs in export sectors at the expense of the rest of the economy in exactly the same way as she claims private sector jobs would be displaced by public sector jobs.

In fact the government's desire to cut the budget deficit is a separate part of their platform. It encompasses two parts. The obsession with the public sector borrowing requirement does not derive from pure monetarism which believes the inflation rate depends on that part of the state deficit financed by money creation only, though some monetarists, e.g. Congdon, stress the links between total borrowing and money creation[6]. The government is responding here to ideas coming from the City of London more than Chicago, however, and to the fact that controlling the money supply was becoming as hard as Keynesian critics had predicted. The attempts to hold down public spending and borrowing reflect the monetarist view that real output and employment are fixed. Hence if the goverment spends more it must displace private spending. This is known as the 'crowding out' hypothesis. Where government spending is financed by borrowing, interest rates are said to be pulled up to choke off private investment. This argument makes little sense logically or empirically: if government investment chokes off pre-existing private investment then new private investment would do the same! Curiously enough the monetarist reasoning which upholds the far-sighted perspicacity of the market leads to the contention that budget deficits have no effect on the private sector, who will adjust their own savings and borrowing offsettingly. The 'neutrality' of government debt is an old classical proposition in economics, denied by Keynesians who believe that there are many circumstances in which it is socially less costly for borrowing to be carried out collectively rather than privately. Prof. W. Buiter, in a recent inaugural lecture at the London School of Economics, has vigorously attacked the Thatcher position on this.[7] In fact using reasoning quite similar to Congdon, he agrees that one may not want the public debt increasing exponentially in relation to GNP, but insists that a soundly run economy will have public debt rising in line with GNP, just as a company will have its own debt rising as its business expands. In particular, Buiter stresses the disastrous way public investment, which is naturally financed by borrowing in all countries, has fallen from 5.1% of GNP in 1972 to 1.7% in 1982 (much of the fall in fact having come under the Labour government!).

The final strand in 'Thatchernomics' is the desire to cut public spending for is own sake, whether or not it leads to a deficit. The government would claim that there is a fixed 'national cake' and that, if the state sector takes more, less is available for private spending. This is irrelevant from the point of view of the macro-economics of job creation, in the short run at least, but Mrs Thatcher believes that state spending is inherently worth less to the economy than private spending. A popular piece of analysis in the 1970s by R. Bacon and W. Eltis argued that the rise of state spending and employment had been a cause of de-industrialisation.[8] It was immediately pointed out that the people employed by the state — very often women — were in different categories from those employed by the industrial sector and that there was no way state employment could be said to have led to a shortage of industrial workers. A more subtle version of that thesis remains, however. Workers are said to resent the high taxes required to pay for the expanded state sector: they do not perceive any value coming to them from this 'social wage' and demand compensating increases in take-home pay. This then makes industry uncompetitive. Leaving aside the fact that social insurance taxation is no higher in this country than elsewhere, there is no evidence, as Riddell concludes, of an expressed desire by the population to see the Welfare State abolished in return for an equivalent cut in taxation and an obligation to make one's own private provision for medical care, etc., far from it in fact.

Ultimately Mrs Thatcher is here expressing the prejudices of her own inner 'Victorian values' in which it is right and proper for those who can to look after themselves. She is against deficits and against the public service spending for instinctive quasi-moralistic reasons. Her analogy of the national and the household budget is quite spurious. Mrs Thatcher may well shiver at the connotations of the word 'mortgage'; but for a real household to be in financial balance, what is required is that its income plus its borrowings equal its outgoings. Households do not purchase their houses or consumer durables out of current income any more than governments can dispense with borrowing.

Many have seen the influence of another guru, F.A. von Hayek, a thinker far more conservative than Milton Friedman. Hayek believes that there is no place for ethical principles in economic policy beyond upholding of the sanctity of property, an ethical principle he considers to be axiomatic. Milton Friedman often criticises state actions on the grounds that they actually end up being anti-egalitarian. But for a Hayekian, all this is would be irrelevant: if the rich wish to give money voluntarily to the poor, the state cannot stop them, but if not, the state should not do so itself, which would be deviating from the task of defending property rights. It is unlikely that Mrs Thatcher derives her ideas in a direct way from Hayek, but we can see from the recent honour conferred on him that she finds his rejection of moral concern in economic policy in accord with her own thoughts.

On balance the government does not seem to have been directly following a particular model or theory in its thinking or its practice. What the government has been most concerned about is to create a new atmosphere, in its view of 'enterprise' but which others would see as reflecting greed and lack of social compassion. The attack on the unions is part of this: there is a clear desire to strengthen employers against workers, but also to turn the workers towards pursuing their own private interests as individuals rather than collectively with their workmates. David Deaton (Chapter 3) documents the way in which legislation has been introduced to encourage opposition by union members to activities of their unions. The desire to do this reflects one of the ambiguities of the monetarists' position which oscillates between insisting that the world is full of markets which operate perfectly so no government actions are needed, and the view that says the world is not like this but that the state should intervene to make it so.

The failure to implement the strictly economic objectives, which we will discuss below, derives as much as anything from the fact that strict monetarism was never the real issue. In other words, as William Keegan has put it, Mrs Thatcher's experiment has not really been an experiment, for that implies a willingness to learn from experience. It has been an act of faith based on certain ideological gut feelings. We can, however, draw some lessons from it.

The Economic Record 1979–84

How do we set about evaluating the performance of a government? What we really want to get at is what the best available alternative might have produced. Implicitly or explicitly we must take the following approaches:

1. Comparing the actual state of the economy in 1979 and 1984.
2. Comparing the actual state now with the situation that might have arisen under alternative policies, either an extrapolation of Labour policies or by making comparisons with other countries and assuming that the difference between UK performance and that of other countries is due to the Thatcher policies.
3. Comparing the actual turn-out of events with promises.
4. Comparing economic forecasts in 1984 with prospects as seen in 1979 before the election.
5. One could compare the 1979–84 period with 1974–9.

Any realistic comparison will have to be a mixture of all these approaches.

There can be no objective conclusion. There is, as we have seen, room for total disagreement about what causes what in the economy, and at the same time this government's record is characterised by the extraordinary divergence between its relative success on inflation and its total failure with respect to unemployment.

Supporters of the government point to the fall in inflation from its peak of 20% in 1980 and the resumption of output growth in 1982. Critics point to the fact that output fell during the period 1979–81 at an unprecedented pace, and has barely reached 1979 levels, while unemployment continues to rise. Though the government points to its success in holding down the public sector borrowing requirement, critics of both Keynesian and monetarist persuasions have argued that this is irrelevant to the country's real needs, and show that the money supply has not been particularly well controlled. Monetarists say the government has not been tough enough, while Keynesians say it shows the futility of trying to regulate the money supply and insist that it is the recession, not the monetary control, that has brought the inflation rate down/

Whatever one may believe about policy and the effects of policy there is no doubt that the economy experienced an absolutely unprecedented slump under the Thatcher administration. Industrial production fell by 18% between 1979 and 1981, after which time it has first flattened out and then begun to recover somewhat. Between 1929 and 1932 industrial production only fell by 10%. In 1983 industrial production had begun to grow again quite rapidly, with growth of manufacturing output rising from 2% in 1983 to 4% in 1984, but the absolute level is still significantly below 1979 levels. Manufacturing industry which had been 28% of Gross Domestic Product (GDP) in 1970 fell from 25% of GDP in 1979 to 21% in 1982. GDP clearly fell somewhat less, and by some measures (statistics differ) it had just got back to its 1979 level by 1983 (see Figure 2.1).

Unemployment, which had doubled between 1973 and 1976 from 3% to 6% and then stayed around that level, had actually begun to fall in 1979. It then began a precipitous rise to 11% in 1981 and 13% in 1983 (on OECD standardised definitions). The actual number out of work has risen to 3 million, and the proportion of 15–24 year olds out of work is 23%. The OECD forecasts no fall in unemployment at all in 1984 or 1985.

We may add to this the fact that British industry has for the first time ever moved into deficit in its trade in manufactured goods. The balance of payments is of course held up for the time being by North Sea oil.

What achievement can be set against these dismal results? The answer is the fall in inflation and above all the claim that a long-lasting recovery is on the way. As we have noted, the government puts the blame for the fall in economic activity and the rise in unemployment on factors beyond its control (but it has been quick to claim the credit for the recovery — even when none has existed). Let us then examine the claims in the government's own terms. The most obvious comparison to take here is to look at the reduction in inflation in the UK and to compare it with that in other OECD countries. The result one gets depends crucially on the time period one chooses and the exact group of countries one compares with. If we compare 1979 and 1983 consumer price increases in the UK and the OECD as a whole we find that in the UK they fell from 13.6% to 4.6% while in the rest of the OECD they fell from 9.8% to 5.3%. But the government claims that the inflation rate was accelerating in

Figure 2.1: Britain's Relative Economic Performance

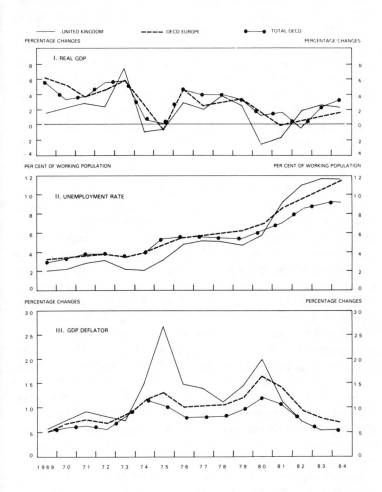

Source: OECD

1979 and so one should take the peak of inflation: for the UK this is 21% for the second half of 1979 or for the full year 1980. The lowest recorded inflation was for the first half of 1983, just under 4%. But it has been rising since then and is expected to flatten out at 5% in 1984–5. For the whole OECD, peak inflation was 12–13% in late 1979 and 1980, falling to a low of 4.3% in early 1983, also staying around 5% for the next couple of years.[9]

What can one conclude? The reduction is enormous; Mr Lawson implies that he wants it brought down even further. The achievement would be even more substantial if inflation ended up close to zero, but this seems very unlikely. Wage increases (in 1984) are running around 7–8%. The interpretation is highly subjective. Between 1975 and 1978 the Labour government brought the inflation rate down from 24% to 8% with a rise in unemployment from 2% to 6%. One might indeed ask whether there is anything at all remarkable in having 5% inflation with 13% unemployed. For workers to be demanding close on 10% wage increases in these circumstances suggests a less than total eradication of the inflationary mentality. The nature of the achievement clearly depends on how it was brought about and what else might have happened. All the forecasts for inflation made in early 1979 showed a major rise on the way and all the indicators were that some kind of anti-inflation policy was going to be needed. Forecasts made immediately after the 1979 election indicated that the VAT increases would add another 3 percentage points to what was already expected to be an inflation rate over 10% without policy changes. Peter Riddell argues that that any government would have had to act somewhat like Thatcher. But would the price have been the same in all circumstances? Defenders of the government, as we have seen, vary between those who say a necessary price was paid and those who say that the recession was caused by other factors than government policy and did not itself play a part in the reduction in inflation. In order to get at least part of the answer we need to see just how severe the monetary squeeze put on by the government has been.

Studies have been carried out by the OECD secretariat and by Alec Chrystal of the movement of the money supply and monetary targets over the last ten years or so. OECD figures show that in the period when Denis Healey was trying to control the money supply, 1976–9, although his targets were slightly less restrictive than under Thatcher the actual outcome was not significantly less, and the outcomes were closer to targets than under Thatcher. Alec Chrystal points out that the much-vaunted Medium Term Financial Strategy for monetary policy was effectively abandoned within a year or so.[10] What we have seen is a regular series of forecasts of a very tight monetary policy, predicating very severe financial conditions which never actually materialised in the way intended. If we look for example at the target for the year 1983-4 as seen successively between 1980 and 1983 we see the target rising from 4-8% to 7-11%. As the OECD figures show, sterling M3, the government's preferred measure of the money supply rose by 19% in 1980-1, about twice the rate under Denis Healey. Other 'narrower' measures of the money supply behaved in quite contradictory ways and indicated that monetary policy was in fact very restrictive, underlining the absurdity of the government's claim that the announcement of its monetary policy would bring predictability and stability and hence prosperity to the economy. In 1981 monetarist commentators were debating whether or not there was a monetary squeeze. Christopher Johnson of Lloyds Bank has highlighted the ironic fact that the high interest rates were actually driving the money supply up.[11] Many bank deposits pay interest and so they become more attractive when rates go up; moreover firms were having to borrow money from the banks to pay interest on their past borrowings and this bank credit was fuelling the money supply figures. I shall argue below that the expectation of tight monetary policies was a major factor in the rise of sterling in 1979-81 which wiped out so much of British industry: when the foreign exchange markets became disillusioned with Thatcher's monetarism the pound began to fall again.

The impossibility of actually controlling the money supply figures has led the government to concentrate on its other obsession, the state budget deficit or public sector borrowing requirement (PSBR). Here they have had somewhat more success in terms of their preferred statistic. The PSBR as a percentage of GNP has been reduced slightly less than was forecast in the 1979 strategy, but this ratio has declined steadily. The problem is that the PSBR is as hard to measure as the growth of the money supply. There is no way of getting a meaningful figure without having a theoretical view about how the deficit affects the economy and vice versa. It is generally held that as unemployment pay increases, tax revenues fall and GNP falls, the deficit will automatically increase by a certain amount in a recession, so that if it increases but by less than this we have observed a contractionary policy in place. We therefore may want to measure changes in the 'cyclically adjusted budget deficit' which counts only those changes that are the result of government decisions. We may also want to allow for the effects of inflation. If indeed the main concern of keeping the PSBR down is to avoid a rising ratio of total debt to GNP, we should bear in mind that inflation raises the value of GNP but not of old government debt, or to put it another way it reduces the real value of government debt. So we may want to look at the 'real deficit'. On this measure the UK government has had a surplus for several years. Furthermore, bearing in mind Buiter's comments about public investment, we might sensibly wish to distinguish deficits to finance current expenditure and deficits for investment: in fact the government had a small current surplus in 1981–2, and a negligible current deficit in 1982–3. The field is fraught with difficulties! Looking only at the changes in the PSBR during the 1970s Chrystal argues that the biggest reductions in both actual and 'cyclically adjusted' measures of the deficit occurred between 1975–6 and 1977–8 under Labour. However, if one looks not at the changes but at the actual levels, the Thatcher period stands out as the most contractionary on record. Buiter estimates that this directly reduced demand by about 4% of GDP. The UK has clearly tightened its fiscal policy on most measures more than any other country during the recession. Counting the cyclically unadjusted deficits the average deficit of all OECD countries rose from 2.7% of GNP/GDP in 1979 to 4.3% in 1983 while for the UK the deficit fell from 3.2% to 2.7%.[12]

The reduction in the deficit has been achieved by a rise in taxation rather than a cut in government spending. The OECD estimate that total taxes including National Insurance contributions rose from 34.7% of GDP in 1979 to 39.1% in 1982. The previous Labour government had brought the levels down from a previous high point of 36.5% in 1975. Public expenditure was scheduled to fall from 1980 to 1984. Instead expenditure has risen in real terms, though the government's method of presenting its plans in cash terms when prices are unpredictable have actually led one observer to regard this method as a major affront to parliamentary scrutiny.[13] There has been a big shift in the distribution of public spending, however. Riddell shows that in real terms over the period 1978–9 to 1982–3 defence expenditure rose by 17%, law order and protective services by 27%, and spending on agriculture by 33%. Meanwhile overseas aid spending fell by 19%, that on housing by 56%, on education and science 1%. However, health and personal social service spending rose by 13% and social security by 20%. The latter figure is clearly an involuntary response to increased poverty. There was a 17% rise in spending on industry, trade and employment. A detailed examination of the Thatcher government's industrial and trade policies as revealed in papers provided by the government to the NEDC shows that the gap between rhetoric and reality has been almost total in this area. The rise in aid to industry has slowed down since 1982, but when we look at the detailed figures this all comes from cuts in regional aid (which Labour was reducing before 1979) and in subsidies to nationalised industries. Discretionary aid to the private sector has remained very important under Mrs Thatcher, especially for electronics, and many aspects of Labour's successful microelectronics programmes have been continued unbroken. (A 1983 DTI document refers to the sucess of policies inaugurated in 1978!) Industrial aid is scheduled to fall in the future, but so far Mrs Thatcher's government has been extremely generous to private industry both in terms of grants and also in a willingness to countenance protectionism on trade policy rather than encouraging competition from imports which her official ideology would call for.

Apart from cuts in subsidies to state industries and in education, the aspect of central government spending that has been most badly affected is investment. As has been noted, Buiter estimates that public investment continued to fall as a share of GDP from 2.8% in 1979 to 1.7% in 1982. There was once a time when we contrasted the state of British cities favorably with the United States or even France. Nowadays, arriving in London from Paris or Toronto is like arriving in Mexico City or Madrid. Public services deteriorate even when small amount of additional cash are spent. Schools and hospitals are being closed because there is not enough cash to run them. It has to be stressed that actual cash cuts, if any, are quite small. What we see however is a change of atmosphere, in which the aim of public spending management is seen as cutting back as much as possible rather than providing the best possible service for the public. We have not really seen many cuts in the Welfare State so far, as Michael Meacher notes.[14] As Devereux and Morris point out, plans to cut expenditure have been fudged or deferred, so far at least, but now one detects a new 'optimism'.[15] The government has declared its deliberate intention, in real terms, to keep overall spending constant while national income rises. Pensions and other benefits are planned to stay constant while incomes rise and public sector wages are actually to fall in real terms from 1984 to 1987. Moreover, amid the overall constancy defence spending is expected to rise, as are health, social services and social security, albeit less fast. Most other categories of state spending are forecast to fall in real terms. Given the problems created by the relatively modest public expenditure cuts so far, this is a recipe for quite unprecedented social tensions in the late 1980s. What makes the picture even more disturbing if one disagrees with the government's premises, is that if economic growth falters the government is determined to cut state spending even more. Thus the higher the level of unemployment, the worse the provision of social infrastructure!

The government's social philosophy has so far been better illustrated by its tax policy than its spending policy. Within the general rise in taxation the Thatcher government has deliberately shifted the burden from the rich to the poor. If we compare the increase in the share of family income taken by all taxes between 1978-9 and 1983-4, we find that for a married couple with two children earning 75% of average earnings the tax bill has risen from 21% of overall earnings to 24%, while for a similar family earning 500% of the national average the bill has been cut from 50% to 43%.[16]

Privatisation is another area where we can see the claims of expediency and principle in conflict. This has clearly been pursued more to distort the PSBR figures than for any reasons of industrial logic. There is a micro-economic case for the breaking up of certain state monopolies to increase competition, or for the encouragement of competition against existing state corporations. There is no good case for selling off state assets whole to private monopolists, often below their true value, yet this is what Mrs Thatcher prefers. Kay and Silberston, accepting the case for more competition in the economy, nevertheless conclude in their recent discussion that the current privatisation policy is merely a substitute for policies to increase competition.[17]

By the standards of the 1970s in the UK, and of the rest of the OECD in the 1980s, the Thatcher policies have thus represented a significant extra element of deflation, but I would agree with Chrystal in suggesting that the domestic effects of these policies alone cannot account for the severity of the UK recession. Between the second half of 1979 and the first half of 1981 real GDP fell at a rate of 1.5-2% per annum, after which time it steadied. For the rest of the OECD it rose at about the same rate as the UK fall. This fact alone is enough to dispose of the world recession as an explanation of our domestic problems. Something special has to be invoked. What is more, the fall was overwhelmingly concentrated on the industrial sector. Mrs Thatcher would like us to think that this was just the result of 40 years of unsound industrial chickens coming home to roost — all in 18 months! There is a much more convincing explanation in the steep rise in the pound. By 1979 there had been some rise in the value of the pound from the low of 1976, but between 1979 and 1981 a combination of additional inflation and the pound moving up (instead of down to compensate) raised UK costs relative to the rest of the world by about 40%. This is the period when we see manufacturing production plummetting by 18%. The service sector which is less directly exposed to foreign competition did much less badly, hence the lower fall in overall GDP. One wants to ask whether, as Chrystal argues, the pound was doomed to go up because of North Sea oil or whether appropriate monetary policies could have held it down without promoting a further inflationary explosion, as Keegan argues. The immediate answer has got to be that policies could certainly have been found to keep the pound down. This is clear both from *a priori* reasoning and the Norwegian experience of the same period. Norway's effective exchange rate rose by a mere 4% in 1979–81; GNP continued to rise and unemployment remained at 2%!

The UK government could have announced its willingness to sell pounds at a rate of $2 throughout 1979–81. Having done so for a while would have created the expectation that the rate would stick there. It might have had to create a lot of money as well as expectations: intervention in the foreign exchange markets requires appropriately accommodating internal policies, or at least the conviction in the market that they would be forthcoming. Another result would have been lower interest rates! But the British government did everything it could to give the impression it would not stop the pound rising because of its obsession with keeping the UK monetary growth down. Chrystal argues that in period between 1976 and 1979 the authorities formed the view that they could not keep the exchange rate down without allowing the money supply to expand. They were probably right. For a monetarist this poses a quandary which is likely to be resolved by keeping the money supply down and letting the exchange rate go up. Monetarists, after all, believe that the exchange rate has no long-lasting effect on competitiveness. They believe the 'real' economy is determined by supply-side factors and, as with the unemployment-inflation trade-off, they believe the exchange rate only affects inflation. This was an assumption of the forecasting model used by the London Business School, home of the government's chief economic adviser Terry Burns. He and his colleagues argued that a rising pound would just hold down inflation. It most certainly did not: the peak rate of inflation in 1980 coincided with the fastest acceleration in the rise of the pound. British competitiveness was severely affected by the rising pound, and there was no fall in inflation in this period. What completely invalidates the monetarist argument is that the fall in inflation occurred after the pound also had begun to fall. Common sense and econometric evidence suggests that if the pound had been held down in 1979–81, inflation would not necessarily have been that much higher.

The monetarists have one further argument, however: suppose, they say, you had to expand the money supply drastically in order to keep the pound down; would that not have pushed the price level up? Not necessarily. First, what was needed was not so much a drastic rise in the money supply as a declared willingness to let the money supply expand, and in particular a willingness to keep interest rates down to make the currency unattractive to speculators in the event it did not rise in value. Keeping interest rates down would have been valuable in any case for the domestic economy. Secondly, sterling balances built up by international speculators are held for quite different motives from money held by the general public. It is quite true that if a government runs a gigantic budget deficit financed by printing money to hand as cash grants to its citizens they are likely to spend that money and push prices up. Additional sterling deposits acquired by international banks are not the same thing. We can add one more point to this: we noted the 20% per annum rise in the money supply in 1980–1. Monetarist theory tells us that monetary expansion feeds through into prices with a lag of about two years. In fact 1983 was the low point of infation, confirming the point we got at the outset from Brown and from Hendry and Ericsson: there is simply no short-term correlation between the money supply and inflation that is close enough to justify using such a link as a basis for economic policy.

Since 1981 the pound has come right down again, not far enough to restore our competitiveness against European currencies, but an exchange rate of £1 = $1.12 shows that the foreign exchange speculators have finally realised what Mrs Thatcher's anti-monetarist critics were saying five years ago!

I think we need to admit that the inflation rate was due to accelerate in 1979–80. Peter Riddell argues plausibly that a Labour government would have had to introduce some counter-inflation policies. It is taking a long time for the lesson to sink in that some form of incomes policy is inevitable: people who say that incomes policy cannot control inflation by itself are beginning to see that monetary policy alone cannot either. The lessons of 1975-9 which were part success, part failure, could have been learned; no doubt some tightening of fiscal policy would have been needed in the face of reluctance to accept an incomes policy. But with a lower exchange rate we could have taken this more gradually and not seen such a large chunk of the economy destroyed.

In my view what we have seen over the last five years has been a government pursuing fiscal policies that were far too tight and threatening draconian monetary policies which combined with the effects of North Sea oil pushed up the value of the pound. Chrystal is quite right to point out that the Thatcher government did not in fact impose a much tighter monetary squeeze than Denis Healey: it was no more competent at regulating the money supply than anything else. Therefore one can say North Sea oil was to blame as he does, but this is to ignore the fact that one can offset these pressures by relaxing monetary policy, as Norway did with the result that she is expected to have 3.25% unemployment and 6.5% inflation in 1984! To be sure Norway has subsidised some of its manufacturing industries in a haphazard way which has led to some distortions in the economy, but we in the UK have not been without distortions!

The last point to take up concerns the prospects for the future. UK economic growth in 1983 was actually above the OECD average and the government points to impressive gains in manufacturing productivity. Can things continue to improve on such a scale as to compensate for the losses in the meantime? I personally doubt it. The OECD forecasts that the growth rate will decline again over 1984-5 and that it will not lead to any significant fall in unemployment; ironically the productivity gains which must help employment in the long run may have the opposite effect in the short run unless action is taken to increase demand. Part of the productivity gains do little more than offset the losses in 1980-1: others simply come from the closure of the least efficient plants with no change in the working practices of the remaining ones. There is generalised evidence from the slowdown in productivity growth across the Western world since 1973 that low levels of economic activity are not conducive to rapid productivity growth. There is no doubt that greater 'realism' has been injected into some wage and manning bargaining, but what is striking is just how limited this has been. One reason for this has precisely been the recession.

Anecdotal evidence is accumulating of factories where workers agree to manning arrangements that had been defended with the somewhat short-sighted goal of preserving jobs, only to find that even so the firm goes broke. The continuing ability of the Japanese economy to make productivity gains in the 1970s comes from the low levels of unemployment and the fact that workers displaced from one activity can often be relocated within the same firm.

We conclude that the monetarist experiment failed to control the money supply and public spending, and controlled inflation only by a monumental recession which occurred almost by accident through the exchange rate. The government denies all these failures, and that high levels of public spending are unavoidable in a civilised society. If the recovery aborts, the future may bring cuts more savage than those of 1979–84.

Notes

1. W. Keegan, *Mrs Thatcher's Economic Experiment* (Allen Lane, London, 1984).

2. A. Chrystal, 'Dutch Disease or Monetarist Medicine? The UK Economy under Mrs Thatcher', *Federal Research Bank of St Louis Review*, vol. 66, no. 55 (1984), pp. 27–37.

3. P. Riddell, *The Thatcher Government* (M. Robertson, Oxford, 1983).

4. Ibid., and W. Keegan, *Mrs Thatcher's Economic Experiment*.

5. A.J. Brown, 'Friedman and Schwartz on the United Kingdom' and D. Henry and D. Ericsson, 'Assertion without empirical basis: an econometric appraisal of Friedman and Schwartz' in *Bank of England Academic Consultants' Panel Paper no. 22*, 1983, pp. 9–101. See also M. Friedman, and N. Schwartz, *Monetary Trends in the United States and the United Kingdom*. (University of Chicago Press, Chicago, 1982).

6. T. Congdon, 'The analytical foundations of the Medium Term Economic Strategy' in M. Keen (ed) *The Economy and the 1984 Budget*. (Basil Blackwell, Oxford, 1984).

7. W. Buiter, 'Allocative and Stabilisation Aspects of Budgetary and Financial Policy', *Centre for Economic Policy Research Discussion Paper no. 2* (1984).

8. R. Bacon and W. Eltis, *Britain's Economic Problem: Too Few Producers* (Macmillan, London, 1976).

9. OECD, *Survey of the UK Economy* (OECD, Paris, January 1984).

10. A. Chrystal, 'Dutch Disease' and OECD, *Economic Outlook*, no. 35 (July 1984).

11. C. Johnson, 'The Failure of Monetarism', paper presented to the Manchester Statistical Society, December 1982.

12. Data from *Economic Outlook*.

13. Kay, J. (1982) 'The new framework for public expenditure planning' in J. Kay (ed) *The Economy and the 1982 Budget*. (Basil Blackwell, Oxford, 1982).

14. *Guardian*, 20 July 1984.

15. M. Devereux and N. Morris, 'The Chancellor's Arithmetic' in M. Keen (ed.).

16. P. Riddell, *The Thatcher Government*, p. 71.

17. J. Kay and Z.A. Silberston, 'The New Industrial Policy — Privatisation and Competition', *Midland Bank Review* (Spring 1984), pp. 8–16.

3 THE LABOUR MARKET AND INDUSTRIAL RELATIONS POLICY OF THE THATCHER GOVERNMENT[1]

David Deaton

Philosophy

The central concern of the Thatcher government has been to defeat inflation. But as important in understanding its policies is its free-market philosophy. The neo-classical vision of the economy is one in which the free exchange of goods and labour promotes enterprise and full employment. The invisible hand ensures that self-interest is channelled through competition to ensure a harmonious outcome. In such a model state activity, excessive taxation, or the combination of workers into trade unions or employers into cartels are threats to the essential harmony. To achieve such a harmonious outcome the state is largely passive: it should establish a judicial system to enable the rules of the free market to be observed, it should ensure a stable currency, and it should provide by itself only those collective goods such as defence which the free market cannot provide.

But how the government should behave in a free-market economy is one thing; achieving such an economy is more difficult. Either the government accepts that the world differs from the model and accomodates to the existence of powerful organised groups, or it tries to bring about a change in society to match the model. The Thatcher government to all intents pursued the latter strategy. As we have seen in Chapter 2, it rejected the idea of an incomes policy and instead sought to bring down inflation by tight control of the money supply. It aimed to restore the profitability of industry by loosening the burden of the state through reducing taxation and employment protection provisions. Its attitude to trade unions had three main elements: there needed to be some redress of the balance of power between employers and organised labour in order to restore profitability; wages when set by collective bargaining needed to take more account of economic conditions; and trade unions needed to be more responsive to the wishes of their members. In terms of unemployment the Thatcher government denied the role of governments in creating jobs either through the expansion of demand or direct intervention in the labour market: the government can only create the right conditions and free the labour market from impediments. Trade unions were one such impediment but there also existed a variety of government-sponsored impediments to market forces' operating in the labour market.

Trade Union Policy and Industrial Relations Legislation[2]

The recession has had an impact on labour practices and the power of trade unions, but it was the Thatcher government's policy to reform trade unions and industrial relations through a series of legislative measures. In order to put these measures into context it is necessary to consider the historical development of legal policy in the labour area.

The legal rights of trade unions to organise and take industrial action are enshrined in a number of statutes which grant trade union immunities from the rigours of the common law. As one authority has put it:

> without the immunities the unions could not lawfully have fulfilled their basic function of counter-balancing the employer's dominance over the individual employee. The immunities were in essence the British legal form of basic democratic liberties, the equivalent of what in other countries took the form of positive rights to strike guaranteed by legislation or the constitution.[3]

By the 1950s British industrial relations had assumed its 'voluntarist' character. Legal regulation was minimal. This left great scope for regulation through collective bargaining. Employers had no general legal duty to recognise or bargain with unions, there was no legally protected right to organise in trade unions, and collective agreements were not enforceable as legal contracts. Moreover, the unions who adopted numerous other political and legislative objectives did not press for positive rights in respect of agreements, organisation, recognition, bargaining and strikes. They relied 'not on state support but industrial self-help'.

But in the last twenty years the legal framework of industrial relations has been transformed by a rapid succession of reports, statutes and case law. The background to this was the feeling that Britain's persistent economic decline was in major part due to a failure of its industrial relations system. The strategy of the Donovan Commission, which reported in 1968, was to encourage individual managements to reform their industrial relations procedures and payment systems. To this end it recommended the establishment of a procedure for employers' recognition of trade unions, the registration of collective agreements, and the setting up of a public agency with special responsibility for promoting reform. But this strategy of reform was to be 'accomplished if possible, without destroying the British tradition of keeping industrial relations out of the courts' (para. 190). Neither the Labour government, whose White Paper *In Place of Strife* contained 'penalty clauses' with criminal sanctions against employers, unions and unconstitutional strikers, nor the Heath government, which came to power in 1970, were happy with this tradition.

The Industrial Relations Act 1971 sought to reform collective agreements and bargaining structures by legal means. The Act provided that written collective agreements would be presumed to create legal relations in the absence of an express clause to the contrary, and also for a legal procedure for determining which union should operate in a particular 'bargaining unit'. The other major aim of the Act was to restrict trade unions by creating a new range of civil liabilities known as 'unfair industrial practices'. The Act failed to have an impact on industrial relations for two reasons. Unions almost universally boycotted the new procedures, and most employers were reluctant to enforce civil liabilities. The Act gave rise to a series of major crises in which small employers used the Act and caused considerable embarrassment to the government. Management indifference and union hostility towards the Industrial Relations Act severely limited its effect. Indeed it created a climate in which any attempt to achieve voluntary restraint on pay was doomed to failure. Nevertheless the individualist orientation of the 1971 Act was to be revived by the Employment Acts of 1980 and 1982.

The 1974-9 Labour government repealed the Industrial Relations Act and passed the Employment Protection Act in 1975, which established a number of rights for individuals and trade unions including time off for trade union activities and the right not to be penalised for taking part in such activities. It allowed unions to refer recognition disputes to the Advisory, Conciliation and Arbitration Service (ACAS) with the threat against the employer of an arbitration award, and required employers to consult unions over redundancy questions.

The Labour government's industrial relations legislation was part of a broader strategy whose stated aim was to bring about a 'fundamental and irreversible shift in the balance of wealth and power in the favour of working people and their families'. However, as two observers have noted, 'the new laws were indicative not of a transfer of power but rather of the encouragement which the government offered to trade union leaders to assist in the maintenance of social and economic stability'.[4] Nevertheless, the incoming Conservative government pledged itself to 'redress the balance of power between employers and trade unions and between individual liberty and collective organisation'. This carried very much the free-market ideology of its economic policy with its individualistic emphasis on employees and employers rather than trade unions.

The major pieces of legislation enacted by the Conservative government were the Employment Acts of 1980 and 1982 and the Trade Union Act of 1984. These statutes imposed secret balloting procedures on trade unions, made the operation of closed shops more difficult, removed certain legal immunities from trade unions, and amended the unfair dismissal provisions. Together with other policy measures they also attempted to introduce more flexibility into the wage determination process.

Balloting

The Employment Act 1980 tried to encourage trade unions to take more decisions by secret ballot. To this end public money was made available to finance the cost of trade unions' holding ballots for the election of officials and shop stewards, the calling of strikes, changes in rules and mergers. Most trade unions were hostile to this form of government interference and very few applied for the available funds. The government response was to try compulsion. The Trade Union Act 1984 required unions to elect members of their executive committees by secret ballot. Unions who did not hold secret ballots before calling strike action ran the risk of losing their immunities from civil liabilities. Unions were also obliged to hold secret ballots every ten years if they wished to operate a political fund. The government's keenness to see an increased use of the ballot is based on the assumption that it represents the best means of ensuring democracy, but there is no doubt that the government believed that the minority of trade union activists and leaders are more militant than the non-active majority. However, there is little evidence for the view that workers are less likely to vote in a ballot for strike action than their leaders.[5]

The Closed Shop

It is over the issue of the closed shop that the conflict between individual and collective rights is most acute. The Conservative party has long been opposed to the closed shop which it sees as an infringement of individual liberties and associated with restrictive practices and militant trade unionism. Supporters of the closed shop, including many employers, argue not only that there is a collective right to ensure that individuals do not 'ride free' on the benefits of union organisation, but also, more pragmatically, that it contributes to smooth inter-union and union-management relations, and that there is no general link between the closed shop and restrictive practices or union bargaining power.[6]

But the government in its legislative programme has avoided a head-on confrontation over the closed shop. Under the 1980 Act new closed shops must have at least 80 per cent support amongst those involved to be immune from the unfair dismissal procedures. This Act also grants non-unionists who were employed at the time the closed shop came into operation exemption from compulsion to join it, and extends the statutory conscience clause from religious belief to 'objection on the grounds of conscience or deeply held belief'. Existing closed shops were virtually untouched by the 1980 Act though the Code of Practice associated with it called for periodic reviews of them. However, the 1982 Act went much further. Under this Act dismissal on the grounds of non-membership of a union would be regarded as unfair unless the union membership agreement had been approved by a secret ballot with 85 per cent support amongst those voting. The 1982 Act also provided for an increased level of compensation for an unfair dismissal from a closed shop and provided for retrospective compensation for those unfairly dismissed from closed shops between 1974 and 1980.

Immunities

The individualistic nature of the common law in Britain means that only by virtue of various immunities can trade unions organise and take industrial action without being liable to legal action by those affected. The two Employment Acts remove certain of these immunities from people who picket at places other than where they work (except, in certain narrowly defined circumstances, trade union officials and dismissed workers), from those taking sympathetic, secondary or political action, and from those taking action in support of practices which stipulate that only union labour should be used. The 1982 Act exposes trade union funds to suits for damages where the union has authorised or endorsed an unlawful dispute, which more or less means any dispute other than one directly between an employer and his employees.

Unfair Dismissals

The unfair dismissal legislation was the only successful and surviving part of the Heath government's Industrial Relations Act. The Thatcher government has retained the main provisions but has used them as a means of attacking the closed shop. However, it has been argued that unfair dismissal legislation unduly restricts the freedom for the employer and indeed discourages small employers in particular from taking on more workers.[7] The 1980 Act changed the emphasis of the legislation by placing the onus on the worker to show that the employer acted unreasonably.[8] It also reduced the maternity entitlement, and excluded from the legislation those working for small employers with less than two years' service. Thus, even the floor of individual employment rights, which protect workers irrespective of whether they are trade union members, has been undermined by the government's labour legislation.

GCHQ

Apart from general legislation in the labour field, the most direct attack on trade unions came in 1984 with the government's attempt to ban trade unions in its Communications Headquarters at Cheltenham (GCHQ). The government's stated concern was with disruption to GCHQ's monitoring activity which it considered a vital defence service. It offered £1000 to those who voluntarily gave up their trade union membership with the threat of transfer of those who refused the offer. The civil service unions in reply offered to conclude a non-strike and disruption agreement. The government declined what many trade unionists regarded as an overgenerous offer. In July 1984 the ban was declared illegal in the High Court because of the government's failure to consult the unions. However, this decision was reversed on appeal. Ironically, in August 1984 fifty non-union technicians at GCHQ walked out over a regrading claim, demonstating the naivity of equating disruption with the presence of trade unions. One view of the GCHQ ban is that the government was testing opinion to see whether it could launch an offensive against trade unions in essential services. Another view is that the Cheltenham ban was an act of foreign policy designed to appease the American government which had a shared interest in the work of GCHQ.

An Assessment of Trade Union Policy

Unlike the Heath government's attempt to reform industrial relations with one major piece of legislation which tried to impose a new framework of labour law, the Thatcher government has moved more subtly in this area with a series of carefully thought out measures. But most of the measures have been concerned more with fringe aspects of industrial relations than with the way issues are dealt with in the vast majority of employment situations, though many have tackled subjects which are very much in the public eye such as picketing and strikes with political dimensions. In many of the areas covered by the legislation, such as trade union balloting and the more recent closed shop provisions, it is too early to discern the impact of the legislation. However, it is clear that the spread of the closed shop has been halted[9] and the ability of individuals to win unfair dismissal cases has fallen.[10] In the miners' strike of 1984 and in other disputes the police have been more ready to bring prosecutions against pickets than before the legislation. The most marked change has been in strike activity, which fell to a low level in 1982 and 1983, and a general relaxation of resistance to changes in production methods. There has been a marked drop in the level of union membership and a 'new realism' amongst trade unions in collective bargaining. However, these trends are probably more the consequence of the recession than legislation. Indeed the fall in the level of strike activity has been short-lived as 1984 saw a marked increase in the number of working days lost through strikes, led by the long miners' dispute over pit closures.

Introducing Flexibility into the Labour Market

By 1984 the level of unemployment had been hovering around the three million mark for two years despite a modest recovery in output. Inflation was more or less stable at 5 per cent, and according to the monetarist theory, the economy should have reached the 'natural rate of unemployment' (see Chapter 2). Such a high natural rate may be a reflection of a number of things such as inflexibility in the labour market, high unemployment benefits and an inadequate stock of skills. With a stimulation of demand being ruled out, the major policy measures aimed at reducing unemployment were those designed to make wages more responsible to market conditions.

Under the Employment Protection Act 1975 unions in dispute over recognition could apply to ACAS for an offical investigation which could recommend recognition. Failure by an employer to implement such a recommendation led to the possibility of an arbitration award. Trade unions also had the right under the Act to go to arbitration to secure 'recognised' terms and conditions or in their absence demand the general level for comparable workers in the area or industry. Both these provisions were removed by the Employment Act 1980.

The Standing (Clegg) Commission on Pay Comparability had been set up to assess a number of public-sector wage claims. While the Conservative government agreed to honour recommendations arising from investigations under way, the very idea of such a commission was at odds with the government's market orientation. The method of determining pay in the public sector by comparison with similar jobs in the private sector ran contrary to the principle of employers' ability to pay wage increases and was in conflict with its attempts to control public expenditure through cash limits. Mrs Thatcher in her statement announcing the abolition of the Clegg Commission said, 'pay needs to be negotiated with full regard to the country's economic circumstances'.

In 1983 there were 27 Wages Councils which fixed legal minimum rates of pay for some 2.7 million low-paid workers. The government regarded them as a hindrance to the free working of the labour market and has declared its intention to abolish them. In the meantime the Secretary of State for Employment has attempted to influence the level of settlement by writing to Wages Councils urging them to consider the employment implications of their awards. He has also used his power to appoint the 'independent' members of the councils in a way that would influence wage increases granted. In response to the employers' criticism that the three independent members of the Retail Trades Wages Council were 'mainly interested in the social implications of the awards', Norman Tebbit replaced all three when their terms of office expired. The effectiveness of Wages Councils has also weakened by a reduction in the number of inspectors by a third leaving only 119 to police wages in the industries covered.[11]

Another action designed to free the labour market from constraints on wage determination was the abolition of the Fair Wages Resolution in 1982. The purpose of the Resolution, which is a House of Commons resolution rather than a statute, was to ensure that firms undertaking government contracts provided fair wages and conditions of employment. The history of the Fair Wages Resolution goes back to 1891 when the first resolution was introduced by a Conservative government and the strengthening of the subsequent ones owes as much to Conservative as to Labour administrations. The decision to abolish the resolution ran contrary to the wishes of many employers as well as unions, and is in conflict with international conventions. The desire to abandon the Fair Wages Resolution seems to reflect the government's determination to contract out public services, which it is argued can only be made cheaper at the expense of lower wages for the people employed on such contracts.[13]

Thus not only did the Thatcher government abandon the idea of an incomes policy, but it took steps to dismantle a range of government sponsored wage-fixing arrangements. Some of these such as the ACAS recognition procedure and the Clegg comparability commission had been established by the previous Labour government; others such as Wages Councils and the Fair Wages Resolution had been part of the fabric of British industrial relations since before the First World War.

Free-market economists point not only to institutional constraints on wage flexibility as a cause of high unemployment but also to the level of unemployment benefit and payroll taxes such as the employers' National Insurance Surcharge. The Thatcher government has, however, shown little inclination to tackle unemployment by reducing the level of benefits except in two areas. Shortly after coming to power, the government announced that the earnings related supplement (ERS) to unemployment benefit would be abolished in 1982. This had been paid since 1966 to those in receipt of unemployment benefit for the first six months of an unemployment spell. The effect of ERS had been to increase the level of unemployment benefit relative to earnings and, so the argument goes, to induce unemployed workers to take longer searching for a job. The result would be a higher level of unemployment for the same level of job vacancies. An analysis of unemployment and benefits over time by Maki and Spindler[13] seemed to confirm this argument and suggested that unemployment in Britain was 30 per cent higher than it would have been in the absence of ERS. This influential study has been heavily criticised, however, particularly because of the difficulty of seperating the effect of unemployment from other variables which exhibited a similar trend. An alternative approach by Nickell, using the General Household Survey, concluded that ERS had increased the unemployment duration of recipients by 25 per cent but aggregate unemployment by considerably less than this.[14] Atkinson concluded in his review of the evidence that there was 'little ground to suppose that the introduction of ERS led to an "avalanche" of claims or that its abolition [would] dramatically reduce the level of unemployment'.[15] Indeed since the abolition of ERS there has been no discernible effect on unemployment.

The second area in which benefits have been adjusted is in respect of those on strike. In the 1980 Budget, measures were also taken to reduce the financial support to the families of those on strike by adjusting the tax provisions and by assessing benefit on the assumption that the striker was in receipt of £12 strike pay per week.[16] One measure which was generally welcomed as encouraging employment, however, was the gradual reduction and the eventual abolition in 1984 of the employers' National Insurance Surcharge which amounted to a payroll tax and a disincentive for employers to hire more workers.

Training Policy[17]

The government's stated policy in the area of training stands in marked contrast to other aspects of its economic and industrial policy. Whereas the government has attempted to promote private enterprise and market solutions in most areas, its *New Training Initiative* White Paper of 1981 effectively dismissed the idea that the financing of industrial training was the responsibility of employers. Instead the government has committed itself to spending roughly a billion pounds per year on the training of nearly half a million school leavers.

Free-market economics provides a theory (known as the human-capital theory) which argues that there would be an adequate amount of training without state intervention. Human-capital theory distinguishes between general and specific training. General training is that which increases the productivity and hence the earnings potential of an individual under a wide range of employers. An individual has the incentive to finance the investment in general training (i.e. someone would be happy to pay to be trained in secretarial skills because it enhances her/his earnings ability). Specific training is that which increases the productivity of an individual in a single employment. Hence the employer has has the incentive to finance the specific training of his/her employees and the power to reap most of the benefits (the same individual having acquired secretarial skills at her/his own expense would not be prepared to pay to be trained to use the particular data processing system which only one company uses). But there are problems with the application of this theory. Individual workers may be unable to borrow money to finance their training even when it represents a sound investment, and both individual workers and employers have to forecast the demand for skills with some accuracy if the amount of training overall is to be optimal. An economy subject to fluctuating demand will exhibit considerable uncertainty and this will tend to result in an under-investment in training. The deficiency of the capital market means that employers must step in to finance general training as well as their own specific training, but in doing so they run the risk of generating benefits which will be shared by other firms not contributing to the costs.

During the 1960s and 1970s training policy was aimed largely at these problems by concentrating on the training for those occupational skills which were both costly and highly transferable between firms. The Industrial Training Boards (ITBs), set up under the Industrial Training Act 1964, were designed to increase the amount of training by imposing a payroll levy on employers in their industries, and by paying a grant to those firms which provided training to an acceptable standard. While the ITBs achieved a considerable amount of success in raising the quality of apprenticeship training, they failed to attain their quantity objectives. The amount of apprenticeship training has declined since the mid-1960s and has proved to be particularly vulnerable to the recessions of the 1970s.

Apart from trying to maintain the quality improvements in training achieved by some of the ITBs, the 1981 *New Training Initiative* articulated two main aims: first, the provision of a period of planned education, training and work experience for all workers under 18 years of age, and second, the provision of widespread opportunities for adults to acquire new skills.

The first aim of providing a universal system of youth training involves a major change in the direction of training policy away from the previous policy of training in depth for key skills. The Youth Training Scheme (YTS), intended as a first step on the way to a system of universal youth training, became fully operational in September 1983. Its main provision is to guarantee to all unemployed 16- and 17-year-old school leavers a year's vocational training and work experience. The government's justification for such a policy of universal youth training is stated in terms of both economic performance and individual opportunity. It is argued that new technology will have a major impact on the demand for skills, with a decline in unskilled and semi-skilled work. With large-scale relocation of labour between occupations and industries the workforce will increasingly need a broad vocational preparation for work rather than piecemeal job-specific training. The intention is clearly to emulate the West German system of state regulated apprenticeships which provides an almost universal foundation training for 16–18 year olds and has been given substantial credit for the superior performance of the West German economy.[18]

But the economic value of a system of universal training is greatly reduced in a period of large scale unemployment. The motivation to learn is reduced, what is learnt may not be used, and skills which are not used are likely to decay. There is certainly little evidence that unemployment at present could be reduced by training for jobs which are difficult to fill. Thus in the absence of a policy to create more jobs, the social objectives of the scheme seem to make more sense that the economic ones. A large minority of young people gain few or no qualifications in school and proceed directly to jobs with no serious learning content or unemployment. For them the opportunity to learn skills and to help them to compete for the albeit limited supply of jobs is at least something. Even the predecessor of YTS, the Youth Opportunities Programme (YOP), which provided very little training, was welcomed by many young people for the help it presented them in finding jobs.

The Youth Training Scheme, with its emphasis on training, was designed to improve upon YOP which had been criticised as a means of removing youth from the unemployment register and providing cheap labour to employers. To this end YTS projects would only be accepted by the Manpower Services Commission (MSC) if they met a number of criteria including a work-experience component and at least three months in education and off-the-job training. Such training was to go beyond the need of a particular job by teaching a core of skills which would be transferable within a 'family of occupations'. The MSC would ensure the quality of training by entering into legally enforceable contracts with employers embodying their training plans.

In fact the drive to secure a large number of places for YTS in 1983 was at the expense of training quality. The idea of requiring YTS projects to provide broader occupational training, in particular the occupational families idea, was dropped in the face of employer opposition. The proposal to make training contracts legally enforceable was not realised, so that the MSC's only sanction against a low quality scheme is to close it down. Moreover an assurance was given to employers that initially the inspection of projects would be kept to a minimum. In short the objective of YTS providing high quality training relies on the goodwill of employers. Since the government is committed to the private sector as the principal source of YTS projects, there must be a danger that employers will restrict the training provided to the needs of particular jobs within their own companies. This very much threatens the aim of providing a broad foundation training.

The Youth Training Scheme has been criticised as a device which undermines wages and more traditional forms of employment. By paying trainees a mere £25 compared with an average wage for youths in 1981 of £47, YTS acts to depress the general level of youth wages which some have argued is a major factor in youth unemployment. In addition the Young Workers Scheme subsidises employers who pay young workers less than £50 per week. About 163,000 young people worked under the latter scheme in 1983.

But the impact of both these schemes extends beyond the youth labour market. Employers have an incentive to fill their unskilled and semi-skilled jobs with successive YTS 'trainees' rather than recruit employees. Under the 'additionality' provision, YTS allows companies to receive allowances for two planned employment recruits for every three YTS places. Thus five young people work for an employer at state expense without employment rights in exchange for the company providing three YTS openings.

There remains also the problem of training for key skills. The grant-levy system of the Industrial Training Boards failed to generate sufficient training because they did little to cover the costs of apprenticeship training. YTS does no more than previous schemes in this respect. While it can be used to offset the costs of the first year of an apprenticeship by using the YTS trainees as a pool from which to draw second-year apprentices, no financial assistance is allowed for after this first year outside the industries covered by the few remaining ITBs. Thus the problem of training in depth remains a gap in the government's training policy. Indeed it can be argued that the problem of training in depth has been intensified by the impact of new technology as it polarises skills between a craft-technical élite and the unskilled. It is not sufficient to meet the skill requirements of new technology simply by providing broadly based foundation training.

The second stated objective of the *New Training Initiative* White Paper was to extend the opportunities for adults to acquire new skills. The current system of adult training is centred on the Training Opportunities Programme (TOPS) which provides courses mainly for unemployed adults in skills which are intended to lead to jobs. Since the *Initiative*, it has become clear that adult training policy is to be judged by short-term commercial criteria. Several of the MSG Skillcentres have been closed because they were judged to be cost-ineffective and the new Skillcentre Training Agency has been charged with putting adult training provision on a break-even basis during 1984. The main justification for this commercial approach is the low rate of employment of adults who have passed through TOPS courses (the placement rate fell from 70% in 1979 to 30% in 1981). Hence adult and youth policy on training appear to be moving in different directions. It is acceptable to train youths for jobs which do not exist but not adults: longer-term considerations and the provision of opportunities apply to youth but not to adults.

The high ideals of the *New Training Initiative*, which appeared to be one area in which the market was not to be given primacy, have been watered down. YTS has been used as a measure to combat youth unemployment which has meant making it more acceptable to employers and reducing its impact as a provider of broad foundation skills. Meanwhile adult training has fallen prey to the more general commercial approach of the Thatcher government to public services, and in-depth training for key skills has been left largely to individual employers to finance.

Conclusion

The Thatcher government came to office committed to a free-market philosophy and to the defeat of inflation. Its stated intention was to reduce the burden of taxation and shift the balance of power away from trade unions to individual workers and enterprises. Apart from creating the right climate for growth and full employment it denied that the state had any obligation or power to bring them about.

The government has been most successful in bringing down the rate of inflation but this has been at the expense of a dramatic decline in manufacturing industry and a large rise in the level of unemployment. However, the fact that the government was re-elected in 1983 despite the level of unemployment does suggest that it has succeeded to some extent in its aim of abrogating the responsibility of the state for maintaining a high level of employment.

In the past five years the power of trade unions does seem to have been weakened, but this is largely due to the recession rather than the industrial relations legislation which the government enacted. Moreover, the shift in power has not been between unions and their members which was the stated intention of much of the legislation.

The aim of making the labour market more flexible has only been partly achieved. There is evidence to suggest that wages are now determined with more emphasis on the ability of employers to pay and less on comparability and fairness. However, the government is still concerned that real wages have failed to adjust in response to the high levels of unemployment.

The government's argument is that because of the legacy of inefficiency in the British economy, the benefits of its policies and the returns for harsh years of recession are only just beginning to come through. Certainly there is some evidence of a recovery and that industry is now 'leaner and fitter' than five years ago. But the prospects for a decline in the level of unemployment seem bleak and it looks as if the new era of prosperity, if it materialises, will be highly selective in whom it benefits.

Notes

1. The author is indebted to Roy Lewis and Peter Nolan for helpful comments on an earlier draft of this chapter.

2. For a more detailed discussion of labour legislation see R. Lewis, 'Collective Labour Law' in G.S. Bain (ed.), *Industrial Relations in Britain* (Blackwell, Oxford, 1983).

3. Ibid., p. 363.

4. See R. Lewis and B. Simpson, *Striking a Balance* (Blackwell, Oxford, 1981), p. 18.

5. See *The Royal Commission on Trade Unions and Employers' Associations* ('Donovan Report') (HMSO, London, 1968), paras. 426-30; H.A. Clegg, *The Changing System of Industrial Relations in Britain* (Oxford, Blackwell, 1979), pp. 226-7 and R. Lewis, 'Collective Labour Law', p. 390.

6. For evidence on this question see S. Dunn and J. Gennard, *The Closed Shop in British Industry* (Macmillan, London, 1984).

7. M. Andrews and S. Nickell, 'Unemployment in the United Kingdom since the War', *Review of Economic Studies*, XLIX (1982), pp. 731-59, using time series analysis, found that 'the impact of unfair dismissal legislation in 1972 had caused a rise in unemployment of over 1 percentage point by 1977' (p. 745) but they stressed that the result should be treated with some scepticism unless more evidence was found to support it. Using the survey data, W.W. Daniel and E. Stilgoe, in *The Impact of Employment Protection Laws* (PSI, London, 1978), found that an insignificant number of small employers regarded employment legislation as a factor inhibiting recruitment.

8. Strictly speaking, the burden of proof is neutral between employer and employee, whereas under the Employment Protection Act 1975 it was up to the employer to show that the action was reasonable. But, as Lewis and Simpson point out, 'he who makes a claim must prove it' (*Striking a Balance*, p. 30). For a detailed study of the working of unfair dismissal legislation see L. Dickens *et al.*, *Dismissed* (Blackwell, Oxford, 1985).

9. Dunn and Gennard, *The Closed Shop*.

10. Dickens *et al.*, *Dismissed*.

11. E. Maclennan, 'No to Norman?', *New Society*, 65 (1983), pp. 322-3.

12. C. Pond, 'Back to the Sweatshop', *New Society*, 62 (1982), pp. 508-9.

13. D.R. Maki and Z.A. Spindler, 'The Effect of Unemployment Compensation on the Rate of Unemployment in Great Britain', *Oxford Economic Papers*, XXVII (1975), pp. 440-54.

14. S. Nickell, 'The Effect of Unemployment and Related Benefits on the Duration of Unemployment', *Economic Journal*, LXXXIX (1979), pp. 34-49.

15. A.B. Atkinson, 'Unemployment Benefits and Incentives' in J. Creedy (ed.), *The Economics of Unemployment in Britain* (Butterworth, London, 1981), pp. 128-49.

16. This sum is periodically adjusted in line with inflation and stood at £15 in August 1984.

17. For a more detailed discussion of training policy see R.M. Lindley, 'Active Manpower Policy' in Bain (ed.), *Industrial Relations in Britain*, pp. 339-60 and P. Ryan 'The New Training Initiative after Two Years', *Lloyds Bank Review* 152 (1984) pp. 31-45.

18. S.J. Prais, *Productivity and Industrial Structure* (Cambridge University Press, Cambridge, 1981).

4 LOW PAY

Steve Winyard

Introduction

1979 marked a watershed in government policies on low pay. Before Mrs Thatcher's victory at the General Election, successive Conservative and Labour administrations had expressed a concern for the low paid and operated, albeit with varying degrees of commitment, policies to improve their relative position in the earnings 'league'.[1] The Thatcher government however, with its neo-classical vision for the economy, has sought reductions in the earnings of the low paid. In this it has been highly successful. Between 1979 and 1984 wage inequalities widened markedly; the low paid fell behind whilst those at the top of the pay structure enjoyed rises well above the average. Furthermore, changes in the direct tax system reinforced these trends. The burden on the low paid increased whilst those on $2\frac{1}{2}$ times average earnings and above enjoyed tax cuts.[2]

In the first section of this chapter we will look briefly at the 'principles' that have guided government action on low pay since 1979. We will then examine the evidence from the Department of Employment's *New Earnings Survey* on the extent of low pay in 1984 and trends in earnings inequality. The third section focuses on the main policy initiatives taken by the government over the past five years, the weakening of the wages council system, the abolition of the Fair Wages Resolution and Schedule 11 of the Employment Protection Act 1975, privatisation, the introduction of the Young Workers Scheme, and the erosion of women's employment and equal pay rights. All of this must however be set against the dramatic rise in unemployment; from 1.3 million in May 1979 to well over 4.5 million in mid-1984.[3] This more than anything else has weakened the bargaining position of the low paid and ensured that many employers have been able to make cuts in wages. In the final section we attempt to draw up a brief 'balance sheet' for government action. Even if the deal on offer to workers is a transfer from the dole queue to the sweatshop, is this taking place? Also what have been the costs to individuals and families of the poverty that low wages so often bring?

Priced out

As we saw in Chapters 2 and 3, the Thatcher government is closely wedded to a free-market philosophy. As monetarists they believe that a market economy is self-stabilising and that as long as the money supply is controlled, there will be full-employment and non-inflationary growth. Their theory of unemployment is little different from the neo-classical theory that was so influential in the inter-war period. It is argued that 'there is a "natural rate of unemployment" which is consistent with real forces and with accurate perceptions'.[4] The real forces referred to here are, for example, the extent of competition in the economy, the degree of wage flexibility, the efficiency of the labour market, entrepreneurial skills and technology; all the factors that will affect the supply and demand for labour. As long as the labour market is allowed to operate freely, prolonged unemployment cannot occur since wages will adjust to ensure an equilibrium. If there is mass unemployment it will be the result of monopolistic restrictions by trade unions which prevent the real wage from falling.

This view of the main causes of unemployment differs markedly from that held by previous post-war administrations, although it should be noted that there was a growing lack of confidence in Keynesian explanations and strategies amongst Labour Ministers after 1975.[5] What is new about the Thatcher government is the strength and consistency of their argument that a major cause of unemployment is the high level of wages. Since 1979 there has been a succession of statements from Ministers putting forward this belief. The general case has been put by the Prime Minister:

> In some industries workers have persistently demanded, and have been able to secure, wages which put prices up to a level the customer won't bear. If excessive wage demands are granted, one of two things will happen. Either workers price their products out of the market and lose their jobs, or, if they are in a monopoly industry and can hold the country to ransom, end up by destroying the jobs of others.[6]

More recently the Chancellor of the Exchequer at the 1984 Conservative Party Conference placed the blame for unemployment on 'the determination of monopolistic trade unions to insist on levels of pay that priced men out of work altogether'.[7] Also at fault is the wages council machinery which 'has operated in some cases to price people out of jobs. In particular these councils have done damage to the job opportunities of young people.'[8]

The converse has also been argued; if wages can be reduced, more jobs will be created. It is this belief that has inspired the government's policy initiatives in this area. How effective have they been? Have wage levels fallen and the number of low paid jobs increased? It is to these questions that we now turn.

Low pay: the evidence

In order to assess the extent of low pay in 1979 and 1984 we need a definition of 'low pay'. Two broad approaches have been used in the past. The first is linked to the idea of a 'living wage'; a person is low paid when his/her take-home pay is below the poverty/subsistence line as specified by government through the level of social security benefits. The second is based on some notion of a 'fair' relationship to average earnings; a person is low paid when his/her earnings fall too far below the national average.

In the absence of any clear statement from the government as to what it understands by the term 'low pay', the subsistence approach takes us closest to an official definition. This approach was considered by the National Board for Prices and Incomes when it was asked to identify pay levels which were 'too low to maintain a reasonable standard of living.'[9] The Board suggested using the Supplementary Benefit scale rates as an official yardstick of need. A person is low paid when his/her earnings are less than the amount required to provide a net income equal to that which would be received by a household of conventional size, consisting of a wage earner with a non-earning partner and two dependent children, on Supplementary Benefit. In the period from November 1983 to November 1984 (1983–4) this gave a figure of £105.45 per week.

Whilst those in full-time work are not entitled to claim Supplementary Benefit, the government does recognise that the incomes of many low-paid workers are insufficient to meet family needs and require 'topping up'. Thus Family Income Supplement (FIS) can be claimed by those with children if their income from full-time work (more than thirty hours per week) falls below certain levels. From November 1983 a worker with two children is eligible for FIS if his/her earnings are less then £95 per week. In November 1984 this level will be raised to £100. This FIS eligibility level can therefore be taken as an implicit poverty line for the working poor. However these benefit-related definitions of low pay are unsatisfactory in a number of respects.[10] First, the level at which SB is set is inadequate to meet normal day to day requirements. Secondly, benefit-related definitions of low pay assume a certain family type (the two-child two-parent family), and this is becoming increasingly uncommon. Thirdly, such an approach tends to undermine the legitimate claims of those in different circumstances, particularly women and young people.[11]

Because of these difficulties many organisations prefer to relate low pay to the distribution of earnings as a whole. The National Board for Prices and Incomes (NBPI) and the Royal Commission on the Distribution of Income and Wealth (RCDIW) both defined the low paid as those falling into the bottom tenth of the earnings distribution (the lowest decile). This definition was equivalent in 1983–4 to £94.10 per week. In recent years the TUC has used two-thirds of average male manual earnings (£101.80 per week in 1983–4) as its minimum wage target. The Low Pay Unit has preferred to use two-thirds of the median earnings of full-time male workers (manual and non-manual) giving a figure of £107.07 for 1983–4.[12]

To justify its choice of two-thirds of average earnings rather than some other proportion, the Low Pay Unit has referred to the European Social Charter administered by the Council of Europe. This specifies that workers shall be provided with what is described as 'fair remuneration'. The Council of Europe defines this according to a 'decency threshold' which they set at 68 per cent of the combined average (mean) earnings of men and women.[13] This gives a figure for 1983–4 of £108.32 a week in Britain. Moreover, the survey of attitudes carried out by MORI in 1983 for the *Breadline Britain* programmes found that two-thirds of those interviewed supported the idea of a national minimum wage, while 57 per cent of these thought it should be set at £90 per week or above. Updated to 1983–4, this is equivalent to £100 per week.

These different definitions thus give figures for low pay ranging from £94 to £108 per week in 1983–4. In this chapter we will use £105 as our cut-off point since this is derived from the Government's own Supplementary Benefit scale rates. Table 4.1 shows the numbers and proportions of workers earning below this figure in April 1984 according to the Department of Employment's New Earnings Survey.

**Table 4.1:   Proportions of Adult Workers* Earning Low Wages,†
April 1984**

	Including Overtime		Excluding Overtime	
Full-time men	million	%	million	%
Manual	0.9	17.1	1.4	26.8
Non-manual	0.4	8.5	0.4	9.7
All men	1.3	13.2	1.8	18.9
Full-Time women				
Manual	0.7	71.4	0.7	76.8
Non-manual	1.4	41.4	1.4	42.7
All women	2.1	48.3	2.2	50.5

*Employees on adult rates
† Less than £105
Source: *New Earnings Survey 1984*

Almost three and a half million full-time workers, two-thirds of
them women, had total earnings (including overtime pay) which fell
below the £105 per week definition of low pay in April 1984. The
majority of low-paid men (around three-quarters) were manual
workers. In the case of women around two-thirds of low-paid
women worked in occupations that are classified as non-manual
(such as shopwork and hairdressing). The *New Earning Survey* provides rather less information about part-time workers. They are,
however, much more likely to be low paid than full-timers; some
three-quarters of part-time female workers and over half of part-
time male workers received less than the hourly definition of low pay
(£2.62 per hour). In total, taking account of earnings from overtime, $6\frac{1}{2}$ million workers were low paid in 1984, just under one-third
of the workforce.

How has the position changed since 1979? Using the 1979 Supplementary Benefit scale rates we arrive at a low-pay definition of £60
per week.[14] Applying this to the *New Earnings Survey 1979* shows
that a significantly smaller proportion of the workforce was low
paid than in 1984. In the case of male manual workers the figure was
9.6 per cent compared with 17.1 per cent in 1984. For women workers the difference is smaller; 66.6 per cent in 1979 compared with
71.4 per cent in 1984. It should, however, be noted that the New
Earnings Survey 1984 changed the definition of 'adult worker' and
this will have caused a small overstatement of the extent of change in
the case of men and understatement of the change for women.[15]

Another indication of the deterioration in the position of the low paid since 1979 is given in Table 4.2. As a result of government policies and the economic recession there has been a significant widening of wage inequalities.

Table 4.2: Dispersion of Full-time Gross Weekly Earnings of Full-time Men aged 21 and over as Percentages of the Corresponding Median: 1979–84

	Lowest decile	Lower quartile	Upper quartile	Highest decile	Mean
1979	66.6	80.3	125.1	156.9	108.0
1980	65.9	80.1	126.5	161.6	109.9
1981	65.6	79.8	129.5	167.7	111.1
1982	64.5	79.0	129.8	168.1	111.0
1983	64.1	78.8	129.8	169.7	111.5
1984	61.6	77.2	130.6	171.5	111.3

Source: *New Earnings Survey*, 1984 Part B, Table 30

In 1979 the lowest paid tenth of male workers (the lowest decile) earned 66.0 per cent of the average (median) male wage. By 1984, their relative earnings had declined to the equivalent of only 61.6 per cent of the average. By contrast, the highest paid tenth of male workers (the highest decile) earned 56.9 per cent more than the average in 1979; by 1984 their 'differential' had increased to 71.5 per cent above the average. A similar pattern can be observed for women. In 1979, the lowest decile earned 69.4 per cent of the female average, while the highest decile earned 158.6 per cent of that average; by 1984, the lowest paid women had seen their relative earnings decline to 66.2 per cent of the average, whilst the best paid tenth had enjoyed an improvement to 166.3 per cent of the average. Indeed, the earnings of the lowest paid tenth of manual men are significantly lower now than in the 1930s when a major earnings survey was carried out.

Finally it should be noted that changes in the tax system have widened inequalities still further. Whilst taxation has increased for most households since 1979 the greater part of the increased burden has fallen on those on or below average earnings. A family on half average earnings has seen its tax burden more than double since 1978–9 compared to a 6 per cent increase for those on average earnings.[16] A family on five times average earnings has enjoyed a 14 per cent *cut* in their tax bill over the same period. Added to this shift, the Low Pay Unit (in conjunction with the Civil and Public Services Association) has shown that since 1979 the cost of living facing the low paid has risen by over 4 per cent more than that facing the average household (as indicated by the official Retail Price Index). This is the result of high increases in the price of necessities (such as housing, fuel and food) relative to price rises of other retail items.[17]

Policy Initiatives: 1979–84

Changes on this scale in the distribution of earnings over such a short period are unprecedented. As Guy Routh has noted in his seminal study: 'The outstanding characteristic of the national pay structure is the rigidity of its relationships.'[18] As regards the deterioration in the position of the low paid two factors have been at work. First, there is the impact of economic recession. This has created a buyer's market for labour and an increasing number of employers have used it to implement real wage cuts. Secondly, the Government has taken a number of policy initiatives designed to restrain wages and particularly those of lower-paid workers. It is these initiatives that we now examine.

As we saw earlier, the wages council system has been singled out for criticism by Ministers on the grounds that it is 'pricing workers out of jobs'. First established in 1909 by a Liberal government, wages councils are independent tripartite bodies made up of employer and worker representatives together with three independent members. There are currently 26 separate councils covering over 2.7 million workers (approximately one-eighth of the workforce). However, over 90 per cent of workers covered by wages councils are in just three sectors: hotels and catering, retailing, and clothing manufacturing. The minimum rates are set by a process of negotiation between the two sides with the independent members acting in an arbitration and conciliation role. The independents normally seek to reach an agreement between the two sides rather than using their casting vote in favour of one side rather than another. The councils represent a form of wage negotiating machinery, with the difference that, once agreed, the minimum rates are backed by the force of law.

The government's main criticism of the wages councils is that they fail to take sufficient account of 'ability to pay' when setting the statutory minimum rates. In an exchange of letters with the chairmen of the two retail councils between 1980 and 1983 the Minister repeatedly spelt out this view and attempted to secure reductions in the proposed increases in the minimum rates. Unsuccessful, he wrote in the following terms concerning the proposed April 1983 increase:

> I have received many letters from small and large businesses alike about these proposals. It is abundantly clear that, if not modified, the proposals will have damaging effects on employment in the retailing industry. I trust you will give the most serious consideration to the representations on this point that you will no doubt receive.
>
> Should the Council ignore the representations and confirm the proposed increases I would be driven to conclude *either* that the Council does not recognise any links between wages and jobs, *or* that it does not see it as part of its responsibilities to take this clear connection into account when making proposals about minimum wage rates. In that event I would be glad to know which view the Council takes.[19]

In polite replies the two independent chairmen told the Minister that his letter would be considered by the council together with other representations at its next meeting. Perhaps not surprisingly, at the next opportunity the government appointed new 'independent members' with more 'realistic' attitudes to these two wages councils. Similar pressures have been applied to a number of the other major wages councils.[20]

In sharp contrast, the Low Pay Unit (LPU) has consistently argued that the statutory minimum rates are too low. In their evidence to the House of Commons Employment Committee, the Unit pointed out that the minimum rates for men in 1983 were between 25 and 40 per cent of male average earnings. For women the legal minima ranged from 41 to 62 per cent of women's average earnings. The Unit also argued that the rates do take account of ability to pay. 'As in any negotiating mechanism, market forces are reflected in the relative strength of employers' and employees' representatives, although it will be the aim of the Independents to ensure that neither side takes "unfair advantage" through their position as monopoly buyer or seller of labour.'[21]

In addition to putting downward pressure on the level of settlements in the wages council sector, the government has also significantly weakened the enforcement machinery. In 1980–1 it cut the number of wages inspectors by one-third. There are now 120 'outdoor' inspectors to police the wages of over 2.7 million workers; on average each inspector has responsibility for 23,000 employees in 3,300 establishments. In all of Wales there are only five wages inspectors.[22] The fact that most establishments covered by wages councils are small and scattered geographically (such as newsagents or grocery shops) means that even visiting those firms who are most likely to be underpaying is a daunting task.

In 1978, ACAS recommended an improvement in the inspection rate to make the enforcement machinery more 'credible'. 'These proposals will require an increase in the numbers of Wages Inspectors and supporting staff, but are essential to ensure that all employers comply with the legislation.'[23] Since then, however, the number of establishments inspected by visit by the wages inspectorate has fallen and, as we have noted, the number of 'outdoor' wages inspectors has been cut. This is at a time when the number of employers found to be underpaying their staff was rising; from 31 per cent in 1979 to 37 per cent in 1983.

While the proportion of employers found to be underpaying the minimum rates has grown in recent years, the number of prosecutions has fallen. In 1983, out of nearly 10,000 employers found to be in breach of the Wages Orders, only two were prosecuted.[24] This low prosecution rate is due in part to the reduction in wages inspectorate staff. A prosecution may tie up a single inspector for months, so there is greater reluctance to take cases as far as the courts. The result is to reduce further the effectiveness of the enforcement machinery and to make more possible a 'financial' decision on the part of employers to continue underpaying their staff.

In addition to weakening significantly the wages council machinery, the government is considering its total abolition. It is currently prevented from doing this by UK ratification of ILO Convention 26 which requires signatory governments to 'maintain machinery whereby minimum rates of wages can be fixed'. However, in 1985 the Convention has to be ratified for a further five-year period and the government has indicated that it might renounce this commitment 'if it seemed that the wages councils reduced opportunities for employment'.[25] Support for such a move is not, however, as strong as might be expected. The CBI has come out in favour of retention, as has the Institute of Personnel Management. In both case there is concern that abolition will lead to a competitive spiral of wage undercutting which reduces economic efficiency.[26]

The second major policy initiative by the Thatcher government was the abolition of the Fair Wages Resolution (FWR) in September 1983. This left Britain for the first time in nearly in century with no general provision in government contracts requiring contract firms to pay either 'the going rate' of pay to their employees or, more specifically, collectively bargained pay rates. The resolution was an old parliamentary decree, originally conceived in response to a committee report on the 'sweated trades' under the 1891 Conservative government. It was designed to raise the standard of contract work done for central government by stipulating that firms offer workers the accepted pay rates for their trade. The 1946 form of the resolution extended its scope to cover other conditions of employment in addition to wages. Its introduction was not party political. Indeed, in urging acceptance of the measure Harold Macmillan said:

> . . . the time may come when the bubble is broken, when we shall have some new economy drive . . . with the Treasury trying to cut down the expenditure of Departments by forcing them to take contracts brought down somehow or another to the lowest possible figure. When that happens this motion will be . . . once again the great protector of the standard of life of the mass of the wage-earning classes and of the long built up traditions of co-operation between industry, both from the employing and from the working side.[27]

Rejecting these 'one nation' sentiments, and in the face of very considerable opposition, the government went ahead with abolition. It did so for two main reasons; first, because it believed that the FWR impeded free competition in the tendering process, and secondly, because the resolution was seen to be disruptive of normal pay bargaining. Some of the strongest opposition to abolition came from employers who argued that the only people to benefit would be 'the cowboys and the black economists'.[28] A proliferation of companies employing cheap labour, poorly trained and ill-equipped for the work, was predicted. Even the CBI favoured retention of the FWR in a modified form.

Abolition of the FWR has also been important for the government's programme of privatisation and contracting out of public sector services. In the words of the Secretary of State for Social Services: 'We remain committed to more contracting out where that saves the NHS money. That is not a doctrinaire policy; it is common sense.'[29] With fair wages protection it would be much harder to achieve these public expenditure savings. Without it, contractors can cut wages in order to undercut other tenders.

The most immediate effect of abolition has indeed been wage cuts for large numbers of workers on public sector contracts. For example, shortly after September 1983, many contract cleaning firms reduced the wages of staff employed on government work, by an average of 15 per cent.[30] However, the experience of cheaper services has often been unsatisfactory. The example of Wandsworth council's difficulties with its private refuse service, resulting in heavy fines against the employer for poor standards of work, is well documented. In other cases low pay has been accompanied by high staff turnover and deteriorating standards. Of the 74 refuse collectors originally employed by contractors in Milton Keynes last summer, only eight were left with the firm by January 1984.

Contracting out for cheaper services has also had its effect on the wages and conditions of those directly employed by local authorities. It has been estimated that for every case of a local authority service being offered to a private contract firm there are twelve cases of savings being made via an 'in-house' tender from public sector workers. As one leading Birmingham city councillor has put it: 'A hint of privatisation has been seen to concentrate the minds of DLOs [Direct Labour Organisations] very effectively . . .'[31] Often public sector workers have been cornered by the tendering process into accepting substantial job losses, pay cuts and reductions in fringe benefits. In effect, some local authorities have used the example of contracting out in other areas as a lever against nationally agreed rates of pay and conditions of work.

In addition to the Fair Wages Resolution, another fair wages protection which the Conservative government abolished was Schedule 11 of the Employment Protection Act 1975 (EPA), repealed under section 19 of the Employment Act 1980. This was introduced in 1977 to establish and maintain fair competition through the elimination of wage undercutting throughout the economy. In its relatively short life some 2,000 Schedule 11 claims were made to the Central Arbitration Committee of ACAS, a substantial proportion on behalf of relatively low-paid workers.[32] However, the Conservative government argued that the Schedule was being used as a means of circumventing the restrictions of pay policy, that it could disrupt agreed pay structures, and that it did not 'allow for all the considerations which should help to determine terms and conditions of employment to be fully considered, for example, market prospects, profitability, labour efficiency, prices'.[33] Abolition has denied 50,000–60,000 low-paid workers each year the opportunity to raise their wages through comparison with the terms and conditions of workers in the same trade or industry.

A third set of initiatives to reduce wages has been directed specifically at younger workers. As was noted earlier, the priced-out argument has been applied most frequently to this group. First there is the Young Workers' Scheme, introduced at the beginning of 1982. This initially offered employers a subsidy of £15 per week for each person aged under 18 whom they employed at a wage of less than £40 a week. Employers who were paying between £40 and £45 were entitled to a subsidy of £7.50 but those who paid more would receive nothing. The employer did not need to demonstrate that a new job had been created in order to qualify for the subsidy; he could cut the wages of the young workers he already employed, or substitute young workers for older workers at the lower wage levels.

As the Low Pay Unit has commented: 'since employers are not required to take on additional responsibilities but only to cut the wages of young people, take-up of the scheme has been enthusiastic'.[34] However, as a means of job creation the YWS has not been successful. A study commissioned by the Department of Employment during 1982 showed that 90 per cent of the jobs for which a subsidy was paid would have existed anyway, and another 4 per cent of the jobs were created at the expense of adult workers. There is also evidence that the highest take-up of the scheme has been amongst firms covered by wages councils, and that employers are claiming the subsidy by illegally underpaying the minimum rates.

A less obvious but nevertheless important downward pressure on young workers' wages has been the level of allowances paid under the Youth Opportunities Programme, and more recently the Youth Training Scheme. These have tended to set a 'going rate' for the wages of 16–18 year olds and in 1984 many firms were paying just a little over the £25 received by YTS workers. Finally, the government has exerted considerable pressure on wages councils to reduce their awards for young people. The Agricultural Wages Board and the Licensed Residential and Restaurant Wages Council did so in 1983, and held young workers wages at the previous year's levels.

The fourth set of initiatives to reduce wages and conditions of employment have concerned women workers who, as we have noted, form the majority of the low paid. However here the government has been constrained to a significant extent by membership of the EEC and in particular Article 119 of the Treaty of Rome and the Equal Pay Directive. In the absence of these treaty obligations it is likely that the Equal Pay Act (EqPA) would have been eroded. Cetainly the Government's response to the 1982 ruling of the European Court of Justice that the EqPA was in breach of European law was far from positive. The initial proposals for amending the Act fell short of the European ruling in at least five significant respects.[35] The final version that was approved by Parliament in 1983 was little better. As Jo Richardson MP observed in the debate on the amendment, 'the regulations are riddled with holes, and there is no way in which they can help any woman to achieve the objective which is apparent in the judgment of the European Court'.[36]

In addition to failing to bring forward any positive proposals to narrow the gap between women's and men's earnings, the government also made a number of changes to legislation and regulations which eroded the rights of women workers. Maternity leave and sick pay provision, protection against unfair dismissal, and childcare facilities in particular have been cut. However as Jenifer Dale has noted, 'there has been no wholesale attack on rights . . . as yet Tory fantasies of a family policy where women know their place — in the home — remain fantasies'.[37]

A Balance Sheet

Who has gained and who has lost from these policy initiatives? The government has sought to lower wages in the economy believing that this will help to increase employment. As we have seen, they have had considerable success in achieving wage reductions towards the bottom end of the distribution. However, as Peter Holmes has noted in Chapter 2, there is no sign as yet of the beneficial impact on jobs. The true level of unemployment is in the region of 4.5 million and still rising. Furthermore a recent simulation of the effects of the abolition of the wages councils, using the Treasury model, has shown that after five years there is no significant impact on employment.[38] Whether the pricing-out theory is presented in terms of particular industries and groups of workers, or the economy as a whole, it is seriously flawed.[39]

The costs of the Conservative government's policy to reduce

wages have been high. There is a clear connection between low pay and poverty. The most recent DHSS statistics on the number living in or on the margin of poverty show that in 1981, of the 9.1 million people under pension age living in low-income households (defined by the DHSS as 140% of the Supplementary Benefit level) over 40 per cent were dependent on a full-time wage earner.[40] Even among those living on incomes *below* the Supplementary Benefit equivalency level (a total of 1,690,000 people under pension age), over two-thirds of a million were dependent on at least one full-time wage earner. This number represents an increase of nearly 40 per cent since 1979, so that the families of the low paid were the largest group among the non-pensioner poor.

When pensioners are included in the picture of poverty, the number of persons dependent on low wages, as a proportion of all low income households, appears to fall quite sharply. For example, of the 2,810,000 people living below Supplementary Benefit level, only 24.2 per cent would then be dependent on a low wage. However, such figures neglect the fact that poverty in old age is often caused by poverty during a person's working life: the low paid are unable to accumulate assets and therefore tend to remain in or near a state of poverty when retired. This phenomenon will be exacerbated by the fact that the low paid are also more likely to suffer periods of unemployment: low paid, unskilled manual workers are six times more likely to be unemployed than the average male worker.[41]

These figures relate to 1981 but the overlap between low pay and poverty is likely to be significantly greater in 1984. Unfortunately the government has stopped publishing on a regular basis estimates of the numbers in poverty so the true position cannot be established. Nevertheless some indication of the escalation of poverty amongst the low paid is given by the numbers dependent on Family Income Supplement. In April 1984 there were 210,000 families with children whose earnings were so low that they were claiming FIS. This compares with only 96,000 in 1978. And since FIS take-up is thought to represent only half the numbers actually eligible, we may assume that well over one-third of a million families with children are now living *in* poverty through the effects of low wages, in addition to several hundred thousand people without children. These people are bearing the costs of the government's continuing belief that wage cuts create jobs. The beneficiaries are less evident.

References

1. C. Thomas, 'Low Pay and Incomes Policy' in R. Chater *et al.* (eds.), *Incomes Policy* (Oxford University Press, Oxford, 1981).

2. R. Smail, 'Setting Record Taxes Straight' in *Low Pay Review*, 18 (1984).

3. A. Walker, 'The Level and Distribution of Unemployment' in L. Burghes and R. Lister (eds.), *Unemployment: Who Pays the Price?* (CPAG, London 1981) and Unemployment Unit, *The Missing Million* (Unemployment Unit, London, 1983).

4. M. Friedman, *Inflation and Unemployment* (Institute of Economic Affairs, London, 1977), p. 15.

5. A. Deacon 'Unemployment and Politics in Britain since 1945' in B. Showler and A. Sinfield (eds.) *The Workless State*, (M. Robertson, Oxford, 1981).

6. *Hansard*, 4.5.80, Col 185.

7. N. Lawson, *The Times*, 11 October 1984, p. 4.

8. *Hansard*, 27.7.81, Col 901.

9. National Board of Prices and Incomes, *General Problems of Low Pay*, Cmnd 4648, para 17.

10. D. Byrne *et al.*, 'Low Wages in Britain', *Low Pay Review*, 16 (December 1983).

11. F. Bennet, 'A Family Wage', *Low Pay Review*, 4 (March 1981).

12. Low Pay Unit, 'Cheap Labour: the Current Crisis', *Low Pay Review*, 20 (1984).

13. S. Winyard, *Fair Remuneration?*, (Low Pay Unit, London, October 1982).

14. C. Pond, 'Low Pay in the 80s', *Low Pay Bulletin*, 30 (December 1979).

15. Department of Employment, *New Earnings Survey 1984*, Part B, (HMSO, London, 1984).

16. C. Pond, 'Taxation: a Political Liability', *Marxism Today*, vol. 27, no. 2 (Februray 1983).

17. C. Pond, 'Price and the Poor', *Low Pay Review*, 9 (1982).

18. G. Routh, *Occupation and Pay in Great Britain* (Cambridge University Press, Cambridge 1965), p. 147.

19. *Hansard* 31.3.83 Col 243–244.

20. 'Wage Settlements', *Low Pay Review* 15 (September 1983), p. 16.

21. *Minutes of Evidence taken before the Employment Committee*, HC 491 (July 1984).

22. *Hansard* 2.2.83, Col 102.

23. ACAS, *Toy Manufacturing Wages Council*, Report No 13 (HMSO, London, 1978), p. 13.

24. Department of Employment, 'Minimum Wage Enforcement', *Employment Gazette* (HMSO, London, October 1984).

25. *Hansard* 21.2.84 Col 679.

26. Low Pay Unit, *Who Needs the Wages Councils?* (Low Pay Unit, London, 1983).

27. *Hansard* 14.5.46 Col 841.

28. Incomes Data Services, *Report No. 147* (London, May 1983).

29. *Hansard* 13.7.82, Col 839.

30. *Minutes of Evidence taken before the Employment Committee.*

31. A Coombs, *Local Government Studies*, vol 9, no. 2 (1983).

32. L. Dickens *et al.*, *A Response to the Government Working Paper on Amendments to Employment Protection Legislation*, (IRRU, University of Warwick, November 1979).

33. 'Working Paper on Schedule 11 of the Employment Protection Act', *Department of Employment Gazette*, (September 1978).

34. Low Pay Unit, *Who Needs the Wages Councils?*, pp. 37–8.

35. D. Byrne, 'An Act of Inequality', *Low Pay Review*, 13 (May 1983).

36. *Hansard* 20.7.83, Col 494.

37. J. Dale, 'Women and Social Policy', *Critical Social Policy*, 8 (Autumn 1983).

38. H. Neuburger, *From the Dole Queue to the Sweatshop* (Low Pay Unit, London 1984).

39. H. Neuburger, *Unemployment: Are Wages to Blame?* (Low Pay Unit, London, 1983).

40. DHSS, *Low Incomes in 1981* (DHSS, London).

41. A.B. Atkinson, 'Low Pay and the Cycle of poverty' in F. Field (ed.), *Low Pay* (Arrow Books, London, 1973).

SECTION TWO: THE WELFARE STATE

5 SOCIAL SECURITY POLICY

Doreen Collins

Since social security accounts for nearly 30 per cent of public expenditure any government desirous of curtailing the latter must devote considerable attention to the former. As is now well known, social-security expenditure has proved difficult to control but the effort to do so is raising fundamental issues about the purposes and methods of income maintenance in modern society. In order to explain this, a brief word about the past may be helpful in order to draw attention to the significance of changes which, considered separately, may not appear to be of great importance or to involve large sums.

It is worth remembering that the British social-security system is a very old one of which a major characteristic has been the increasing use of a system of national insurance as opposed to a means-tested scheme. As the years rolled by, the national insurance system came to cover all the main circumstances of loss of income and effectively to include the whole population. The recasting of the social services in the late 1940s is generally held to have been a watershed and the reform of income maintenance services which then took place has remained as the basis for future developments. Even then, change came primarily through the extension of existing services, their greater rationality and more coherent pupose together with the addition of a family allowance system (now child benefit). Above all, it was intended that these services should express a generosity of spirit, provide good quality services and be available as part of a concept of the social rights of citizenship to set alongside longer established political rights and supported by the obligation to manage the economy so as to ensure full employment. In the field of social security, the great architect of post-war reform, William Beveridge, saw that these ideas meant services that would be universal over the population, comprehensive over needs and which would rest primarily on the notion of social insurance. He postulated that the provision of comprehensive health services was a necessary precondition for effective income maintenance services. Although the Beveridge Report spoke of the importance of a partnership between the state and the individual, in which the former's responsibility

67

would be limited to the coverage of basic needs, it nevertheless implied a considerable extension of collective commitment both because of the wider responsibilities involved for central government, including the take-over of much administration, and because of the intention that benefits should cover basic human needs. In this approach to social security, means-tested benefits were intended to have a residual role. Services were subsequently structured on this conception but grew steadily more complicated as new benefits were added to the national insurance scheme and special means-tested benefits introduced to deal with newly identified forms of poverty. A remarkable change was the growth of occupational benefits, not available to all in the labour market, let alone to all citizens, which concentrate primarily on payments in retirement and sickness and whose value reflects previous earning capacity rather than an abstract concept of human need.

Although it is common to talk of the post-war consensus, in fact there has been a lively debate for many years about the value of the Beveridge system in which the ends and means of social policy, the extent of individual and family responsibility, the importance of voluntary action and of private saving have vied with the values of collectivism and the goal of lessening inequalities. As living standards began to rise in the 1950s it became possible to look forward to a new type of affluent society in which, at most, pockets of poverty would continue and a better-off, better-educated and healthier population could increasingly look after its own need for replacement income.[1] Thus the traditional values of freedom and liberty received a new airing rather than a stress on freedom from want, deemed to be more or less achieved. The rediscovery of poverty in the late 1950s[2] suggested that this assumption was premature but the argument was complicated by the introduction of a relative, rather than absolute, standard by which the existence of poverty should be judged and this period saw the debate shift to include the much broader question of the responsibility to lessen, if not eliminate, social inequalities. Whilst a large measure of agreement proved possible in the provision of educational and health services, discussion over income levels has been much more confused. It became broader as questions of earnings differentials, methods of pay determination, the extent of low pay and the effects of the taxation system were added to the objectives and methods of the social security system but their interrelationship and the extent to which these matters should be considered within an all-embracing framework of 'fairness' remain highly contentious. Against this background, dissatisfaction with the extent to which social security services have been able to meet the demands and expectations of society has made it possible to react either by urging greater redistribution through existing mechanisms or their limitation to more restricted purposes. Whilst the inclination of the government since 1979 has been to adopt the latter point of view, the extent to which it has managed to do so is less clear cut.

Social security schemes grew out of the recognition of the circumstances in which income becomes inadequate for needs and the refusal of these social realities to disappear is the primary reason for the stubbornness of this item of public expenditure to respond to the wishes of the current government. Old age and ill health are the big money spenders, as they always have been, and this remains true despite the rapid rise of unemployment in recent years and the fact that unemployment support has always been the emotive issue in the history of British social security. Probably the most complex issues to handle relate to family poverty which has so many causes. It may arise from family break-up or because a family never existed or the size of the family may be too large for the wage to support or the breadwinner may only be able to work part-time. Family poverty is a deeply emotive question for many people because it touches on matters of individual responsibility, the welfare of children, the nature of modern marriage and the functions of the family as a social institution. The relative importance of the different reasons why cash support from the community is required is shown in Table 5.1.

Table 5.1: UK Social Spending by Type of Benefit. (%)[3]

	1970	1981
Sickness	26.3	21.2
Invalidity/Disability	7.8	8.5
Employment Injury	1.3	1.1
Old Age	43.2	40.2
Survivors's Benefits	3.5	2.0
Maternity	2.1	1.5
Family Benefit	8.6	9.6
Placing & Vocational Guidance	0.5	1.2
Unemployment	3.9	11.8
Housing Benefits	0.2	0.9
Miscellaneous	2.0	1.4
Total	99.4	99.0

Despite the dramatic rise in unemployment costs, social security remains primarily about the elderly, the sick, the disabled and their dependants. Thus the hard facts of demography continue to be the prime determinants of need. The number of over-65 year olds in the UK has grown by over 2 million since 1961 and, although it is not expected that this group as a whole will increase greatly during the next 15 to 20 years, there will be a significant increase in the number of really old people who require considerable support from family and community in personal services and whose pensions, it must be assumed, will require boosting through some form of index-linking if they are to retain a worthwhile value in money terms, let alone maintain living standards in real terms should community wealth increase. The present debate[4] on pensions, portable, occupational, index-linked, is in part a reaction to these facts and a desire to canvass the possibilities of spreading the load away from statutory schemes onto other shoulders.

Pressures on social-security costs also come from other factors. The real standard of living of social beneficiaries has to increase in some measure if real standards are rising generally whilst new problems have come to the fore, such as the growth in the number of single-parent families, and old ones have required a new look. The improvement in the system of child support is one example.

The result of such factors is that there is a built-in momentum towards growth in social security but it still remains the case that the proportion of Gross Domestic Product spent on it in the UK is relatively small in West European terms. A possible hypothesis, somewhat ironic, is that the British method of providing social security and health care has helped to check rather than encourage expenditure in comparison with other methods of provision and, if an ideological dislike of collectivism leads to the adoption of methods more akin to those found elsewhere, the rate of growth of social security coverage might well turn out to be greater rather than less, although the distribution of benefits and costs would doubtless change.

A weakness in the social-welfare debate until the 1970s was its indifference to the relationship between social goals and economic capability and this may have been assisted by the particular form of social provision which encouraged an oversimplistic Left/Right divide in which one side saw any suggestion of change as an attack on the hard-won gains of the poor, who could only be protected by all-embracing public services supported by differential taxation, and the other the monster of state control battening on the productive energies of the nation. Yet it was a Labour government which began the process of braking public expenditure and the present Conservative government that now recognises that slowing its rate of growth, or at best its stabilisation, is the most that can be hoped for in view of the massive social responsibilities it contains. A number of policies pursued by the government, such as raising the earnings limit and the taxation of short-term benefits, were also the intention of the Labour government. Thus the rhetoric of party manifestos is likely to exaggerate differences in a field where there is more agreement than it is comfortable to acknowledge.

The tone of the 1979 Conservative manifesto was set by Mrs Thatcher who stated that the central political question for her is 'people and how they want to live their lives'. The document argued that the social balance had tilted too far in favour of the state at the expense of individual freedom. Thus the role of the state was seen in terms of helping people help themselves and of encouraging personal responsibility. Of five major tasks set before the electorate, the most specifically 'social' referred to the support of family life, help to home ownership, raising standards of education and concentrating welfare services on the effective support of the old, sick, disabled and those in real need. In elaborating this goal, prime stress was laid upon home ownership and it is here that the really dramatic changes in social policy have occurred. Quality of, and choice in, education would be tackled, the quality of health and welfare services maintained through the better use of resources, notably through simplifying and decentralising and cutting back bureaucracy. Spending through the NHS would not be cut but a place would be found for the private sector as an extra resource for health care. More would be done to help people stay in the community through helping them and their families to provide care and voluntary and self-help groups working in partnership with the statutory services would be encouraged. The social security system required simplification whilst income tax often acted as a disincentive to work at the lower levels of pay. A tax credit system was seen as the long-term answer and, in the meantime, the system would be simplified, the incentive to work restored, the poverty trap reduced and more help given to those in greatest need. By reducing tax and taxing short-term benefits, through the strict enforcement of rules concerning job acceptance and through a drive against fraud and abuse, the incentive to work would be restored. The child benefit scheme was approved and one-parent families recognised as a group requiring special help. The elderly would benefit through the curb on inflation, the reduction of taxes and the aim of abolishing the earnings rule. The conditions of eligibility for pensions for war widows would be improved and a start made on a more coherent system of benefits for the disabled. Thus social goals for government were derived from the broad process of rolling back the state, thereby allowing individuals more freedom and control over their own lives, rather than through the pursuit of further collective endeavour. At the same time, existing services were to be maintained and, indeed, improved through efficiency and active encouragement given to individuals and the voluntary sector to participate in their work.

By the time of the 1983 manifesto certain differences of emphasis may be perceived. Although helping people and their families fulfill their own expectations was stated to be the major purpose there was a good deal more discussion of functions that the state would undertake. Unemployment was singled out as a prime issue and much made of the special measures of training allowances to encourage self-employment and job creation for the long-term unemployed. However, a new stress was to be found on the duty to protect the most vulnerable, notably the pensioners, and to preserve the standards of the NHS. It was untrue that the government wished to dismantle the Welfare State but it did wish to increase personal freedom and responsibility by giving more choice to individuals and families and to improve standards in the public services.

The 1983 manifesto reiterated that the right to own a home is essential to its view of the good society and further extensions of the right to buy were envisaged together with a stress on the problems of the inner cities. Little new was added to the policy for social security, with which this chapter is concerned, beyond the issue of maintaining the pension rights of those changing employment. However, the aim of helping people to stay in familiar surroundings when sick or elderly had become important and this included the necessary extension of powers and finance for health authorities in order to enable patients requiring long-term care to move into more informal surroundings than those of hospital. The voluntary and private sectors were important elements in the provision of health and welfare care and opportunities for individual volunteers were noted. A brief reference was made to the fact that, in its capacity as an employer, the government was fulfilling its commitment to equal opportunities for men and women in the public services.

Whilst the main thrust of social policy remained the same, the brashness of the earlier manifesto had softened. The government was at pains to point out the developments that had occurred in the public services, that its responsibility to the weak remained and to suggest ways in which services might be maintained despite limited finances. There is here at least an implicit recognition that social issues of poverty, inner-city decay, of long-term care of the elderly and disabled have to be tackled as the responsibility of the public sector. Thus the essential dilemma of Conservative social policy was exposed. Cutting public expenditure and taxation leads to greater freedom and choice for the individual but because so much public expenditure is directed to social ends it is difficult to avoid hurting the most vulnerable members of society. The way out of this impasse is to concentrate upon those 'who cannot help themselves' but this leads to the quagmire made up of the definition of need, investigation of individual circumstances, means-testing and the drawing of arbitrary lines between those who qualify and those who do not. Furthermore, any significant change of direction in a social security programme must cause considerable confusion and difficulty for current recipients but because problems are spread over many people in very varied circumstances much of the hardship goes unrecorded.

Consequent upon taking office, the government proceeded to introduce a number of changes in social security benefits both to contribute to holding public expenditure and to begin to express a different emphasis in social responsibility. The following account is indicative of policy changes, not a comprehensive discussion of all the changes made. Although certain restrictions came in November 1979 as immediate measures, the 1980 benefit rates were more illustrative of Conservative thinking. Child benefit received but a limited uprating and continued to lag until 1983. Since there is no legal, as opposed to moral, obligation to maintain its value it is a benefit particularly vulnerable to austerity measures. Retirement pensions were only increased to compensate for price changes whilst unemployment and sickness benefits were increased by 5 per cent less than this to compensate for their exemption from taxation. Whilst tax was levied from April 1982 the restoration of the 5 per cent cut was left until November 1983. Prescription charges were also increased.

1980 also brought an important change in the method of

determining long-term benefit increase. Since 1975, benefits had been linked to the larger of the increase in earnings and prices but in 1980 the link with earnings was dropped and in consequence the rise in benefits was about 6 per cent less than it otherwise would have been. Even so, government reserves the right to determine when and how to honour the more limited pledge[5]. A further change came in 1983 when the method of calculating price changes became based on the actual increase between May and May for use the following November instead of a mix of the actual price increase for the previous six months and a forecast of the price increase for the ensuing year in a calculation year from November to November. Since the evidence is that earnings are currently outstripping inflation[6] it must be the case that the gap between earners and long-term beneficiaries is widening. The consequence of this process will be important in later years amongst the very old whose relatively depressed condition will lead them to make particularly heavy demands on other types of services.

Another form of retrenchment has been to remove sickness benefit from the National Insurance scheme altogether. At first it became subject to certain restrictions but from 1982 the first eight weeks of benefit became a statutory charge on the employer in exchange for a relief in insurance contributions. Legal minima exist for benefits but they no longer have to include dependants' allowances and the standard of living of those off sick for short periods is now the responsibility of employers' sick pay schemes.

The growth of social security benefits has always been tempered by the recognition of the importance of maintaining the willingness to work. Government is hostile to interference with minimum wage levels so it has to act through policy on unemployment benefit and the income tax threshold. Cuts in short-term benefits were followed in 1982 by the abolition of the earnings-related supplement, eligibilty rules concerning periods of interruption of employment were tightened and reductions made in the amount of benefit payable to the holders of occupational pensions who were over sixty years old. The Prime Minister has refused to promise that, in the future, unemployment benefits will be compensated for inflation.[7] By 1981, unemployment benefit, without earnings supplement, was running at 33 per cent of net average earnings[8] whilst Table 5.2 shows the varied condition of the unemployed.

Table 5.2: The Unemployed and their Benefits, 1982[9]

Benefit Received	
Unemployment only	448,000
Unemployment + supplementary	231,000
Supplementary only	1,100,000
None	321,000

Work incentives for pensioners were planned through the abolition of the earnings rule but this has not yet been done for reasons of economy although the limit has been increased after an initial period of freeze. Rules for the preservation of pension rights have been changed to encourage men over sixty to take low-paid jobs.

Changes were made, too, in the payment of Supplementary Benefit. A general cut of 1 per cent in benefit levels was made in 1981 because of a previous overestimate in inflation and the policy of only compensating for future price increases adopted. Reductions were made in benefits payable to the families of strikers and help with winter heating costs limited to households which contain an old person over seventy, a severely disabled person or a child under five. The long-term unemployed are excluded from the more favourable benefit rate unless over sixty years old.

Parallel with changes which work to the disadvantage of recipients have been those designed to improve the relative position of some groups of beneficiaries. The long-term Supplementary Benefit rate operates after one year not two, extensions have occurred in mobility allowances for disabled people, the rules eased for benefits for those suffering from occupational deafness, for eligibility for maternity grants, for single parents to claim child benefit, the premium given to the single parent for the first child has been raised, more benefits included in the Family Income Supplement and greater assistance with fuel bills provided for those who are eligible. Single mothers claiming one-parent benefit for a first or only child should no longer be asked questions about their sex lives. Taxation changes, too, have been designed both to assist the most vulnerable and to increase the incentive to work for low-earning families. The 1983 Budget increased the income limit for the age allowance as well as personal allowances. Nevertheless, it has been estimated that the poverty trap, whereby the loss of benefits which occurs as income from work rises offsets any increase in earnings, still catches 122,000 workers.[10]

From details such as these it is possible to build up a picture of current policy which seems entirely consistent with the views expressed in 1979. A shelter is provided against inflation but increases in real standards are a matter for government discretion, a clear distinction is drawn between the value of benefit and wage for those who can work and special protection is provided for certain groups, notably single parents and families on low wages. The curtailment of the operation of the National Insurance scheme in favour of means-tested benefits has led, as it must, to an increase in the clients of the Supplementary Benefit system, notably in non-pensioner groups. By 1983, one-eighth of the population had become dependent on Supplementary Benefit, 3 million more than when the government took office, and this long-term shift in the balance between National Insurance and Supplementary Benefit as a means of income maintenance must surely be one of the significant changes brought by the Conservative administration.

Table 5.3a: Supplementary Benefit Client Groups (Thousands)[11]

	1979	1980
No. recipients regular weekly payments in Dec.	2850	4270
Pensioners	1720	1780
Unemployed		
with NI	80	285
no NI	486	1437
Sick & Disabled		
with NI	52	83
no NI	155	157
NI widows		
under 60	19	20
One parent families not in other groups	306	415

Table 5.3b: Family Income Supplement Recipients[12].

1979	1983–4
80,000	175,000

An early announcement from the 1979 government was of the intention to replace the Supplementary Benefits Commission with a

Social Security Advisory Committee allowing the administrative functions to be merged into the DHSS with the use of local benefit officers to assess individual claims and retaining a right of appeal. Thus came to an end a policy first established in 1934 with the creation of the Unemployment Assistance Board, designed to establish a national system of means-tested benefits but at one remove from normal political processes in order that the needs of the clients might be seen and catered for less emotively than hitherto. The independence of its descendants, the National Assistance Board and the Supplementary Benefits Commission, had enabled it to produce reports of social significance and to perform an evaluative function for the changing circumstances and needs of the poorer social groups and it is not yet obvious that an advisory committee will carry on this tradition with such good effect. Simplification of administration was also an intended aim together with stronger measures to prevent abuse. In the case of National Insurance, simplification is primarily a matter of more efficient administrative systems to ensure the maximum collection of contributions with minimum cost, comprehensive record keeping and effective payment methods. Computerisation holds out the dream of great efficiency but it may be worth pointing out that collection problems are normally more difficult as more people become self-employed, any possible growth in contracting out and in alternative insurance schemes makes an individual's insurance record more complex, whilst payment systems cannot advance too far beyond public acceptability. Since contributions are a form of tax it is attractive to argue that they could simply be merged into the inland revenue system and this may well be part of the long-term aim of introducing a tax credit system which amalgamates income tax and social security. Modern methods make this mammoth change feasible for the first time but this does not in itself mean that the older arguments for their continued separation no longer hold. Contributions make insurance costs visible to the community, a single record system raises questions of data privacy, the consequences of a single error are greater for the individual and it will be even more important to handle changes in individual circumstances without serious time lags. With a greater variety of schemes, greater mobility, including international mobility, there will be more complexity and more appeals from individuals so a new administration will not necessarily save large sums. Some relatively minor changes have occurred so that, for instance, new mothers receive child benefit monthly and more benefits can be paid directly into bank and giro accounts. Payment of Supplementary Benefit by cheque posted to the recipient has, however, brought considerable losses.

Administration of a means-tested system is a different matter but the concept of public service as a safety net means that heavy reliance must be placed upon it. As a method, means-testing runs the risk of stigmatisation and requires a specially trained staff to investigate and assess claims; it is more time consuming for staff and tends to increase the possibility of staff and clients seeing themselves as belonging to two different camps and acting accordingly. As Table 5.3 shows, the big increases have come in the unemployed, especially those ineligible for National Insurance, one-parent families as well as in low-wage families, and they are all groups whose circumstances require time if they are to be considered properly, but staff numbers have remained practically stationary despite the increase of work.[13]

Many believed that social security benefits, during the 1960s and 1970s, had become too complicated. One had been piled upon another until neither administrator nor applicant understood the position or knew how to find a way through the maze. One of the purposes of the Social Security Act 1980 was to simplify the benefits system. A number of entitlements ceased to be discretionary and were given precise legal form whilst fewer categories were used for beneficiaries. It was agreed that recipients should be given more information about how their benefits were calculated and that the code concerning discretionary benefits should be published. In theory, therefore, it has become possible to know one's rights and it is certainly more important, for extra benefits are not given unless they are asked for. A recent study has made plain that neither staff nor applicants understand what benefits are available.[14] It is now agreed on all sides that take-up is a serious problem and DHSS statistics confirm this. Whilst there is nearly 100 per cent take-up for retirement pensions, child benefit and the death grant, means-tested benefits present a different picture. Only 75 per cent of non-pensioners and 67 per cent of pensioners claim and it is estimated that at any one time 810,000 pensioners and 580,000 non-pensioners are leaving £760 million unclaimed. About 70 per cent of single parents were claiming the extra one-parent benefit in December 1981.[15] Appeals, too, are on an upward trend. 50,639 in 1979 had grown to 56,084 by 1982.[16] All in all, it does not seem that the government can yet claim that it has solved the problem of combining the policy of directing resources to those in greatest need with efficiency and, if the present system is considered as a necessary transition between a decaying old system and a more up-to-date one, many of the currently poor are paying the cost. It seems probable that greater efficiency would lead to more, not less, expenditure in this section of the social security system.

The effects of these changes are difficult to assess in any helpful way. Crude income figures suggest that overall the population is more, rather than less, reliant, is more heavily taxed and that its standard of living has not increased but, of course, many factors besides government policies will have contributed to this position.

Table 5.4a Income of UK households by Source (%)[17]

	1979	1982
Wages & salaries	66	62
Income from self-employment	8	7
Rents, divis, int.	7	8
Private pensions, annuities	5	7
Social security bens.	12	13
Other transfers	2	3

Table 5.4b: Direct Taxes as Percentage of Household Income

	1979	1982
Income taxes	14	15
N I contribs.	3	4
Pension scheme contribs.	2	2

Table 5.4c: Real Household Disposable Income per Head (1980–100)

	1979	1982
	99	99

Furthermore, between 1978–9 and 1981–2, disparities of income increased but it must be remembered that the manifestos made no promise of equality.

Table 5.5: Shares of Personal Income After Tax[18]

	1978–9	1981–2
Top 10%	23.4	25.5
11–20%	16.3	16.4
21–30%	13.5	13.2
31–40%	11.3	10.8
41–50%	9.3	8.8
51–60%	7.7	7.3
61–70%	6.4	6.3
71–80%	5.1	5.2
81–90%	4.1	4.0
Lowest 10%	2.9	2.4

In 1984, the Treasury announced[19] that public expenditure as a whole was broadly stable allowing for an annual price rise of 5 per cent but within this the social security budget has been consistently above target. It is demand led. Population structure and employment opportunities are two of the most obvious factors affecting demand but, within broad limits, individual decisions can be affected by government. A considerable effort has been made to make work more attractive than non-work but, unless jobs are available, good training facilities provided, adequate child-care arrangements made for women and single parents, individuals may have no choice but to seek social support. With large-scale unemployment endemic it is impossible to measure the effectiveness of the changes in benefit on the willingness to work. Early retirement has been another fashionable policy in recent years and is succeeding in that there has been a dramatic fall in the number of over-sixties who are economically active. The proportion of men aged 60–64 in this category fell from 69.6 per cent in 1981 to 59.6 per cent in 1983 and now only 21% of women in this age group are economically active.[20] Whether this really expresses 'freedom of choice' for the individual may be open to doubt. This result is only possible through a combination of redundancy payments and earlier pension provision and may well have an, as yet unknown, knock-on effect on demand for health care, leisure and educational facilities. One conclusion may be that freedom of individual decision is a concept more readily applied to the young, mobile and trained members of society than to the typical clients of the social security system. There has been an attempt to switch benefits away from those people deemed to be attached to the labour force towards those who cannot work, although this policy is disguised by the scale of unemployment, some pushing of public expenditure onto employers and some transfer from central to local government accounts through the housing benefit system. A deliberate attempt has been made to favour the most vulnerable groups amongst the social security population with a consequent rise in the number of means-tested beneficiaries. Such a trend, if it continues, would indeed be a reversal of that gathering pace during the twentieth century to categorise circumstances of loss of income and pay benefits on standard conditions of eligibility. So attractive has this been in the past that increasing numbers of people were incorporated into the National Insurance scheme through 'blanketing-in' arrangements in order to get away from the disadvantages of assistance services. The recent reports that the government is interested in bringing the child benefit system into the tax system in such a way that only poorer families benefit[21] would be consistent with its policies but would probably cut across two existing attractions, namely that it is universal and paid directly to the mother.

A policy of residual responsibility for central government is only practical if the bulk of the population covers its needs in a different way. No clear policy has yet emerged to explain how this is to be done but it would clearly be a long-term policy involving the abolition of both the National Insurance and Supplementary Benefit schemes at least in their present form. The Secretary of State has four major reviews in progress to cover retirement pensions, housing benefit, Supplementary Benefit and benefits for children and young people but these cannot be a substitute for an overview of the role of public provision in the future. It is intended that this will be done by a coordinating committee which will also relate social security provision to the taxation system but, so far, a wry comment from the Beveridge Report about another age seems apt: 'In all this change and development, each problem has been dealt with separately, with little or no reference to allied problems.'[22] The public role, however, must now be seen in conjunction with the enhanced role of occupational welfare implied in the withdrawal of the state. In such an emerging partnership, the use of a tax-credit system for the public sector may prove to be the best hope of providing a service which is both acceptable and efficient. Such a balance would seem to be perfectly in accord with the statements of the manifestos but so far most attention has been paid to short-term considerations of curbing the public sector with consequent turmoil for many recipients. The serious thinking is yet to come.

Notes

1. E.g. I. Macleod and J.E. Powell *The Social Services — Needs and Means*, (Conservative Political Centre, London, 1949); W. Hagenbuch, 'The Rationale of the Social Services', *Lloyds Bank Review* (July 1953); A. Peacock, *The Welfare Society*, Unservile State Papers (undated but based on a lecture delivered in 1960).

2. E.g. B. Abel-Smith and P. Townsend, *The Poor and the Poorest*, Occasional Papers on Social Administration (G. Bell & Sons Ltd, London, 1965).

3. Eurostat, *Basic Statistics of the Community 1982-3*. Derived from Table 3.32. The figures relate to functions not schemes.

4. E.V. Morgan, *Choice in Pensions*, Hobart Papers (Institute of Economic Affairs, 1984); T. Congdon, 'Pensions, property and the great divide', *The Times*, 21 June 1984; 'Looking forward to better pensions', *The Times*, 8 August 1984; 'Why state pensions should be on the road to oblivion', *The Times*, 15 August 1984. See, too, the report on DHSS consultative document on portable pensions, *The Times*, 17 August 1984.

5. Hansard 976 HC Official Report (5th series), col 903 (Patrick Jenkin, 20 December 1979).

6. Wages up 7.8 per cent in previous year, prices up 5.1 per cent: *The Economist*, 18 August 84. p. 81.

7. Hansard HC Official Report (5th series), cols. 151-2 (5 July 1983).

8. *Social Trends* (1984) p. 76.

9. *Ibid*.

10. K. Slack, 'Digest of Social Administration', *Journal of Social Policy*, vol. 12, part 4, p. 532.

11. DHSS, *Social Security Statistics* (1983), p. 185.

12. *Social Trends* (1984), p. 75.

13. Staff in local DHSS offices increased from 63,152 in July 1979 to 63,401 in January 1982. Hansard 17 HC Official Report (5th series), Col. 461.

14. Policy Studies Institute, *The Reform of Supplementary Benefit*, (PSI, London, 1984).

15. DHSS, *Social Security Statistics* (1983), p. 261.

16. Ibid., p. 182.

17. *Social Trends* (1984), p. 72.

18. *The Economist*, 11 August 84, p. 24.

19. Cmnd 9143, *The Government's Expenditure Plans 1984-5 — 1986-7*.

20. *The Times*, 26 July 84.

21. *The Times*, 16 August 84.

22. Cmnd. 6404, para. 3.

6 THE THATCHER GOVERNMENT AND THE NATIONAL HEALTH SERVICE

Robert Elmore

> To use the stonework of the NHS as the building
> material for a new society is to risk breaking up what
> remains, with all its imperfections, a formidable
> monument to social imagination without any certainty
> that the new structure will ever get beyond the planning
> stage of rhetoric.
> Rudolf Klein[1]

Any analysis of the NHS which is divorced from the political, economic and social context is likely to be arid. Although there are many who would prefer to regard the provision of health-care services as essentially a technical problem, the possibility of doing this — always a dubious proposition in any event — has become a political impossibility now that the uneasy consensus which had existed for some thirty years has been shattered. The approach of the Thatcher government towards the NHS is in many ways equally as radical as that of the Attlee government which created it. Yet the initial Conservative radicalism has had to be modified in order to encompass a number of issues which had not been adequately considered beforehand. Any social policy which is to succeed — at least to the extent of being policially acceptable — needs to satisfy the criteria of feasibility, legitimacy and support;[2] failure to satisfy any one could bring the policy into jeopardy. The requirement of achieving an appropriate balance between them almost invariably means that policies are modified to cope with the current political and economic realities.

Since 1979 the Thatcher government's approach to the NHS has been characterised by a desperate search for simple solutions — not *easy* solutions — but solutions which are elementary in structure, uncomplicated to operate and which are broadly concerned with two sets of problems: those concerning the structure, cost and control of the NHS; and those concerning its ideological status.

The purpose of this chapter is to examine the way in which the Thatcher government regards the NHS and the manner in which it has dealt with or proposes to deal with the ever-present problems associated with the operation of such a service and which would exist whatever complexion of government held office. These problems are concerned with cost containment, the relationship between central control and local autonomy, the equitable distribution of resources, efficiency and effectiveness and the consequences of clinical freedom. Additionally in the case of the Thatcher government when they assumed office they had to contend with an increasing demand for public participation in health-care matters, not least as a consequence of the operation of Community Health Councils and the increasing militancy on the part of those working in the NHS. There was, too, a declining economy, rising inflation and an increasing proportion of the GNP being allocated to welfare services.

In addition to these inherited problems and issues the Thatcher government saw the NHS in a significantly different way from either previous Conservative or Labour administrations. With the assumption of leadership, Mrs Thatcher in 1975 initiated a process of transforming the policies of the party, especially those concerned with welfare. In essence they embraced a more rigorous market orientation, proposals for a massive reduction of state activity in relation to both the economy and welfare, and the return of many state functions to the private sector. The NHS because of the amount of direct state involvment became an obvious candidate for early attention.

The Conservative Party Manifesto 1979 made scant reference to the NHS. The brief manifesto was seen mainly as a document listing an economic and political strategy into which more specific policies could be fitted. Certainly, there was no doubt about the increasing emphasis of reliance on the market mechanism rather than government intervention in the economy; an increasing reliance on self-help and a preference for replacing the direct financing of the NHS by private health insurance; in short there was a preference for a 'residual' model or a 'safety-net' model of the Welfare State. So the statement contained in the manifesto to the effect that it was not their intention to reduce spending on the health service has to be taken within this context.

During the period the Conservatives have been in office a number of substantial changes have been instituted or are in the process of inauguration. Some, such as the change from the 1974 structure, were generally welcomed; others such as the proposals for the 'privatisation' of the support services and the increasing use of private medicine as proposed in *Care in Action* rather less. Some of the changes may well be difficult to reverse, and especially difficult if the Conservatives are in office for a third term. It is possible a new consensus could be established, especially if the core of patient care is relatively unaffected.

Financing Health Care

Although the Conservative manifesto stated that any radical change in the method of funding the NHS, such as a greater reliance on the insurance principle, would have to wait until the Royal Commission on the NHS had reported, I suspect this was more a statement of prudential calculation rather than a genuine preparedness to learn. In the event the Royal Commission unequivocally did not think the NHS should be funded by health insurance. The Commission was resistent to suggestions that the free use of the NHS should be restricted to those with income falling below a defined level and argued that partial insurance financing would imply an expansion of the private health-care sector. Such an arrangement would have many of the advantages and disadvantages of a system based primarily on insurance funding. However, the Commission argued, 'there would be a danger of producing the two tier system of health care . . . We would have serious reservations about actively encouraging a system in which the richer members of society received better care than the less well off.'[3]

In considering alternative methods of financing health services two interrelated themes were — and indeed still are — apparent in Conservative thinking. Although these are interrelated they need to be distinguished. One theme is concerned with the belief that health care ought to be treated just as any other item of consumption. The other extols the appropriateness and relevance of private insurance in the financing of the National Health Service.

Within the limits of space it is impossible to deal with either of these themes comprehensively but it is important that the broad outlines of each theme are traced. Norman Fowler stated in his address to the National Association of Health Authorities:

This Government's commitment to the National Health Service is clear and unequivocal. As I made clear in July 1982, we are also committed to the present system of financing the NHS. That statement stands as government policy today. And as you will know, it followed detailed consideration of alternative ways of financing the NHS.[4]

Nevertheless argument still continues within the party. For example, even after the Secretary of State's statement of July 1982, that 'The government have no plans to change the present system of financing the National Health Service', a number of constituency resolutions due to go to the Conservative Party Conference in October 1982 were highly critical of this stance[5] and in the following year the Bow Group published a paper 'Beveridge and the Bow Group Generation'[6] where it is argued that Mrs Thatcher was wrong to promise during the general election campaign that the NHS would continue to be financed in its present form. The paper urges Conservatives to question the Party's commitment to the NHS and consider that the NHS should be financed on the basis of private insurance.[7] So that although ministerial affirmations are made the issue is far from being closed.

The nature of the market for health care has long been the subject of debate. In the editorial of the April/June 1984 edition of *Economic Affairs*, the editor, Arthur Seldon, argues forcefully for allowing market forces to have greater impact.[8] This view has been expressed by many authors published under the auspices of the Institute of Economic Affairs (IEA) and has increasingly come to the fore challenging the consensual approach. The IEA can claim a great deal of the credit for influencing the current Conservative policies towards the NHS.

However, it has to be admitted that an undiluted market approach to the allocation of health care services is not generally accepted. At the core of the argument is the view that the operation of markets is more efficient in terms of an optimal use of scarce economic resources. Arguments supporting this viewpoint in respect of the NHS were contained in the Centre for Policy Studies' publication *The Litmus Papers — A National Health Dis-service*,[9] a document published in 1980, that was widely discussed. An additional element in the argument is that the 'market approach' offers greater choice for the 'consumers' or 'users' of the service. It is perhaps this element of the argument which has gained greater credence within the Conservative Party and that leads on to what might be called the private insurance option which clearly is still a runner in Conservative thinking. But before discussing this aspect, it is worth noting that Professor A.J. Culyer, an economist particularly interested in health economics, after considering what might be called the 'strong' arguments for a market approach wrote: 'The main conclusion is that *health care markets are always and everywhere so imperfect that the marketeers' image of the market for health is a completely irrelevant description of an unattainable Utopia*[10] (emphasis in original).

Quite clearly this discussion cannot dispose of the debate satisfactorily but suffice it to say that although this approach is not dominant it does constitute a not inconsequential rumbling from the New Right within the Conservative Party.

Perhaps of more immediate importance is the Thatcher government's attitude towards private insurance. This topic too has been the subject of much discussion. The earliest of immediate relevance is the Jones Report, *Health Service Financing*, commissioned by the BMA in 1967, and reporting in 1970. The committee included in its membership Arthur Seldon and Sir Geoffrey Howe, both of whom have close association with the recent departure from the traditional consensus of Conservative thinking. This report, although it did not constitute the policy of the British Medical Association, was widely discussed. Here the insurance option for financing health was to be based on a threefold scheme: firstly, a range of services to be financed through taxation and which would be for the chronically sick, geriatric care, the long-term mentally ill and mentally handicapped; secondly, a compulsory insurance scheme covering an 'adequate' service financed on a *per capita* basis; and thirdly, 'superior' voluntary insurance where it would be possible to increase the benefits obtainable through higher premiums. Both compulsory and voluntary schemes would be eligible for income-tax relief and membership of a voluntary insurance scheme would confer exemption from the compulsory one. Although this plan was not established it nevertheless emphasises the persistent interest in various forms of insurance funding. Indeed, during the debate following the publication of the Royal Commission's Report, Patrick Jenkin expressed considerable interest in some form of insurance as a method of funding the NHS. After stating that he did not share the Royal Commission's view about the undesirability of changing the basis of financing the NHS, he continued, 'We believe there could be advantages from changing the basis of financing . . . We intend to carry forward our studies on that in order eventually to make up our minds on the issue.'[11]

Of course, as mentioned previously, official policy did not institute any change in the method of financing the NHS as it would be politically and financially impracticable, certainly in the short-term, but increasing encouragement has been given to the development of private insurance schemes and private medical resources. The Chancellor gave a fillip to such developments when, in the 1981 Budget, he introduced income-tax relief for employees earning less than £8,500 whose medical insurance was purchased by their employers through a group scheme. Additionally, in 1982 the government entered into negotiations with BUPA, PPP and Western Provident Association for group discounts for non-industrial civil servants and in 1983 an explanatory notice concerning insurance benefits that were available was circulated to them.[12] Thus, although the official policy is to retain the system of financing the NHS, it is also official policy to give encouragement and aid to facilitate the development of the private insurance sector — and private medicine.

It is worth asking just why a general insurance model was rejected. Two groups of reasons have been offered: that such a scheme would require a new bureaucratic structure to administer it and the cost of administering the NHS in any case bears very favourable comparison with most, if not all, insurance schemes; and, the difficulty of devising methods of ensuring that those who could not pay for treatment need not do so. These are important reasons but perhaps the crucial factor is what might be called the problem of third-party payments. Neither in the NHS nor in insurance schemes is the patient faced with the full cost of treatment; both, in a sense, are free at the point of use and thus, accordingly suffer substantially from the same defects, as critics of the 'free at point of use' elements in the NHS have so forcefully argued. To reduce the demand for insurance benefits certain sanctions are imposed in the form of co-payments (paying only a percentage of a bill) or deductibles (the requirement of the payment of a given lump sum of any bill) to regulate the market.

Another reason the government has for supporting private insurance is the belief that the extent to which patients use private hospitals and pay-beds is not taken into account in assessing health care facilities. A study commissioned by the DHSS and undertaken by the Department of Community Medicine at Sheffield University suggests that the size of the private sector is such in relation to certain kinds of elective surgery that morbidity studies based solely on NHS statistics in respect of these operations may be defective. It concludes:

If NHS resources are to be distributed in proportion to the need for health care in each region, the allocation might have to take the size of the public sector into account. . . . In some regions, as many as 1 in 5 patients who received elective surgery did so privately; if this is ignored then the remaining 4 in every 5 may be better supported than in other regions.[13]

The equitable distribution of services is part of the rhetoric of all governments and political parties and this policy has been incorporated in the several attempts to obtain regional equity although starting quite specifically with the Resources Allocation Working Party (RAWP) only in 1976. The Conservative administration seems to want to include the resources of the private sector in this evaluation. Indeed, in the policy document *Care in Action* (1981) an innovation occurs with the inclusion of a section encouraging 'a more imaginative approach to the possibilities of planning and providing services in partnership with the private sector where it is economical to do so. Interchange or sharing of private sector and NHS staffing may eventually be possible.'[14]

The increasing emphasis on bringing the NHS and private medical resources together is also revealed in the abolition of the Health Services Board which was concerned with phasing out pay-beds from the NHS. Following the successful election in 1979, Patrick Jenkin, Secretary of State, arranged with the Health Services Board that no further pay-beds would be closed and then subsequently, with the Health Services Act 1980, abolished the Board and transferred all the functions of that body to his Department. The increasing involvement of the DHSS with the private sector is further exemplified by the report in *The Times*[15] that Norman Fowler and Kenneth Clark have agreed to the initiation of talks between DHSS officials and American Medical International, Britain's largest commercial, i.e. profit-making, private hospital group. The private group was considering building new hospitals or refurbishing old ones of, say, 100 beds in return for a 30- or 40- year lease from the Health Service and a contract to treat NHS patients paid for by District Health Authorities. The hospital would also treat private patients. At the end of the lease the hospital would revert to the NHS.

The drawing together of the public and private sectors of health care is also made increasingly easy by the terms and conditions of service contained in the contracts for full-time NHS consultants agreed in 1980. This new contract allows full-time consultants to practise privately without a reduction in NHS salary. They may now 'undertake a limited amount of private practice, receiving professional fees up to a limit in gross annual earnings from it of 10 per cent of their gross whole-time salary (including any distinction award, if applicable)'.[16]

In a variety of other ways the Thatcher government is promoting the private health sector which includes facilitating the development of medical insurance schemes, the building of private hospitals and private nursing homes, not least through aid from the Business Start-up Scheme and the encouragement of partnership arrangements. In a paper circulated by the DHSS to chairmen of Regional Health Authorities in February 1983 they were advised of the many ways cooperation could be facilitated. It opened with the following which seems to epitomise the current government's attitude:

> Although the private sector of health care is comparatively small, the benefits to the NHS of a partnership with it are disproportionate to its size. The development of private facilities draws on other sources of finance and increases total health care provision in the country and, in so doing, helps to bridge the gap between the demand for health care and its supply. The independent sector can relieve pressure on the hard-pressed NHS services, either directly or by allowing the NHS to direct resources to other areas.[17]

Perhaps the really remarkable element in all this policy is the total failure of the government to explore the appropriate balance between the NHS or public sector and private medicine, or indeed whether increasing use of private sector health-care facilities could markedly distort the pattern of provision. The benefit structure of private health-care insurance provides finance for a relatively narrow range of medical services, the majority of their expenditure, at least 60%, so Maynard has estimated,[18] being used to finance what has been called 'surgical running repairs', e.g., hernias, haemorrhoids, varicose veins, etc. Private insurance at present, therefore, is primarily concerned with surgery and has little to offer longer-term medical problems.

Given the nature of the private market it is probable, as Rudolf Klein[19] has suggested, that it would be at odds with any attempts to give equal access to health-care resources and he suggests two policy objectives: that the development of the private sector should not impede the development of the NHS; and that the resources mobilised by the private sector should be additional to those of the NHS. These objectives, he argues, are crucial to an efficient functioning of the NHS. The interests of a particular District Health Authority (DHA) may be at variance with the local private sector; and no responsible DHA, given the nature and variability of funding, could ever tie up its resources with a lengthy contract. This would mean, in effect, that the private sector contract, by its very nature, would take precedence over all other aspects of its work in that it would be difficult to redeploy the resources committed if that were required.

Through a series of relatively small policy adjustments, moves towards cooperation with the private sector are being increasingly realised. There are, however, some areas where undoubtedly the government will be forced sooner or later to intervene. With the expanding involvement of the private sector with health care will come the need for the regulation of that sector, not only in regard to cost containment, which on a fee-for-item basis usually escalates dramatically, but with regard to efficiency and effectiveness of both treatment and organisation.

What does become important if this trend is going to be maintained is the development by DHA members of criteria for incorporating the private sector into local NHS operations. There could be three approaches. One would be to ignore the existence of the private sector entirely, but this may not be politically possible. Certainly, at the moment they cannot control the growth of the private sector and to make any local plans without taking into consideration the nature and extent of the market might be less than prudential. A second approach would be to take into account the private sector and reduce those services where the private sector could operate — something that a recent DHSS paper has hinted — e.g., elective surgery and long-stay care. The local market would have to be estimated and this would involve the NHS in the creation of a two-tier service. A third option might be for DHAs to use a local private sector service for meeting short-term local specific needs, for example, reducing an unduly long waiting list for some disability or condition without the need to employ extra staff, including consultants, who would still be in post when the emergency had abated.

Closer cooperation is being achieved for the most part on an *ad hoc* basis. As McLachlan and Maynard write in the Nuffield Provincial Hospitals Trust Study:

> The challenge is to those responsible in the present circumstances for making the rules and regulations to find the right mix with the right degree of flexibility . . . It requires and one hopes for a coherent strategy from statesmen, who are capable of taking a long-term view of the field and of producing policies which will improve the health of the nation.[20]

In respect of the close cooperation with private health insurance and private medicine the Conservative government has not yet produced a coherent policy. If one believes in a market that is self-regulating perhaps that is all that is required, but very few people concerned with health care would subscribe to that viewpoint.

The Support Services and the Private Sector

In addition to encouraging the increasing use of the resources of private medicine, the Secretary of State has become insistent that DHAs should explore the possibility of contracting out to the private sector a range of non-clinical support services. Initially the letters and circulars from the DHSS were merely recommending Health Authorities to explore the possibility, but with the general reluctance of many to consider this issue the DHSS issued Circular HC(83)18 requiring health authorities to test levels of expenditure on support services by means of competitive tendering to determine whether savings could be made. In particular it requested that domestic, laundry and catering services be treated in this fashion. He also required that a timetable indicating the dates for putting out each of these services to tender (and this could include in-service tendering) should be completed by the end of February 1984. In addition, following the rescinding of the Fair Wages Resolution in September 1983, health authorities were informed that 'In seeking tenders for services and awarding contracts health authorities should not specify rates of pay or conditions of service for contractors' staff'.[21]

Such a move is seen as constituting a threat to NHS staff employed on the support services and has engendered a fear that the quality of these services could be endangered if lower-paid staff were employed. All District Health Authorities are required to do this whatever their own judgments. Already the proposals have created a great deal of uncertainty and unrest, and undoubtedly have affected morale. The full consequences of this policy have yet to be seen. Undoubtedly it does not augur well for industrial relations.

This constitutes an additional way in which the Conservative administration hopes both to reduce expenditure on the support services and increase the involvement of the private sector. Although the government has argued that it will leave the financing of the health service unchanged, the ways in which expenditure is deployed could substantially change the nature of the health service with a decreasing number of people being employed by it. Of course, this activity is not limited to the NHS but extends to services in local government and other public agencies.

In their 1979 election manifesto the Conservatives promised to decentralise the NHS and reduce bureaucracy. In common with all political parties it criticised the changes of 1974 and proposed to review the structure. In his first public statement[22] at the BMA Council dinner a few weeks after the Conservative victory and his appointment as Secretary of State, Patrick Jenkin revealed the guidelines which were to inform his approach. First, he wished to make the NHS a more local service arguing that doctors '. . . do not need the torrent of advice which has poured out of Alexander Fleming House in recent years'. Secondly, he emphasised personal responsibility for maintaining health: '. . . The cardinal principle must be to emphasise the individual's personal responsibility for his own health.' Thirdly, some attention was given to health education and preventive medicine and of the 'joint responsibility of the government and the medical profession to see that people know the basic facts about health', though the degree of commitment to this last point seems to be slight, especially as, when in opposition, the Conservatives deliberately seemed to have no policy on preventive medicine.[23] Each of these points gives a clue to Jenkin's approach and is reflected in later action.

Structural and Organisation Changes

The publication of the Royal Commission Report in July cleared the way for the circulation of the consultative paper *Patients First* in December 1979. The proposals contained in the paper had four main elements:[24]

1. a strengthening of management arrangement at local level with greater delegation of responsibility to those in the hospital and in the community services;
2. simplification of the structure of the service in England by the removal of the area tier in most of the country and the establishment of district health authorities;
3. simplification of the professional advisory machinery so that the views of clinical doctors, nurses and of other professionals will be better heard by the health authorities;
4. simplification of the planning system in a way which will ensure that regional plans are fully sensitive to district needs.

These proposals constitute a profound movement in attitude since 1974. In the 1972 White Paper on reorganisation the emphasis was on central planning with the DHSS preparing guidance on national policy objectives and in this process the Department was to have 'close and more regular contact than in the past with the health authorities . . .'. *Patients First* would suggest a reversal of this policy.

While the consultation process was occurring the government introduced legislation giving it permissive power to make organisational changes. Eventually these were announced in July 1980 and were to be completed by April 1983. The main feature of the reorganisation was the abolition of the middle tier, the Area Health Authorities, and the creation of District Health Authorities, confirming the government's emphasis on the creation of local services, simplification and decentralisation. As the Circular insists, 'DHAs should be established for the smallest geographical areas within which it is possible to carry out the integrated planning, provision and development of health services.'[25]

Another requirement was the establishment of management units for each distinctive aspect of the service headed by a unit administrator, a Director of Nursing Services and a senior medical representative. Each management unit was to have a designated budget. The creation of unit management groups and unit budgets was considered to be an essential element in increasing local responsibility and accountability.

The arrangements listed in *Patients First* were all part of the programme to have decisions taken close to the point of delivery of patient care. These moves, coupled with changes in the composition of Health Authorities by reducing the number of local government representatives and the elimination of worker representation (although one member is appointed from nominations submitted by trade unions), marked a fundamental change in values and attitudes.

The proposals for the use of smaller hospitals as opposed to the large district general hospital which had been an integral part of the planning ethos for a decade or more was also an extension of this policy. Dr Gerard Vaughan, Minister for Health, in the Foreword to *Hospital Services, The Future Pattern of Hospital Provision in England*,[26] explained that although there were often sound medical and financial reasons for building large hospitals, there were telling arguments against them in respect of 'their remoteness, complexity and impersonality and the effect these have on the morale of staff'.

In February 1981 *Care in Action*[27] was published in which Patrick Jenkin outlined the government's strategy for the health and personal social services. The importance of this document as a guide to the government's current general approach is confirmed in the Circular *Health Services Development* HC (84) 2 issued in January 1984 which is concerned with resource distribution for 1984–5, service priorities, manpower and planning where it states that

> *Care in Action* remains the general guide to national policies and priorities . . . Authorities should base their planning on identifying and remedying their own most urgent problems and exploiting local opportunities within this framework. Guidance from the Department with implications for resource utilisation, for instance on levels of provision, should (except where it is mandatory, e.g. management cost units, safety provisions and building cost allowances) be regarded as an aid in assessing problems and ordering priorities, to be applied flexibly in the light of local needs and circumstances, rather than as a constraint.[28]

Care in Action was the third in a series of documents concerned with strategic issues. Two earlier documents, *Priorities for Health and Social Services*[29] (1976), a consultative document and *The Way Forward*[30] (1977), which developed the responses to the earlier consultative document, endeavoured to provide for a national planning framework and the redistribution of resources geographically. They were innovative with the introduction of norms concerned with levels of provision and expenditure *per capita*. Although *Care in Action* continued to give high priority to prevention and services for the elderly, mentally ill or handicapped and in this respect constituted a continuity of policy with the previous Labour government, there were discontinuities reflecting the rather different approach of the Conservative government.

Each of the documents emphasises the importance of efficiency and the better use of existing resources to finance priorities and development but, whereas in *The Way Forward* stress was placed on saving resources by improved or innovatory clinical practices, in *Care in Action* the suggestions for improving efficiency are concerned more with the support services, control of staff numbers, hours of duty, stock control and energy saving; that is on saving in the non-clinical sector. This could, of course, be a tacit recognition that it may be easier politically to reduce expenditure and seek efficiency in non-clinical areas than the clinical areas. Yet the fact remains that consultants are the greatest generators of expenditure. As Maynard has argued the decisions of a consultant in the NHS — and the private sector perhaps even more — cost approximately £500,000 per annum 'in terms of doctor, nurse, other workers, drug and bed time'.[31]

What is perhaps more interesting is that national norms relating to desirable levels of provision and expenditure have been dropped as have the resource and planning targets associated with particular priority groups or special priority services, though both priority groups and services are identified in *Care in Action*. This omission is not trivial; it denotes a substantial variation from previous policy. First, it moves away from a central planning and directing stance and replaces it with general expenditure control leaving it to individual health authorities to determine local need. Secondly, it moves from an emphasis on inputs as indicators of performance in the belief that few additional resources will be available and hence, developments, improvements or whatever must be financed by the redeployment of resources at the local level. Thirdly, it would seem to suggest that input norms give no indication of efficiency or effectiveness. Fourthly, following Rudolf Klein, it may be that the government is following a policy of 'blame diffusion, tending to minimise their own task and to emphasise the importance of local decision making, on the rational calculation that there is little point in claiming responsibility for what will almost inevitably be bad news'.[32] *Care in Action* follows the strategy outlined in *Patients First* of devolution, local control and flexibility, but in so doing there is an explicit abandonment, certainly in the short run, of a *national* policy as opposed to supporting local initiatives.

The Search for Efficiency

An important theme running through *Care in Action*, albeit muted, is concerned with self-audit, assessment, monitoring and review.[33] In 1982 Norman Fowler seems to have derived a number of proposals from it with the intention of achieving increased efficiency. He argued that new developments, especially for the very old, should be financed from 'efficiency savings' which could also be used to contribute to the nurses' pay settlement. In addition, four initiatives were launched: the appointment of an enquiry team to look at NHS under-used and surplus land; to employ six firms of professional auditors to examine the accounts of eight selected District Health Authorities; to introduce a series of Rayner-type scrutinies examining various aspects of the health service; and finally, to introduce annual accountability reviews, with the regions reviewing districts, and the Minister reviewing regions.

In 1983 the quest for efficiency was extended when in February Mr Roy Griffith, Deputy Chairman and Managing Director of Sainsbury's, was invited to give advice on the effective use and management of manpower and related resources in the NHS. The survey was undertaken and the NHS Management Inquiry Report (Griffith Report) was presented in the form of a set of recommendations for management action. No supportive evidence was adduced to support the recommendations. The Griffith Report[34] recommended the creation of a Health Services Supervisory Board and a full-time NHS Management Board. The Supervisory Board would exercise general oversight over the NHS and the Management Board, which would be under the direction of and accountable to the Supervisory Board, would plan the implementation of the policies approved by the Supervisory Board, give leadership to the management of the NHS, control performance and achieve consistency over the long term. The Management Board would be responsible for all existing NHS management responsibilities in the DHSS and all Regional, District and Special Health Authorities and Family Practitioner Committees and other centrally financed services. A general manager was to be identified at each Authority level and would be charged with the responsibility for ensuring that the policy objectives set by the Authority are achieved.

In introducing the NHS Management Inquiry Report in October 1983 to the House of Commons Norman Fowler argued that the inquiry team endorsed the main initiatives that the government had undertaken to improve the accountability and effectiveness of the NHS. Nevertheless it was found that the established form of 'consensus management' (decision-taking on a consensual basis) could lead to lowest common denominator decisions and long delays in the management process. In broad terms the recommendations were to be accepted but the Inquiry Report was to be distributed for consultation. However, it was intended that the recommendation of general management would be implemented, initially from April 1984 but later changed to September in the case of Regional Health Authorities and the end of 1985 for District Health Authorities.

The Inquiry Report generated widespread discussion especially about the concept of the general manager; who should hold this post, or perhaps more importantly from which profession should the manager be chosen; what was to happen to the concept of 'consensus management'; could the NHS stand another reorganisation; and would a general manager impinge on clinical freedom? In the event most of the major professional organisations came out in general support of the Griffith Report proposals which, following consultation, were embodied in Circular HC (84)13.[35]

The development of the management function through the appointment of general managers raises a number of issues which have yet to be clarified. Although consensus management is not abolished how it will operate in relation to the general manager has yet to be explored. It is possible that for most purposes no problems will occur but given the nature of the NHS with its reliance on professional bodies the role of a general manager, although in many respects resembling that of one in the private sector, raises issues which are different. There is, too, a question about the role of the authority member. The references to them are extremely sparse and in respect of the lay member quite inadequate. Lay members do a great deal more than represent 'consumers' interests' — and indeed, in so far as an authority is competent that function is a duty placed on *all* members. The role of chairman has in some senses been involved in a subtle but significant change with more *personal* responsibility is being devolved on the holder of this office. Many of these points have been explicitly recognised and will need to be the subject of further inquiry.

The detailed ramifications of the Griffith Report are not yet clear but certain important consequences are emerging which will undoubtedly affect the nature of the NHS. First, there will be a strong managerial direction of the service coming from the NHS Management Board. Secondly, there may well be a substantial reduction in the nature and amount of local consultation and this could affect the role of Community Health Councils. Thirdly, the chairman is placed in a position where independent authority can be exercised in many ways without recourse to the Health Authority. Finally, with its concentration on efficiency it has little to say about measuring effectiveness of provision. As the report states, 'Underlying all that we recommend is the desire to secure the best possible services *for the patient* (emphasis in original). But the health service is not only about patients but about preventive medicine and positive health.

Nevertheless, it has to be said that many of the suggestions in the Report and changes introduced elsewhere are timely. For example, it is little short of amazing that performance indicators (for all the difficulties in establishing them) were not introduced until some 35 years after the creation of the NHS. Apart from the changes in structure which have already been effected and those which are currently under way there have been a number of *ad hoc* interventions which emphasise the government's determination to gain control over the level of NHS expenditure. These have included efficiency savings, a direct cut in expenditure, manpower limits, more rigorous cash planning, refusal to finance pay increases above specific levels. All these activities amount to a formidable effort to maintain cost containment. This suggests that the Government has in no way slackened its belief 'that the government's top priority must be to get the economy right; for that reason it cannot be assumed that more money will always be available to spend on health care.[36]

Conclusion

This brief survey has concentrated on some of those aspects which are likely to have consequences which stretch beyond the difficulties created by the present economic difficulties. It is all too easy to get trapped into arguments about ephemeral matters, albeit important to the individuals concerned, and ignore fundamental changes in structure, management and attitude which may persist even when the economic difficulties may be a matter of history.

The fundamental changes which have been introduced into the NHS since the Conservatives assumed office have been considerable. Moreover, they have been introduced with a speed and urgency which bespeaks a massive determination to effect change. When one compares, for example, the lengthy debates and consultations which preceded the 1974 reorganisation with the speed and manner in which the 1982 reorganisation was brought about, the urgency to turn the NHS into the kind of organisation the Conservatives wanted is immediately appreciated. What, then, are these fundamental changes? They seem to be concerned with five areas: the relationship of private insurance and private medicine to the NHS; the introduction of competition through competitive tendering in the provision of non-clinical services; the development of new forms of accountability and management control; the development of community care; and what has been called the 'domestication' of health and social care. Each of these changes is firmly placed within the overriding ideological values and presuppositions of the 'New Right' Conservatives, though not all of the earlier aspirations have been achieved. The changes occurring within the NHS have to be seen accordingly in this light and not just as methods of ensuring increasing efficiency and cost-containment, even though these are important. It would have been possible to devise methods of achieving change without choosing those selected by the Conservatives. Thus it is not the fact of endeavouring to achieve essential changes but the methods and values embodied in the making of these changes which is the basic issue. There is nothing original in this viewpoint; any political party would have its own perspective on such issues but for many years it was assumed that somehow the NHS was beyond massive political intervention. As Iain MacLeod, former Minister of Health, reflecting this consensus, put it in 1958: 'The National Health Service, with the exception of recurring spasms about charges, is out of Party politics.'[37] This is no longer the case and a fundamental mistake is made to think otherwise, whatever one thinks ought to be the case.

It was widely assumed that the Conservatives would introduce some form of insurance to finance the NHS but that policy has been abandoned: it was seen not to be 'feasible'. What has not been abandoned is the encouragement of private medical insurance and although such insurance has been primarily concerned with treatment in hospital, Norman Fowler has indicated that he would like to see the development of private insurance schemes involving general practitioners, arguing that it was important for patients to have the option of private, or NHS treatment in general practice as they do in hospitals.[38]

The cooperation with the private medical sector has increasingly been advocated. It is now clearly part of government policy and includes not only the use of pay-beds and the resources of private provident hospitals and nursing homes but cooperation with commercial hospitals operating for profit. This is not the place to debate the relevance of the private sector for the NHS or the appropriate mix of public and private facilities, but it ought to be noted that the particular nature of the market for private medical care could militate against obtaining 'the best medical and other facilities available; that their getting these shall not depend on whether they can pay for them, or any other factor irrelevant to the real need.'[39] If the private sector is to be seen as an essential element of health-care provision supplementing or complementing it — the distinction is important — then policy needs to be developed urgently to determine it nature and size. At the moment no such policy has been developed.

It has always been open for Health Authorities to contract with private commercial firms for the provision of support services and, indeed, a number have done that over the years. The government's insistence on competitive tendering can on the one hand be seen as a drive to reduce expenditure and improve efficiency but equally it can be seen as a deliberate move to reduce state involvement in the direct provision of services. With the repeal of the Fair Wages Resolution, it could be seen also as a move against the Whitley Council system. Kenneth Clark stated in an interview that he would like to see that the whole area of review bodies and the Whitley Council be opened up for discussion.[40]

The change in structure and management arrangements again introduces new elements. It has been argued that the attainment of national health goals involves three factors: equity; professional freedom to practise; and budgeting and economic control. It could be that all three are impossible to achieve simultaneously and that choices have to be made to settle for two of the three. It seems that in the arrangements the Conservatives have made for managing the NHS they have implicitly chosen professional freedom and budgetary and economic control to the detriment of equity. Yet, it could be argued that there is substantial support for equity of provision in respect of the NHS. This comes out clearly in a survey reported in *British Social Attitudes, the 1984 Report* where opposition to a two-tier health service has substantial public support.[41] Nevertheless, the new arrangements seem more a move back to the managerialism of the early 1970s without the strategic planning element.

Community care and 'domestication' really need to be considered together. These require the cooperation and collaboration of local authorities, especially Social Services Departments, voluntary associations and families and individuals. The caring and tending of sick, handicapped, elderly and infirm people in their homes or small community units as opposed to hospitals may have much to commend it but the idea of community care has been introduced without much thought given to the consequences of such policies. The notion that it will reduce costs is on the whole false: what is more realistic is that it transfers costs from the NHS to other budgets such as local authorities, voluntary groups, families and individuals. Also the cost in terms of the effects on lifestyle and life-chances needs to be considered. It could be argued that this in part is an attempt to return health problems to the family and individuals and a reduction of the commitment of the state to assist those in need. This whole area is fraught with grave social difficulties which are exacerbated by the under-funding of local authorities to provide adequate and comprehensive programmes of community care. Inevitably, much of domestic care is undertaken by the female members of the family and it could be argued that the consequences of such policies bear unduly on them.

What is happening to the NHS reflects the conflicts that exist in society. Although many of the changes could be explained by a search for efficiency and cost-containment — and that this is an important element cannot be denied — perhaps the changes reflect the deeper disagreements about equality, class, the role of government and the state. What is quite clear is that the changes that have been made by the Thatcher government are the beginning of an increasingly bitter fight about the appropriateness of the present structure of the NHS, in a country beset with the kinds of economic problem which Britain has to face. The 'feasibility, legitimacy and support' criteria in respect of Mrs Thatcher's NHS have yet to be achieved.

Notes

1. Rudolf, Klein, 'Ideologies, Utopias and the Debate about Health Care', *British Medical Journal*, vol. 1 (1981), pp. 332-4.

2. P. Hall, H. Land, R.H. Parker and & A. Webb, *Change, Choice and Conflict in Social Policy*. (Heinemann, London, 1975).

3. Cmnd. 7615, para 21. 23.

4. Norman Fowler, *Address to the National Association of Health Authorities*, DHSS Press Release 83/114 (24 July 1983).

5. Editorial, *Hospital Doctor*, vol. 62, no. 31 (19 August 1982), p. 1.

6. *Beveridge and the Bow Group Generation*, (B.G. Publications, London, 1983).

7. *The Times*, 'Tory group questions NHS Policy' 10 October 1983.

8. Editorial item, *Journal of Economic Affairs*, vol. 4, no. 3 (April–June, 1984).

9. Arthur Seldon (ed.), *The Litmus Papers — A National Health Dis-service* (The Centre for Policy Studies, London, 1980).

10. A.J. Culyer, 'The NHS and the Market: Images and Realities', in Gordon McLachlan and Alan Maynard (eds.), *The Public/Private Mix for Health*, (Nuffield Provincial Hospitals Trust, London, 1982), p. 27.

11. *British Medical Journal*, 26 January 80

12. NHS Unlimited, Committee to Combat Private Medicine, *Memorandum 6 — The Conservatives, The National Health Service and Private Medicine* 1983), p. 18.

13. *The Lancet*, vol. 11 (14 July 1984).

14. DHSS, *Care in Action. A Handbook of Policies and Priorities for the Health and Social Service in England* (HMSO, London, 1981), p. 42.

15. *The Times*, report by Nicolas Timmins, Social Services Correspondent, 21 August 1984, p. 4.

16. Committee to Combat Private Medicines *The Conservatives, the National Health Service and Private Medicine*, p. 8.

17. DHSS, *Co-operation between the NHS and the Private Sector at District Level* — the full text reprinted in *The Health Services*, no. 50, (3 June 1983), p. 6.

18. Alan, Maynard 'The Private Health Care Sector in Britain' in McLachlan and Maynard (eds.), *The Public/Private Mix for Health*, p. 144.

19. Rudolf Klein, 'Private Practice and Public Policy', in McLachlan and Maynard (eds)., *The Public/Private Mix for Health*, pp. 113–14.

20. Gordon McLachlan and A. Maynard in *The Public/Private Mix for Health*, p. 536.

21. DHSS, Letter DA (83) 40, 22 November 83.

22. *British Medical Journal*, 'Tory Health', vol. 1 (9 June 1979), p. 1522.

23. *The Lancet*, Westminster Commentary, 'The New Government's Thoughts', vol. 1 (19 May 1979), p. 1096.

24. DHSS, *Patients First — Consultative Document on the Structure of the National Health Service in England and Wales*, (HMSO, London, December 1979).

25. DHSS, *Health Service Development: Structure and Management, Circular HC(80)8* (DHSS, May 1980), para. 3.

26. DHSS, *Hospital Services: The Future Pattern of Hospital Provision in England*, a consultation paper (DHSS, May 1980).

27. DHSS, *Care in Action*.

28. DHSS, *Health Services Development — Resource Distribution for 1984/5, Service Priorities, Manpower and Planning*, Circular HC(84)2 (DHSS, January 1984), para. 12.

29. DHSS, *Priorities for Health and Personal Social Services in England*, a consultative document (HMSO, London, 1976).

30. DHSS, *The Way Forward — Priorities in the Health and Social Services*

(HMSO, London, September, 1977).

31. Alan Maynard, 'The Private Health Care Sector in Britain', in McLachlan and Maynard (eds.), *The Public/Private Mix for Health*, p. 160.

32. Rudolf Klein, 'The Strategy behind the Jenkin Non-strategy', *Brtish Medical Journal*, vol. 282 (28 March, 1981), p. 1091.

33. DHSS, *Care in Action*, p. 44.

34. NHS Management Inquiry, *Letter to Secretary of State* (Griffith Report) (DHSS, 6 October 1983).

35. DHSS, *Health Service Management Implementation of the NHS Management Inquiry Report*, Circular HC(84) 13 (DHSS, June, 1984).

36. DHSS, *Care in Action*, Foreword

37. Iain MacLeod, 'The Political Divide', in *The Future of the Welfare State* (Conservative Political Centre, London, 1958).

38. Norman Fowler, 'The Next Five Years' interview recorded in *The General Practitioner* (8 July 1983), pp. 43-4.

39. Ministry of Health, *A National Health Service*, Cmnd. 6502.

40. Kenneth Clark, 'A Conservative Outlook', interview in *The Health Services* (20 May 1983), p. 8.

41. Roger Jowell and Colin Airey, *British Social Attitudes, the 1984 Report*, Social and Community Planning Research (Gower, London, 1984), p. 84.

7 EDUCATION POLICY 1979–84

Peter Gosden

Throughout the period of the Heath government, from 1970 to 1974, Margaret Thatcher served as Secretary of State for Education and Science. Thus when she became Prime Minister in 1979 she was unique in at least two respects: she was the only former head of the Education Department to make 10 Downing Street and she was the only modern Prime Minister ever to have had no experience of senior ministerial office outside the Education Office. Since 1979 there has continued to be a great deal of direct Prime Ministerial interest in education.

At the time of the Heath government Mrs. Thatcher acquired something of a reputation in Whitehall for her success in fighting for and winning resources at a time when the Treasury was demanding considerable cuts in public expenditure. The White Paper which was published at the end of 1972 entitled *Education: A Framework for Expansion* represented a government commitment to long-term development which would involve considerable new expenditure.[1] In a debate in the Commons in February 1973 Mrs Thatcher included among the government's achievements in education a general increase in expenditure, the expansion of further and higher education, special measures to improve the primary schools and to increase the provision of nursery education.[2]

By 1979 it was quite clear that public attitudes generally towards the education service and especially towards the schools had undergone a marked change. In 1969 *Black Paper One: The Fight for Education* was published. The rapid expansion and the reshaping of the maintained school system made some measure of reaction and criticism inevitable, while the political party squabbling over comprehensive schools produced some pretty venemous partisan comments on the education system. The oil price crisis of 1973, and the increasing economic troubles of the seventies, along with the failure of a considerable part of British manufacturing industry, have all served to furnish an audience for the sort of criticisms to be found in the Black Papers. It was in fact an expression of the general loss of confidence in the nation's political, social and financial institutions which has occurred. After becoming Prime Minister, James

105

Callaghan held a series of meetings with senior Ministers about the work of their departments and, following a meeting with Fred Mulley, a request went to the DES from the Prime Minister's office for a memorandum on the state of the nation's schools. Callaghan is said to have been prompted partly by his policy unit and partly by the Cabinet Office in requesting this report. It is interesting to note that one of the Cabinet Office staff, James Hamilton, then moved across to become Permanent Secretary at the DES in time to take some responsibility for the Department's response. It has been pointed out that through one Minister and another, Labour or Conservative, the strategy then formulated in 1976 has been the strategy which the Department has chosen to pursue since that date.[3] The request certainly gave the DES the opportunity it sought to take a much more active and directive part in governing matters concerning the curriculum.

The Department and the Inspectorate between them produced a document, known as the Yellow Book, which was highly critical of aspects of the very system over whose creation they had themselves presided. What particularly amazed others in the education service was that the document distributed blame and held forth on alleged shortcomings without admitting the DES's own responsibility — indeed it put itself firmly among the critics of its own system. The points made in the Yellow Book had an appeal to populist politicians. In the primary schools the time was said to be ripe for a shift of emphasis away from the newer and freer methods. In the secondary schools comprehensivisation had led to difficulties so that parents felt their children were receiving a less rigorous education than would have been the case in a grammar school. Teachers were, on average, below what was to be expected in good grammar schools. Some teachers were putting too much emphasis on preparing pupils for their role in society and too little emphasis on preparing them for the demands of the labour market. Variations in the curriculum were said to be a cause of concern and the time had come to try to establish a common core to the curriculum for all secondary pupils. The Schools Council's general performance was said to be mediocre. The influence of the teachers' unions had led to a greater political flavour — in the worst sense of the word — in its deliberations so that there now needed to be a review of its functions and constitution. Finally

> It would be good to get on record from ministers, and in particular from the prime minister, an authoritative pronouncement on

the division of responsibility for what goes on in school suggesting that the Department should give a firmer lead. `. . . The Inspectorate would have a leading role to play in bringing forward ideas [concerning the curriculum and teaching methods] and is ready to fulfil that responsibility.[4]

In his subsequent speech at Ruskin College, Oxford, James Callaghan, who was certainly alert to the public mood, expressed some anxieties about the condition of education and launched the 'great debate' but his attitude to much of the Yellow Book was moderate and he did not endorse the bid made by the Department and by the school inspectors to give them a larger role in deciding the objectives of education. In its manifesto for the 1979 election the Conservative Party played fully on many of the hostile points in the Yellow Book. The welcome that had been given to this by Rhodes Boyson was perhaps typical of a considerable section of the Party when he commented that there would be 'a great sigh of relief among parents and Black Paper writers everywhere'.

The manifesto complained that the education system was failing even to provide pupils with the means of communication and understanding so the Party would 'restore to every child' the chance as far as his or her abilities allowed. Higher standards were to be promoted in the basic skills. The Assessment of Performance Unit was to set national standards in reading, writing and arithmetic to be monitored through a system of testing. The Inspectorate was to be strengthened to enforce this.[5] Mark Carlisle, the Conservative education spokesman, elaborated a number of these points. Mixed ability teaching would be discouraged and 'setting' was urged as the most suitable form of internal selection to provide adequately for the different ability groupings. Banks of tests provided by the APU would be used to monitor achievement and would give some indication of standards prevailing in individual schools so that remedial action could be taken as appropriate. 'A' levels should remain as 'tried and trusted landmarks in the educational landscape'. 'O' level standards were to be maintained although some reduction in the number of examining boards and the development of a common grading system were to be encouraged. Schools were to be further stimulated by giving parents more influence. Legislation would be introduced embodying a Parents' Charter which would place a clear obligation on education authorities to take account of parents' wishes when allocating children to schools and requiring all schools to publish prospectuses giving details of their examination and other results. The exercise of true choice required access to adequate information. The principle of the direct grant schools was to be restored by means of an assisted places scheme 'so as to ensure that places in schools of proven academic worth are available to all our ablest children'. Moreover LEAs were to have restored to them their freedom to take up and pay for places at independent schools. The education and training of the 16–19 age group would continue to be a main area of concern for the future. The Labour administration had reacted to the problem of the young unemployed with a proliferation of schemes, grants and allowances without any coherent strategy but a Conservative government would review the relationship between school, further education and training to see how better use could be made of existing resources. 'Throughout education, our aim must be to achieve excellence, variety and flexibility. It is standards, not structure, whish should occupy our thoughts, the needs of the individual rather than abstract schemes of social engineering.'[6] The manifesto itself contained the pledge to repeal those sections of the Education Act 1976 which compelled authorities to reorganise along comprehensive lines.

In this approach to educational issues the Conservatives appear to have reflected successfully sentiments which had an increasing number of supporters in the electorate. In their examination of reasons for the Conservatives' victory in 1979, Särlvik and Crewe have attempted an analysis of the various electoral issues and have pointed out that education became a target for those alleging a general decline in the nation in the 1970s. The claim that the change to comprehensive schools had been accompanied by a deterioration of academic standards seemed to be partly backed by the call for a 'great debate' on education and by the revelations of the inquiry into the conduct of the teaching at the William Tyndale School in Inner London. Thus the Conservative manifesto and campaign emphasised standards, quality and so forth. The aim was to emphasise the need to strengthen the meritocratic element in education which Margaret Thatcher had herself upheld consistently in public utterances while at the DES and subsequently.[7]

Surveys of opinion comparing responses to certain questions in 1974 and 1979 showed quite a strong movement of support for the view that 'changes towards modern methods in teaching children at school' had gone too far. There was also a marked increase in support for the proposal that the government should not establish comprehensive schools in place of grammar schools throughout the country. Investigation also found that there was a very substantial correlation between opinions and voting in the case of comprehensive schools. Indeed Särlvik and Crewe commented that 'one entirely non-economic issue, the question about comprehensive schools, also ranks among the issues with a relatively strong impact on voting change'.[8] Thus when the Conservatives came into office there was some justification for their belief that the policy direction they had indicated in their manifesto had a fair measure of public support.

Mark Carlisle was appointed Secretary of State for Education and Science while Lady Young was appointed as the Junior Minister on the schools side and Rhodes Boyson as Junior Minister for higher education. Carlisle proved to be an amiable office holder but no more than that. Rhodes Boyson's public appearances as education spokesman seemed almost to be filling the vacuum left by his senior. In fulfilment of their electoral pledge, the government passed legislation in 1979 which removed the compulsion placed upon LEAs to reorganise secondary schools on the comprehensive principle and permitted them to withdraw proposals which had already been made.[9]

From the start it has been the Thatcher government's financial policy and its views on political economy which have often done more to colour its education policies than specific aims in the education area itself. By June of 1979 Michael Heseltine, Secretary of State for the Environment and therefore an influential voice on educational finance for the maintained schools, had told local authority representatives that curbs on expenditure were not to be considered as a one-off operation but that they must expect a continuing reduction in resources in real terms over the years. It was clear that the police and the probation services were to be the only sacred cows which were to be allowed to graze unmolested. One local authority representative commented after the meeting that 'we are moving into an age of new miracles, when we are expected to run a service and to maintain standards without any money'. The first Budget of the Thatcher government the next week gave substance to those fears for the rate support grant level was to be reduced by £300 million in England and Wales. Since education accounts for rather more than one-half of all expenditure relevant for RSG, the likely consequences were only too clear.

Since the demise of the Association of Education Committees it has been impossible for LEAs to stand together for any length of time or effectively. The opposite political colouring of the Association of County Councils (ACC) and the Association of Metropolitan Authorities (AMA) has produced suspicions and division which have weakened local government in the interests of the opposing national parties which normally control them. Thus the chairman of the ACC local government finance committee reacted to the cuts by looking forward to 'further discussions with government ministers about next year's position generally and in particular about the burdens that have been forced on local government in recent years which are to be jettisoned'.[10]

The new Education Bill was published towards the end of 1979 and was to emerge after some changes in the Lords as the Education Act 1980. It was intended to fulfil in part the promises contained in the manifesto and also designed to meet the demands of some local government Conservatives to remove from them certain obligations to provide parts of the education service. The 1980 Act was comparatively brief but it was a major piece of legislation because of the way in which it affected the relationships between central government, local government, governors of schools and parents. The enlargement of local options, or enabling such Conservative authorities as wished to effect economies by withdrawing services to do so, was to be achieved by withdrawing the statutory requirements of the 1944 Act regarding provision of transport to school, meals and milk. The first of these was particularly important to the voluntary schools whose pupils are often scattered over a much wider catchment area than are those attending country schools. There was strong opposition from the Roman and Anglican Churches to the possible withdrawal by economy-minded local authorities of a necessary element of the historical settlement of the Dual System problems in the Butler compromise of 1944. The opposition to this change was strong enough for the proposal to be defeated in the Lords so the requirements enacted in 1944 remain unchanged. So far as school meals and milk are concerned, LEAs now have the power to provide these if they wish and on such terms and making such charges as they may think fit. In principle the position has reverted to what it was before the Second World War. The only obligations which remain are to provide such facilities as an LEA thinks fit for children to eat food they bring to school themselves and to provide meals for pupils whose parents were on Supplementary Benefit.[11] In one county where the meals service has been ended — Lincolnshire — this last liability has been reported to have been met on occasion by doing no more than giving bags containing buns and apples to the children involved. Finally the 1944 Act had required LEAs to have regard to the need to provide for children under the statutory school age but didn't actually compel them to do so. This had led to some doubt as to whether LEAs really had a duty or only a power to do so. In keeping with its general tenor, the 1980 Act confirmed that LEAs had the power to provide nursery education but that there was no obligation to make any provision for children under the statutory school age.[12]

By way of positive fulfilment of the manifesto, parent members were to be added to all governing bodies and all types of school maintained by an authority were to have bodies of governors operating under instruments and articles of government approved by the Secretary of State. The actual powers of governors in relation to the running of a school were not clarified and the position remains unsatisfactory, providing ample scope for friction.[13] Parents have also to be offered a choice of school for their children and authorities must arrange for parents not offered their chosen school to appeal, if they wish, to specially appointed appeal committees.[14] Perhaps the most controversial section of this Act was that setting up the assisted places scheme to replace the former direct-grant school arrangements finally abolished by the previous government in 1976. These places can only be held at independent schools which have been accepted as suitable by the Secretary of State and with which he has made 'participating agreements'. The assistance is limited to tuition or other fees. it does not cover the cost of boarding and most of the places are in fact in the former direct-grant day grammar schools which decided to become independent rather than enter the maintained sector as comprehensive schools.[15]

The government looked for an immediate return in the shape of a reduction in expenditure from education authorities and the extent of its hopes was shown in the expenditure White Paper for 1980–81.[16] Explaining the education economies inherent in the reduced rate support grant, Mark Carlisle stated that 80 per cent of the reduction would be achieved from the areas of school meals, milk and transport where 'authorities will be given much greater discretion under the Bill which I have presented to Parliament'. In the event the Lords prevented the cut in transport while few Conservative country councillors found that their own electors wanted to end school meals. Thus the required economies could only fall more haphazardly, producing in some places very severe reductions in capitation allowances for books and other school requisites — the immediate impact of which is less obvious to electors than withdrawal of the meals service.

The only aspect of the Education Act 1980 which would require new expenditure was the provision for assisted places. The total cost of this would eventually be of the order of £50 million annually, but in the early years it would be much less as the numbers of pupils in such places gradually built up from the 5,000 or so offered in the first year. That this was the single item in the Thatcher government's educational policy which required and received additional expenditure made the assisted places scheme itself the object of even sharper resentment among local authorities and the maintained sector. The justification for its existence was after all a public indication of the government's lack of confidence in the very schools for which it was itself responsible and which it felt were incapable of meeting the needs of the brightest children at the secondary stage. More generally others have objected to the scheme on the grounds that when the government is cutting heavily into the funds available for running schools on the grounds that the state lacks the means to continue funding the maintained system at the existing level, it is not good enough for it to find also that the state does after all have the funds for a scheme which channels public money into independent schools.

The only other significant legislation undertaken by the Thatcher government in education has been the Act of 1981.[17] This followed some of the recommendations of the Warnock Committee which had reported in 1978 on special education. So far no great progress has been made in carrying through the reforms envisaged. The extent to which the provisions of this Act are put into effect will no doubt depend upon the resources made available.

One of the arguments deployed by the government in reducing the resources available to the maintained sector of education was the fall in the number of pupils consequent upon the fall in the number of live births from the later 1960s. This resulted in a considerable reduction in the number of pupils in primary and middle schools and in the lower forms of secondary schools by 1980. The reduction was, of course, far from uniform. It was most marked in inner-city areas while in some surburban or semi-rural areas some schools were still growing in size. But in higher education the demands of the large birth cohorts of the early and mid 1960s would continue to be felt until after the mid-1980s. Thus any reduction of funding for higher education could certainly not be explained or excused in terms of reduced client demand. Yet the theories of political economy which the Thatcher government embraced apparently demanded cuts in expenditure here. The Conservative manifesto said little about higher education but what it did say appeared to contradict the economic theory to which the party leadership adhered. 'Much of our higher education in Britain has a worldwide reputation for its quality. We shall seek to ensure that this excellence is maintained.' This was the apparently straightforward undertaking given.

From the late 1960s certain officials in the Treasury had been convinced that the cost of running the universities was too high and, as senior civil servants will, they prepared their case and pushed it as and when the political opportunity arose. The arrival in office of the Thatcher administration, with Carlisle as Secretary of State and Rhodes Boyson as the political junior to whom the care of higher education was entrusted, offered such an opening. When the White Paper was issued in November 1979 it stated that an economy of £100 million was to be achieved in higher education. The method was to be by removing an element of public expenditure which might seem to support overseas students. If they still wanted to come to this country they must pay full-cost fees — in the universities minima of £2,000 in Arts, £3,000 in Science and £5,000 annually in Medicine. Similar fees were imposed in the public sector. The withdrawal of government support from institutions whose commitments could not be rapidly reduced as the number of overseas students fell inevitably produced a financial crisis and major disturbance of work in higher education. A strange way of seeking to ensure that excellence was maintained.

The White Paper also stated that it might be assumed that the level of resources for home students would remain constant for 1980–81. This assumption did not extend any further. A cut of between 8 and 9 per cent in real terms for universities was exacted by the Treasury and announced in 1981. The UGC apportioned the reductions among the universities in a letter received by them at the beginning of July. The cuts were to be fully achieved by 1984 and were to involve getting rid of about one-sixth of the total academic staff by retirement or redundancy. The political thinking which gave the Treasury its chance was perhaps revealed by Rhodes Boyson in an address to the Conservative National Advisory Committee on Education at the beginning of October. He claimed that you could not defend student-staff ratios of 9.3 to one in universities and 8.3 to one in polytechnics compared with 13.6 to one in United States universities, and higher still in other countries. This expensive system had been no more than 'the product of prosperity'.[18] One immediate consequence was to reduce the number of student places in universities just as the cohort of over-18s was approaching its peak.

In September 1981 Mark Carlisle was replaced as Secretary of State by Sir Keith Joseph, Rhodes Boyson moved from higher education to be responsible as Junior Minister for the schools and William Waldegrave came in as Junior Minister for higher education. It has been said that Carlisle's faults were his stubborn defence of education in the Cabinet and his inadequate public performances. One Under Secretary said that he was 'decent and polite and he listened to what you told him — you can't say much more of any Minister than that. And in government terms he delivered a nine per cent cut. What did he do wrong?'[19] It is possible that he was simply expendable when his place was needed for Sir Keith who could hardly have continued much longer at the Department of Industry. The incoming Secretary of State brought with him the reputation for being the high priest of Thatcherite doctrine and his speech to the Party Conference seemed to envisage ever decreasing support for the education service. 'More money does not necessarily mean higher standards' and the need to cut public spending to protect the trading base formed the keynote of his address. Yet he is undoubtedly a person with an entirely genuine interest in education at all levels and the only way in which he can presumably square the contradictory nature of his own beliefs is by continuing to try to convince himself that there is no necessary connection between the provision of resources and the achievement of moderately acceptable standards in education.

The problems thrown up by the ill-considered and sudden cuts imposed on universities had not been foreseen by the government. The actual cost of the redundancies had not been allowed for. The total number of students was not cut initially but simply diverted to the public sector so that for the next two years supplementary votes had to be sought by the DES to meet the additional cost of paying for more student grants than had been allowed for in the estimates. Thus not only in terms of teaching and research, but even financially, the cuts of July 1981 were a mess. When the Cabinet agreed to the university cuts it apparently didn't know that the government then had no means of controlling the numbers entering polytechnics and other institutes of higher education. Thus the question of introducing machinery which would give the government effective control over public sector higher education became more urgent.

Following the dropping of the recommendations of the Oakes Committee at the time of the General Election in 1979, the problem of coordination or control over public sector higher education remained. Education authorities with such institutions had claimed the cost of running them against a pool to which all authorities contributed. As part of its programme for public sector economies the government included in the Education Act 1980 a provision which permitted the total size of this pool to be determined in future not by demand but by the Secretary of State — known as 'capping' the advanced further education pool. Local authorities had for many years developed institutions of their own in higher as well as further education and were naturally reluctant to yield control over these to the central government. The DES finally (in 1981) produced a plan to nationalise some 90 public sector institutions including all the polytechnics and to concentrate higher education work in these.[20] Against the background of these ideas the two local authority bodies, the AMA and the ACC along with the Department eventually agreed to establish the National Advisory Body on a provisional basis. Politically this organisation was headed by a Committee for Local Authority Higher Education whose members were drawn from the AMA and the ACC with the Junior Minister responsible for higher education as its chairman. At the lower level the National Advisory Board consists mainly of persons actually concerned with running the polytechnics and colleges of higher education. This provisional arrangement was confirmed in 1984 when a Voluntary Sector Consultative Council was added so that the remit of the NAB could be enlarged to include the voluntary sector and it was renamed the National Advisory Body for Public Sector Higher Education.[21] When the form of controlling body was under discussion, Rhodes Boyson had commented that it would need to have executive powers to prevent uneconomic courses from being established and to rationalise courses. Undoubtedly it has been mainly a successful centralised instrument for achieving economies and it will now be extending its activity to the voluntary sector having within its orbit 400 or so institutions.

For some years the DES had become increasingly anxious to remove the Schools Council which had been set up in 1964 following the efforts of the then Ministry of Education to set up its own Curriculum Study Group to oversee the curriculum and examinations in schools. At that time the power and influence of the education committees and of the teachers' associations had frustrated these efforts and led to the setting up of the Schools Council for the curriculum and examinations on which teachers and local education authorities were represented. Following local government reorganisation education committees had lost much of their influence, the Association of Education Committees was no more and by the 1980s the teachers' associations were also much less influential than they had been. The anxiety of the Conservatives to be seen to be doing something about standards married happily with the desire of some officials in the DES to be rid of the Schools Council. The Department mounted an inquiry into the Council and after careful consideration Mrs Nancy Trenaman who undertook it recommended that the Council should remain but be much reformed. The DES rejected the findings of its own inquiry and Sir Keith on 22 April 1982 announced the abolition of the Council. Neither teachers' nor local authority organisations were consulted. The Council was to be replaced by two quangos whose members were to be appointed by the Secretary of State, one for examinations and one for curriculum. This followed very closely the evidence that Walter Ulrich of DES Schools Branch had given to Mrs Trenaman in the course of her inquiry. There was no careful justification of the new arrangement in Sir Keith's statement; perhaps all was justified by the claim that the costs of the new arrangements would amount to £2.5 million per year whereas the previous arrangement was costing £3.6 million. It should be noted that all the members of both new bodies are nominees of the Secretary of State and this has now become the general pattern for advisory bodies working under the DES. No longer are local authorities, teachers' associations and the like each invited to nominate to a certain number of places on such committees although they can, of course, hopefully send any suggestions for membership for the Secretary of State to consider.[22]

The functions of the new Examinations Council are to supervise examinations at 16 + and 18 + and in particular to ensure that syllabuses and procedures for assessment at 16 + are in accordance with the national criteria approved by the Secretary of State, to approve new 'A' level syllabuses and any revisions of existing syllabuses, to monitor standards and generally to advise the Secretary of State on how the examination system can best serve the needs of the education service. Sir Wilfred Cockroft, former Vice Chancellor of the New University of Ulster, was appointed chairman of the Council and it has recommended a reduction in the number of examining bodies by process of grouping as well as a fusion in title of GCE 'O' level and the CSE to GCSE although the standard of the GCE 'O' level pass is to be recognisably preserved within the new structure.

The urgency and importance attached to examinations as distinct from the curriculum was perhaps shown by the delay before the appointment of the School Curriculum Development Council. This Council was

> to inform itself broadly of what curriculum development is currently going on, to judge its adequacy and to identify gaps and future likely needs, to stimulate within a modest budget work to meet the identified needs and to promote the dissemination of curriculum innovation, whether stemming from its work or that of others, where means do not already exist.[23]

Sir Keith has taken a close personal interest in the membership of both Councils.

Apparent attempts by the DES to assert itself as the political opportunity has offered in the last few years must be viewed against a context in which local government reconstruction, reform and development in the 1960s and 1970s had had the effect of reducing considerably the influence which the Ministry enjoyed in the local government framework which existed at the time of the passing of the Education Act in 1944. The ending of education grants and the various forms of general or block grant along with the reduction in the influences of education committees and the emergence of local authority corporate management practices and of policy and resources committees on the encouragement of the Department of the Environment have all contributed to make it increasingly difficult for the holder of the post of Secretary of State to discharge the duty laid upon him by the first section of the 1944 Act:

> It shall be the duty of the Secretary of State for Education and Science to promote the education of the people of England and Wales and the progressive development of institutions devoted to that purpose, and to secure the effective execution by local

authorities, under his control and direction, of national policy for providing a comprehensive educational service in every area.

In these circumstances it was hardly surprising that during Sir Keith's first year at the DES an attempt was made to revert to paying education grant as a separate block grant. This failed in the Cabinet committee which examined the proposal being strongly opposed by the Department of the Environment. As the *Financial Times* put it: 'Civil servants in the Environment Department argued that the scheme would break up their controversial system of allocating block grant to councils. . . . Control of education spending would pass out of their hands into the Education Department.'[24] With the Treasury and the government as a whole trying to squeeze local authority expenditure, it has created an impossible situation for the education service and, indeed, for the DES since four-fifths of the service over which it is supposed to preside is financed through the general local authority financial system controlled by the Environment Department and squeezed by the Treasury. In those circumstances presumably any education policy directed away from economy and reduction and towards improvement would be bound to fail.

Within this atmosphere of negative constraint it was impossible for the Secretary of State to take even a minor educational initiative with any success if finance were involved. Following the failure of the education grant proposals in cabinet committee, government backing was agreed for a short Bill to permit the DES to pay grants to authorities for specific activities from April 1985. The grants were not an additional cost to the Treasury since their total value is to be deducted from the Exchequer grant before the balance is distributed as rate support grants. Such specific grants are payable from April 1985. The bill was opposed by the local government associations whose main interest was to preserve their complete discretion over the spending of all grant aid but it was welcomed by some educationists. Sir Keith saw in specific grants a way of providing incentives for LEAs to review their spending priorities in the light of national needs and a way of introducing nationwide changes more quickly. The total amount which can be designated in this way is limited to ½ per cent of planned expenditure on local authority education. This would currently produce a figure of about £50 million.

The constitutional obstacle between its Education Department and local education authorities played an important part in leading the government to use the Manpower Services Commission and thus the Department of Employment vote for its major initiative in the secondary curriculum. Conservative governments have traditionally favoured technical or vocational approaches to the last years of school education for a proportion of pupils. In the autumn of 1982 the government announced its Technical and Vocational Education Initiative by which it offered considerable sums of money to LEAs to develop technical education programmes for pupils of 14–18 in secondary schools. In the first year bids for the money were accepted from 14 LEAs, additional buildings, staff and equipment were provided from MSC funds and pupils began their new courses in September 1983. A much wider scheme was launched the next year although a number of Labour-controlled authorities refused to participate and two, Leeds and Kirklees, even withdrew after their bids for funds had been successful. The government has now indicated that it intends in future to withhold about a quarter of the cost of the further education system from the rate support grant and make this available through the MSC. The Commission, it is proposed, would receive bids from LEA institutions and would pay under contract for courses and teaching of which it approves. In this way the government is hoping to cause FE colleges to teach programmes which will be more in line with the requirements of employment. Local authorities have opposed this strongly, believing that their courses already reflect the needs of employment in their areas. The Conservative manifesto of 1983 stressed the importance of raising technical training in Britain 'to the level of our best overseas competitors'.[25] Given the constitutional difficulty of taking any large immediate initiative through the DES which has grown up in the last two decades and the failure of the Cabinet committee in 1982 to resolve the issue, it was only a matter of time before an administration overcame this obstacle by going round it through another of its Departments.

The *Conservative Manifesto 1983* entitled its education section 'Schools: the pursuit of excellence'. Giving more power to parents was the most effective way to raise standards, it claimed, therefore the government had obliged authorities to take account of parents' choice of school for their children, had given parents representation on governing bodies and obliged schools to publish prospectuses and their examination results. The government had also introduced assisted places to send bright children to some of the best independent schools. But the strongest boast of all was that 'This country is now spending more per child in school than ever before, even after allowing for price rises. As a result, the average number of children per teacher is the lowest ever.' The irony that this should be claimed as an achievement by the Thatcher government could hardly be more obvious.

The government's educational policy has been conditioned primarily by its overall desire to cut public spending. The rapid fall in the school age population indicated that here was an obvious area for economy. Yet the attempt to push home these economies through reducing the general rate support grant met with only partial success. The failure to achieve large savings on school meals, milk and transport as estimated has been discussed. The nature of the constitutional relationship has made it impossible for the government to cut the four-fifths of educational spending controlled by local authorities to the extent that it wished. One of the main effects of the policy has been to move more of the cost of the maintained sector from the taxpayer to the ratepayer. In 1978 about 37 per cent of the cost fell on the rates; in 1985 about 52 per cent will do so. An example of the government's difficulty was the 1980 White Paper's projected 6.9 per cent cut in real terms in education expenditure between 1978-9 and 1982-3; the outcome was a drop of only 1.2 per cent in real terms because authorities largely maintained their levels of spending. In 1981-2 actual expenditure by local authorities was 6.5 per cent above the RSG settlement target and the next year it was 4.5 per cent higher. In both years school meals and milk expenditure accounted for some 25 per cent of the overspend.[26]

The considerable reductions that have occurred in the local education services have to some extent been commented on by the school inspectors in their reports. There has been an especially severe reduction in expenditure on books, school library services have been withdrawn in some areas while in contrasting primary schools more classes are made up of children of different ages. An effect of the 1980 Act has been to withdraw minimum statutory obligations so that much bigger differences in the quality of ancillary services have become apparent.

In higher education it has been possible to cut budgets largely as the government wished since universities are directly dependent on Treasury funds and are probably the easiest part of the education service for the government to control as it desires. The 1980 legislation giving the DES power to control pooled expenditure on public-sector higher education and the creation of the NAB has now gone a long way in increasing central control over local authority higher education.

Perhaps one or two of the more impractical ideas of the last few years ought to be mentioned since they have attracted attention even if they have made no progress. Vouchers for schooling of a stated value which parents could use to send their children to LEA or independent schools of their choice appear finally to have vanished from the Conservative political scene. Loans in place of grants for students have also been set aside as being too difficult to introduce and operate in the system as it exists in this country. The most radical suggestion for higher education came from the Central Policy Review staff which, in seeking economies, suggested that all public funding of universities and other institutions should cease, fees should be set at full cost and as many scholarships might be offered by the state as was felt appropriate. The figure of 300,000 was suggested — the current relevant number of students is about 550,000 in universities and other institutions. Loans, it was thought, might also supplement the number of awards. This proposal was quickly put away as being much too radical especially as an election approached.

Thus the Thatcher administration has found its education policies bedevilled by the contradictory nature of its stated aims, to maintain and raise standards on the one hand but to go on reducing public expenditure on the other — with education regarded as an area where reductions can be made. As with other public services, since the government shied away from the radical sort of approaches of its Think Tank, it can only go on lowering the levels and quality of provision as finance is continually pared down.

Notes

1. DES, *Education: A Framework for Expansion*, Cmnd. 5174 (1972).

2. Hansard, 851 HC Official Report (5th series), cols. 47–56 (19 February 1973).

3. S. Maclure, 'Unrepentant Centralist', *Times Educational Supplement*, 29 April 1983.

4. 'Edited Extracts from the Yellow Book, the DES Memorandum to the Prime Minister', *Times Educational Supplement*, 15 October 1976.

5. *The Conservative Party Manifesto 1979*.

6. M. Carlisle, 'Conservatives Hot in Pursuit of Excellence', *Education*, 20 April 1979.

7. B. Särlvik and I. Crewe, *Decade of Realignment: the Conservative Victory of*

1979 and Electoral Trends in the 1970s (Cambridge University Press, Cambridge, 1983), p. 12.

8. Ibid., pp. 169–71 and 262.

9. Education Act 1979 (1979 c. 49).

10. 'Reaction to the Budget', *Education*, 15 June 1979.

11. Education Act 1980 (1980, c. 20), s. 22.

12. Ibid., ss. 24 and 26.

13. Ibid., ss. 2, 3, 4 and 5.

14. Ibid., ss. 6, 7 and 8.

15. Ibid., s. 17.

16. *The Government's Expenditure Plans 1980–81*, Cmnd. 7746 (1979).

17. Education Act 1981 (1981 c. 60).

18. *Education*, 16 October 1981.

19. Ibid., 18 September 1981.

20. DES, *Higher Education in England outside the Universities: Policy, Funding and Management — a Consultative Document* (1981).

21. DES Press Notice 133/84, 'Sir Keith Confirms Future of National Advisory Body', 31 July 1984 and DES Press Notice 134/84, 'New Council to advise on Voluntary Colleges', 31 July 1984.

22. Hansard, 22 AC Official Report (5th series), cols. 429–36 (22 April 1982).

23. Ibid., cols. 437–8.

24. 'Education Block Grant Scheme Rejected', *Financial Times*, 2 August 1982.

25. *The Conservative Party Manifesto 1983*, p. 30.

26. P. Riddell, *The Thatcher Government*, (M. Robertson, Oxford, 1983) pp. 150–1.

SECTION THREE: POLICE AND LOCAL POWER

8 LAW AND ORDER

John Alderson

The maintenance of law and order is a primary task of government. It was made a major party political issue by the Conservative Party during the general election in 1966. In every general election since that time the subject has figured prominently in Conservative Party election manifestos. Many members of the Party were disillusioned following the failure of the Heath administration of 1970–4 to control the unions, the picketing, the industrial violence and the continuing growth in recorded crimes.

As the Conservative opposition launched their attack on the Labour administration of Mr Callaghan early in 1979 they did so against a background of industrial disorder and the growth in crime which had affected the country under previous Conservative and Labour administrations. Dubbed the 'winter of discontent' by the Conservative opposition, the winter of 1978–9 was marked by considerable disruption of public services through strikes followed by heavy picketing, which was often in defiance of the law.

Turning on the government, Mrs Thatcher referred to the situation as a 'reversion to barbarism'. She labelled society as 'morally, socially and economically' sick and deplored the behaviour of the unions particularly the 'flying pickets who patrolled the motorways'. So far as the growth in recorded crime was concerned the Shadow Home Secretary, Mr Whitelaw, was equally vehement: 'A Government that cannot protect its own citizens from attack in the streets of its towns and cities, that cannot protect property from damage or homes from intrusion has failed to line up to the basic duties of government',[1] he said. Given the chance by the electorate in the General Election called for May 1979, the Conservative Party hoped to do better. Bearing in mind that recorded crime had shown a tendency to rise whatever party was in government and that earlier Conservative and Labour governments had both been beset with industrial disputes and disorder arising from economic change, it posed a considerable challenge.

In their manifesto for the general election of May 1979 the Conservative Party set out their strategy for government in a list of five tasks, two of which were directed towards law and order: 'to restore the health of our economic and social life, by controlling inflation and striking a fair balance between the rights and duties of the trade union movement'; and 'to uphold Parliament and the rule of law'.

The question of picketing during industrial disputes has historically given rise to public disorder of considerable proportions. The Conservative Party manifesto included the following comments:

1979 Election manifesto

> Workers involved in a dispute have a right to try to *peacefully* persuade others to support them by picketing, but we believe that right should be limited to those in dispute picketing at their own place of work. In the last few years some of the picketing we have witnessed has gone much too far. Violence, intimidation and obstruction cannot be tolerated. We shall ensure that the protection of the law is available to those not concerned in the dispute but who at present can suffer severely from secondary action (picketing, blacking and blockading). This means an immediate review of the existing law on immunities in the light of recent decisions, followed by such amendment as may be appropriate of the 1976 legislation in this field. We shall also make any further changes which are ncessary so that a citizen's right to work and go about his or her business free from intimidation or obstruction is guaranteed.

This part of the manifesto also promised compensation for those losing their jobs as a result of closed-shop agreements and other safeguards, as well as secret ballots for union decision-making.

On the subject of the fight against crime, the 1979 Manifesto declared:

> The number of crimes in England and Wales is nearly half as much again as it was in 1973 [the last year of previous Conservative government]. The next Conservative government will spend more on fighting crime even while we economise elsewhere.
>
> Britain needs strong efficient police forces with high morale. Improved pay and conditions will help chief constables to recruit up to necessary establishment levels. We will therefore implement in full the recommendations of the Edmund Davies Committee. The police need more time to detect crime. So we will ease the weight of traffic supervision duties and review cumbersome court procedures which waste police time.

'Surer detection means surer deterrence', was the axiom with which the manifesto approached its penal proposals.

We also need better crime prevention measures and more flexible, more effective sentencing. For violent criminals and thugs really tough sentences are essential. But in other cases long prison terms are not always the best deterrent. So we want to see a wider variety of sentences available to the courts. We will therefore amend the 1961 Criminal Justice Act which limits sentences on young adult offenders, and revise the Children and Young Persons Act 1969, to give magistrates the power to make residential and secure care orders on juveniles.

We need more compulsory attendance centres for hooligans at junior and senior levels. In certain detention centres we will experiment with a tougher regime as a short, sharp shock for young criminals. For certain types of offenders we also support the greater use of community service orders, intermediate treatment and attendance centres. Unpaid fines and compensation orders are ineffective. Fines should be assessed to punish the offender within his means and then be backed by effective sanctions for non-payment.

Many people advocate capital punishment for murder. This must remain a matter of conscience for Members of Parliament. But we will give the new House of Commons an early opportunity for a free vote on this issue.

The Conservative Party's proposals to deal with problems of disorder and illegality arising from industrial disputes, and with crime, were subsumed under the three slogans, 'Trade Union Reform', 'The Fight Against Crime' and 'Deterring the Criminal'.

Trade Union Reform

One of the first tasks which the new Conservative administration set itself was to enact legislation governing the conduct of trade disputes and in particular to control the growing problem of mass secondary picketing. The Employment Act 1980, which came into force on 1 August 1980, was described in the preamble as 'An Act to provide for the payment out of public funds towards trade unions' expenditure in respect of ballots, for the use of employers premises in connection with ballots, and for the issue by the Secretary of State of Codes of Practice for the improvement of industrial relations; to make provision in respect of exclusion or expulsion from trade unions and otherwise to amend the law relating to workers, employers, trade unions and employers associations; to repeal Section 1A of the Trade Union and Labour Relations Act 1974; and for connected purposes'.

So far as maintaining the rule of law on the picket lines was concerned, considerable reliance was placed on the effectiveness of the Code of Practice on Picketing. Hammered out by negotiation between the Secretary of State for Employment, James Prior, and the Trades Union Council, the Code did not impose legal obligations. Some felt that to rely on voluntary cooperation was insufficient and others even argued that the criminal law should be more widely invoked instead. In other words more legal teeth were required to check the probelm of secondary picketing. Experience had shown that the police could not effectively enforce the criminal law offences for intimidatory and violent picketing where pickets numbered many hundreds, or even thousands.

The Act provided that some forms of secondary picketing would result in the loss of trade union immunity from civil action. Redress available to injured parties, particularly employers whose trade was damaged by secondary picketing, was provided in the form of an action for damages to be preceded by application for an injunction stopping unlawful picketing. Pickets and their trades union officials who disobeyed the information would find themselves in contempt of court and liable to fines or imprisonment.

In 1982 the new Secretary of State for Employment, Norman Tebbit, put forward a Bill to further control trade union powers and privileges, doing so without consultation with the unions. It was a much tougher and more far-reaching piece of legislation than Mr Prior's 1980 Act. The preamble to the Employment Act 1982 described it as 'An Act to provide compensation out of public funds for certain past cases of dismissal for failure to conform to the requirements of a union membership agreement; to amend the law relating to workers, employers, trade unions and employers associations, to make provision with respect to awards by industrial tribunals and awards by, and the procedure of, the Employment Appeal Tribunal; and for connected purposes'. It came into effect on 28th October 1982.

The 1982 Act introduced novel measures for punishing trade

unions where they were found to have been responsible for breaches of the civil law, e.g., official but unlawful secondary picketing, by removing their immunity granted under previous legislation (Trade Union and Labour Relations Act 1974). Damages could now be awarded against trade unions for action in tort amounting to sums from £10,000 to as much as £250,000. It was to be a powerful disincentive to unlawful picketing. Funds could not only be sequestered but union officials were to be made more accountable for their actions. A further step had been taken towards fulfilment of the intentions set out in the election manifesto.

The Fight Against Crime

On taking up office in May 1979 the Conservative government inherited two important reports which had been prepared at the instigation of the previous Labour administration. The first was the report of the Committee of Inquiry on the Police 1978 known as the Edmund-Davies Report, dealing with police pay and conditions, and the second was the report of the Royal Commission on Criminal Procedure 1981. Both were to figure prominently in the legislative programme which was to follow. The Conservatives had promised full implementation of the Edmund-Davies Report to achieve 'strong and efficient police forces with high morale'. They further believed that such implementation would help to bring police forces up to strength and beyond. The so called 'fight against crime' was seen to be spearheaded by bigger police forces concentrating on the detection of crime.

Within a few days of the formation of the Conservative government, on 9 May 1979, announcements had been made of accelerated pay increases for the police costing some £550 million. This was in line with the manifesto and some six months ahead of the Edmund-Davies Report's recommendations. The question now remained about what the government were to do with the report of the Royal Commission on Criminal Procedure.

The terms of reference had required the Commission to produce a balanced judgment. In his statement in the House of Commons in February 1978 the then Labour Prime Minister, James Callaghan, said there was 'a balance to be struck between the interests of the whole community and the rights and liberties of the individual citizen'. The time had come 'for the whole criminal process, from investigation to trial, to be reviewed with the fundamental balance in mind'.

The Royal Commissioners had not been unanimous, and a minority were clearly uneasy about the extension of police powers and subsequent control of those powers. But they were agreed on the need for clarification of the processes of criminal investigation whilst at the same time removing arrangements for the prosecution of offenders from the responsibility of the police by the creation of a new system of Crown prosecutions. In this way it was felt the desired balance would be achieved. The ensuing legislation, The Police and Criminal Evidence Bill, introduced into Parliament in November 1982 was intended in the words of the Home Office 'to improve the balance of criminal justice and to underpin public confidence in the police'. There was no mention of the important recommendation of the Royal Commission for the setting up of an independent system of criminal prosecutions.The Bill was widely criticised both within and without Parliament. It proved to be one of the most contentious pieces of proposed legislation of the first Thatcher administration. It occupied the Standing Committee in the House of Commons for more than forty sittings and many amendments flowed from the Committee's deliberations. The Bill fell with the dissolution of Parliament for the General Election in June 1983.

Deterring the Criminal

In the run-up to the General Election of 1979 the shadow Home Secretary, William Whitelaw, had declared, amongst other things, that a future Conservative government would introduce tougher measures for dealing with young criminals: a more spartan regime based on the principle of a 'short, sharp shock'. The manifesto had promised considerable changes in dealing with violent offenders and a wider variety of options for sentencing by the courts.

The main thrust of the new Government's penal measures, the Criminal Justice Bill, was introduced into Parliament in December 1981. When the Bill was debated in Parliament fears were expressed that the new provisions could result in an increase in the use of custody for young offenders. But this was precisely what many Conservatives wanted. The Party had always expressed doubts and even hostility to the Children and Young Persons Act 1969 which the Labour government of that time had designed to keep as many young offenders as possible out of custody which many believed only reinforced their criminal tendencies.

The new Bill which became the Criminal Justice Act 1982 abolished imprisonment and borstal training for young adults, and substituted a determinate sentence of 'youth custody' for offenders aged 15–20 years sentenced to longer than four months' imprisonment for offences for which an adult person could be sentenced to imprisonment. Detention Centre sentences were reduced to a minimum of three weeks and a maximum of four months. The original Bill was amended to require that certain criteria, e.g., serious offences, public protection, offender unable or unwilling to respond to non-custodial penalties, be satisfied before sentence. Special establishments were to be designated and equipped for the purposes of youth custody and after some pressure it was agreed that young offenders should not be housed in adult prisons.

Provisions were included for the wider use by the courts of sentences to day-attendance centres set up under earlier Acts of Parliament. Offenders sentenced to supervision could in future have conditions imposed by the courts including 'curfews'. Persons subject to care orders, i.e. children and young persons who committed further offences, could be removed from home for up to six months subject to certain criteria. Parents or guardians were made liable to punishment by fine for the offences of children and young persons. Changes were made in the scope of suspended sentences so that part of a sentence of imprisonment could be suspended. Powers were given to the Home Secretary to order early release in appropriate cases where the offence was not for a serious or major crime, and to reduce the minimum period for eligibility for parole. The Home Secretary, William Whitelaw, said of the new Bill in November 1981, 'I want to emphasise that our objective is to introduce a new sentencing framework for young offenders better reflecting the realities of the 1980's — less optimistic realities perhaps than the ideals on which the existing framework was based.'[2] At the same meeting he referred to the problem of prison overcrowding: 'If the growth in the size of the prison population were to be maintained at past rates the cost of building and refurbishing prisons to provide adequate accommodation for the numbers of prisoners in the system would far outstrip what the nation could possibly afford.' (His successor Leon Brittan in 1984 was to announce a prison building programme costing £250 million.) Clearly William Whitelaw hoped that the Criminal Justice Act 1982 would not only sharpen up sentencing for young offenders, 'reflecting the realities of the 1980s', but that it would go towards reducing the prison population already proportionately the highest in Europe.

Other Legislation

In April 1980 the Home Affairs Committee produced its report recommending the immediate repeal of the 'suspected person' provisions of section 4 of the Vagrancy Act 1824, known colloquially as the 'sus' law. There had been a growing concern among many over a number of years alleging police abuse of powers to arrest and prosecute persons on mere suspicion. The repeal of such powers did not fit into the government's intentions to strengthen the police in their fight against crime and the police, particularly in London, were against its repeal. The all-party Home Affairs Committee's report, however, made out a powerful case for repeal and the government acceded to its recommendations. To give back a little of what it had taken away the Government clarified and strengthened the law and police powers for dealing with attempts to commit criminal offences by steering through Parliament the Criminal Attempts Bill in the following session.

Another importance piece of legislation, The Prevention of Terrorism (Temporary Provisions) Act 1976, which had been enacted by the Labour government when Roy Jenkins was Home Secretary following indiscriminate bomb attacks by the IRA in Birmingham in 1976 resulting in over 20 persons being killed and many injured, was reviewed by Lord Jellicoe at the Home Secretary's request. Unease had been expressed concerning the arrest and detention of people not subsequently charged and of their deportation within the United Kingdom, i.e. to Northern Ireland. After a far-reaching inquiry Lord Jellicoe recommended that the Act should remain in force 'so long as it effectively reduces terrorism, as I believe it does, [and] it should continue as long as a substantial terrorist threat remains'. He recommended that the Act should be renewed annually for a maximum period of five years. The government accepted the report.

These, then, were the main measures designed by the Conservative Government of 1979–83 to strengthen the rule of law, to fight crime and to deter the criminal: a law and order programme of considerable proportions and of much importance. They had also provided time for a debate on the reintroduction of capital punishment, a motion which on a free vote had been well defeated — 362 against, 243 for.

The Employment Acts

The vast majority of industrial disputes carried on as usual without illegality on the picket lines. The Code of Practice for Picketing was generally well observed and gave coherence which was previously lacking. The police continued to enforce the criminal law in appropriate cases and employers were reluctant to invoke the new civil law. In the last six months of 1983, however, in a bitter and protracted industrial dispute involving the National Graphical Association and Mr Eddie Shah of Messenger Group Newspapers the efficacy of the government's Employment Acts was to have its first real test. The secondary picketing of the newspapers' premises at Warrington, Burnley and Stockport, was in breach of both the code of picketing and of the civil law. Mr Shah sought and was given an injunction to restrain the picketing. The union was found to be in contempt of the court order and heavily fined and Mr Shah used the new legislation to claim damages from the union. Union funds were sequestered and in the ensuing claim Mr Shah was awarded a total of £125,000 in damages including a sum of £25,000 exemplary as punitive damages.[3]

During the early stages of the miners' strike which began in March 1984 and in which unlawful secondary picketing was taking place, the National Coal Board sought and was granted an injunction against the National Union of Mineworkers but stopped short of invoking the full rigour of law, seeking no action to enforce the injunction and making no claim for damages in spite of the continuance of unlawful secondary picketing. The government came under pressure to press the NCB to invoke the new civil law but it declined to do so saying that the dispute was a matter for the NCB. In any case the police, with their newly created public order tactics and organised through the National Reporting Centre at New Scotland Yard were holding firm and deploying huge numbers of officers to ensure that miners wishing to work were given protection. After five months of the strike over 4,000 miners had been arrested on criminal charges connected with breaches of public order.

Once again it was left to a small private firm to move where the British Steel Corporation had hesitated. Miners picketing the Port

Talbot steelworks, and using violent and intimidatory tactics against a private haulage firm, Richard and George Read, were in breach of the new legislation. The hauliers secured a high court injunction ordering the cessation of the unlawful picketing which the South Wales branch of the NUM failed to comply with. In the subsequent application for contempt of court the NUM branch was fined £50,000 and sequestration of the union's funds was ordered.[4] In neither of the first two cases brought under the new legislation was it necessary to imprison union officials, thus avoiding their martyrdom, and in both cases the unlawful picketing was halted. The new law was not only beginning to show its teeth but it was able to succeed where the police and the criminal law had, at least partly, failed. As the government entered the Parliamentary recess in July 1984 it could claim that the new laws were at least in part succeeding. The question still remained however that in spite of every cause which the NCB and the BSC had had to invoke the new law the management had drawn back, and many wondered why.

Policing

By the middle of 1981 the government's implementation of the Edmund-Davies Report on police pay and conditions had had its intended effect. Wastage of experienced police officers had been stemmed, police recruiting both in quality and quantity was at its highest since the years of depression in the 1930s. Police morale was higher as the Government made it quite clear that priority in expenditure was to be given to the police over others, including education and other social services. But all was not well in the inner cities where the police were confronting a growing problem. If the government had hoped that the better paid and more numerous police would be able to keep the inner cities' depressed areas under control, they were soon to be disappointed. Perhaps it had not occurred to them that things were coming to a head.

On 10 April 1981 disorders, street violence amounting to riot, arson and looting began in Brixton, South London, and lasted for three days. The Home Secretary moved with speed to set up an inquiry under the Police Act 1964 and asked Lord Scarman to carry it out. As police authority for the metropolis the Home Secretary was in a tight spot. The government and the Conservative Party as a whole, which had set so much store on its 'fight against crime' philosophy found itself facing scenes of the worst public disorder within living memory.

Hardly had Lord Scarman begun his inquiry into the Brixton disorders than further riots broke out in the depressed city areas of Liverpool, Manchester and the Midlands. The consequences included damage to property counted in millions of pounds, hundreds of young people in custody, and many police and members of the public injured. The government were faced with problems of law and disorder which they could hardly have envisaged on taking office. The Police were found to lack the necessary training and equipment for putting down large scale riots and the Home Office responded quickly by making available plastic bullets, CS gas, protective clothing, and protected vehicles. Much now depended on Lord Scarman's report.

The Home Secretary had informed the House of Commons on 13 April 1981 that in setting up the Scarman inquiry he had deliberately widened the terms of reference to go beyond the immediate causes of the disturbances to include the underlying causes. Speaking in the House of Commons on 16 July 1981, he praised the police for the manner in which they had contained the riots by saying: 'It must . . . be my first duty as Home Secretary to reassure the public that the police will have the full support of the government, and the necessary resources, to tackle street violence,' Significantly, he went on to express views about law and order which had not hitherto been part of the government's law and order strategy. 'Many of the young people committing criminal violence on the streets in recent weeks live in inner city areas, which suffer relatively from a range of disdvantages, including serious unemployment over a number of years.' He went on:

> The complexity of the issue has to be recognised rather than reduced to a matter of simple slogans (*sic*). We must, therefore, be prepared to acknowledge some measure of failure in our society, particularly as regards young people. We have to work to minimise the sense of frustration that is evident, and try to prevent it turning into violence.

Nothing like this understanding had appeared in the election manifesto where the rhetoric was much more combative. Lord Scarman's report was published on 25 November 1981.[5] On the day of publication the Home Secretary announced to the House of Commons that the government accepted the general principles it set out for policing policy. There should be more consultation by the police of the public including the setting up of new consultative bodies. The police should be trained to be more sensitive in dealing with people of all races and classes in society, and a new system for complaints against the police should be introduced. Efforts should be made to recruit more policemen from ethnic minorities and racial discrimination and prejudice within the ranks of the police should be declared a police disciplinary offence. The Home Secretary acted promptly to change policing policies in accordance with Lord Scarman's recommendations, though he was persuaded by the police not to make racial prejudice a specific disciplinary offence, believing that the offence could be dealt with under existing provisions. This was regarded by some as a dilution of the Scarman recommendation.

But Lord Scarman had not only focused his attention on the police but ranged widely over the problems of urban decay, neglect, and disadvantage. One of the government's responses was the initiative of the Secretary of State for the Environment to visit areas of substantial deprivation in Liverpool to enquire of the underlying problems of urban disorder. A Merseyside Task Force was set up under the Minister's direction to seek new ways of tackling the inner city problems, and to take account of the need to tackle disadvantage among the ethnic minority groups. When faced with the realities of widespread civil disorder and Lord Scarman's authoritative pronouncements, the government had been obliged to refine their approach to the problem of crime and disorder.

Meanwhile, criminal statistics continued to reveal that in spite of the government's efforts more crime continued to be reported to the police. Serious crimes reported to the police, which stood at some 2.5 million in 1979 when the government took office had risen to some 3.25 million by 1982. The rate of detection of crimes as a proportion began to show a decrease falling to some 36 per cent of the total.[6]

The Prisons

It has often been said by experienced politicians that 'there are no votes in penal reform'. The Conservative Party manifesto had nothing to say on the subject. It should have been obvious however that to increase the numbers of the police with accent on the detection of crime and at the same time to call for more and longer sentences of imprisonment would have a serious effect on a prison system already under great strain. William Whitelaw said that, when he became Home Secretary in 1979, among his objectives was a programme of prison reform. New and improved penal establishments and a strengthened prison service with high morale and improved management, together with a more rational use of custody as a punishment appeared to be among his hopes. In October 1980 he faced a prison officers' dispute which was to last until February 1981. The prison officers working to rule virtually brought normal operations to a halt and the refusal to admit prisoners above the numbers for which a prison was certified produced an unprecedented prison crisis. The Home Secretary sought and was given exceptional powers by Parliament. These included power to release prisoners before expiry of sentence or awaiting trial and to prohibit the use of imprisonment by the courts for non-payment of money, powers which he did not use. Police cells were full to overflowing and there was great concern about the effect of the strike on the humane treatment of the prisoners. It is important to note, however, that although the prison population fell by over 4,000, there was no noticeable, or at least no measurable, impact on crime — a fact which prison reformers were quick to point out. As the prison officers' strike was resolved the Home Secretary still faced the inevitable problem of prison overcrowding. In May 1983 he was able to claim an increase of 2,000 more places in prisons with 3,000 more in the pipeline. Capital expenditure had doubled, four new prisons were under construction and six more being planned. The numbers of prison officers had or would increase by 15 per cent. In his own words: 'If the prison population remained at the present level we should, given the continuation of the present programmes, and the substantial numbers of additional staff crack the overcrowding problem 10 years from now.'[7] As the 1983 election was called, the prison crisis was still a problem for the Government with over 45,000 inmates and no end to the increase in sight.

The 1983 Election Manifesto

Under the heading 'Law, Democracy and The Citizen', the Conservative Party manifesto still spoke of 'the war against crime' and listed its achievements. 9,000 extra police and more if needed —

better paid and equipped than ever before. More police back on the beat and a claim that street crime was being reduced and public confidence improved in some of the worst inner-city areas.

The Police and Criminal Evidence Bill would 'help the police to bring criminals to justice' whilst laying down rules for the proper treatment of suspects. It was promised that more courts would be built. The Criminal Justice Act 1982 had provided the promised flexibility in sentencing powers and further attendance centres for 'young hooligans' were to be provided. The prison building programme under way would provide 4,800 more places and increases in staff would be implemented. The Party also committed itself to the setting up of an independent prosecution service which it had failed to do during its first term in office.

So far as the Employment Acts were concerned, it was pointed out that they were succeeding in their purpose and that further legislation was to follow concerning secret ballots for the appointment of officials, consideration of trade union levy for political funding and a curb on the legal immunity of unions to call strikes without a secret ballot. The Merseyside Task Force operation following the riots of 1981 was claimed to be a success and a model for further similar initiatives in inner cities.

In his first year of office as Home Secretary, Leon Brittan published a working paper entitled 'Criminal Justice' in which he set out the Governments initiatives. Giving evidence to the House of Commons Home Affairs Select Committee on 23 January 1984 Leon Brittan said, 'on taking office I decided that we needed a strategy which would enable us to establish and pursue priorities and objectives in a deliberate and coherent way. Such a strategy is now in place.' The document sets out for the first time a comprehensive statement of the interdependence of all the facets of the system of criminal justice and the prevention of crime. The Home Secretary stressed that his policy had three main themes: public confidence; efficiency and effectiveness; balance. The strategy with its three main themes, it was said, 'represents a coherent approach to the problem of crime, and a commitment to action. This was to be the direction in which the Home Office would go forward under the new Conservative government.' In his first speech as Home Secretary at the Conservative Party Conference on 11 October 1983, Leon Brittan reminded his audience of some of the Conservative government's achievements. 10,000 more police officers, more officers on the beat, community policing schemes, all of which he believed 'is likely to have a far greater impact on crime as it affects *most* people than any changes in the sentencing pattern'. However he went on to stress that life sentences 'may indeed mean life'. He would not authorise release even after 20 years if such a release posed a risk to the public. For certain kinds of murders, i.e. of a police or prison officer, terrorists, sadistic child murders, and murder by shooting during robbery, no less than 20 years would be served. This brought him into conflict with the Parole Board who felt that their own role was being usurped without being consulted. He also promised to get some of the inadequates and drunks out of the prison system, and to reduce the period of imprisonment from one year to six months for consideration of parole. These measures, he hoped, would help to reduce the prison population.

The much publicised Police and Criminal Evidence Bill introduced by his predecessor would be reintroduced with important changes. The critics of the original Bill considered that police powers to arrest, detain, and search and seize all manner of confidential documents from doctors, social workers and others were much too sweeping. Further criticism had been levelled at the length of time persons could be kept in police cells without charge and to a widening of police powers to stop, search and detain suspects. He later announced that the recommendation of the Royal Commission on Criminal Procedure, that a prosecution service independent of the police be set up, would become the subject of a Bill. Experiments were also continuing in the use of tape recorders during police interrogations. Safeguards for innocent but suspected members of the public would be strengthened through a new Code of Police Practice. Hardly had the new government had time to put forward its unfinished legislative programme than a widespread dispute affecting the mining industry broke out in March 1984. With a large majority of the miners on strike but a significant minority at work the scene was set for a major disruption. As the dispute continued without solution there were scenes of violence and disorder both on the picket lines and elsewhere. Within a few months over 5,000 miners faced criminal charges as the newly equipped and organised police support units were transferred to troubled areas from elsewhere. It was the most serious threat to public order to face the government for ten years. But whereas the miners' strikes and mass secondary picketing during Edward Heath's period as Prime Minister in the early 1970s had found the police both tactically and strategically lacking, the new operational deployment from the

National Reporting Centre at New Scotland Yard enabled Mrs Thatcher's government to ride out the storm more successfully. It soon became clear, however, that whilst the new police stategies might contain the situation at considerable cost, no solution to the fundemental problem was to accrue.

Conclusion

There can be no doubt that the government's promised legislative programme as set out in its 1979 General Election manifesto and to a lesser extent the manifesto of 1983 have been largely carried out. The Employment Acts 1980, 1982 and 1984 have done much to denude the trade unions of much of their power and influence. It is true that the TUC, having lost its right under a convention of consultation directly with the Prime Minister, withdrew some of its participation in industrial affairs. On the other hand where the threat of sequestration of union funds hangs over each union it has done much to curb secondary picketing in small scale disputes. Private employers have used the new laws successfully on at least two occasions. On the other hand, where the disputes have affected nationalised industries such as the coalfields and steel there has been a nervousness and hesistancy about invoking the new powers. The criminal courts have, therefore, become very busy as ordinary union members are caught up in picketing, assembling and travelling, but the union officials and their funds have not been made subject to the new civil law. Perhaps the lesson is that, if sufficient people with sufficient determination defy the law and the police, neither the criminal nor the civil law offer a complete solution. That has to be found in other avenues.

The government's promise to raise the strength and quality of the police has undoubtedly been fulfilled. With over 10,000 more officers, better equipped police forces and units highly trained in public order duties have resulted from government policies. Where cuts have been made in other services the expenditure on the police has risen from some £1 billion to over £2½ billion.[8] As the 1979 manifesto recorded, 'The next Conservative government will spend more on fighting crime even while we economise elsewhere'.

Expenditure on the prison service has likewise increased dramatically from some £200 million to over £600 million, and capital building programme for prisons is the most extensive this century, amounting to some £250 million at current prices over the next seven years. The prison population in 1979 was 42,200, in 1983 43,500 and a steady increase is projected. With more crime being committed and a more efficient police, plus greater use of penal custody, these facts may well ensure that Britain will continue to house a larger prison population *per capita* than most European countries. It is hoped at the Home Office however that the admitted appalling prison overcrowding will be considerably eased.

It is difficult, if not impossible, to measure the success of the government's law and order programme against the events which have occurred during their term of office since some events might have occurred in any case. It can be pointed out, however, that the inner-city riots of 1981 and the miners' dispute of 1984 have provided spectacles of anything but law and order. Similarly the criminal statistics show that recorded crime continues to rise with the occasional levelling out before rising again. Britain, as well as some other western countries, still awaits deliverance from morbid levels of crime and the prospects of spasmodic disorder on a wide scale.

Notes

1. *The Guardian*, 1 June 1983.

2. William Whitelaw, Home Secretary, in his speech to the Annual General Meeting of the National Association for the Care and Resettlement of Offenders, 10 November 1981.

3. Raymond Hughes, Law Courts Correspondent of the *Financial Times*, 31 July 1984.

4. Editorial assessment, *The Times*, 31 July 1984.

5. Lord Scarman, *The Brixton Disorders: 10–12 April 1981* (HMSO London, November 1981).

6. Home Office Criminal Statistics, HMSO 1982.

7. William Whitelaw, 'Prisons: No Easy Way Out', *The Times*, 5 May 1983.

8. Home Office, 'Criminal Justice — A Working Paper', May 1984.

9 THE CONSERVATIVES AND LOCAL GOVERN- MENT, 1979 AND AFTER

Mike Goldsmith

Since the return of a Conservative government led by Mrs Thatcher in 1979, local government has been at the very centre of the political stage, higher on the political agenda than at any other time this century. Debates on local government have frequently made front page news; television programmes have been devoted to the subject, and whole page advertisements defending local government have appeared in prestigious journals. Ministers and local politicians have accused each other of bad faith and even worse practice; academics and public lawyers have claimed that the constitution is threatened and that important liberties are at stake.

But throughout most of this century, and arguably throughout its history, local government in Britain has received little attention and has consistently been regarded as an administrative backwater, largely concerned with the delivery of a number of relatively minor local services, an agent of central government with only limited discretion over what it did. What has brought about the change, and why has local government become one of the most politically sensitive issues of the 1980s?

The answers to these questions lie in the kind of changes associated with the growth of Welfare State services generally in Western developed societies and in the stresses and strains which this growth has placed upon governments, especially in terms of their ability to finance an ever increasing level of service. These strains have been made particularly severe by the deep recession which Western countries have experienced since the mid-1970s. The stresses and strains gave rise to what O'Connor called 'the fiscal crisis of the State', a crisis which Britain shared along with other Western European countries and with the United States.[1]

The crisis in Britain, however, was in some respects both more severe, and further aggravated by some of the policies adopted to deal with them. And, as far as Welfare State services were concerned, local government in Britain was at the centre of the crisis. The reason for this lies in the very large part which local government in Britain plays in the delivery of governmental services, a part far larger than its counterpart elsewhere. By any criteria, local government in Britain is large: local authorities are large in area terms: the Highlands Region of Scotland is 9,700 square miles, almost as large as Belgium. They are larger in population terms: the Greater London Council area has just under seven million residents. There is nothing like the small French *commune* to be found in Britain. And in expenditure terms, they are massive. In 1981 local government spent £33.5 billion, more than the GDP of Norway. Local government also provides a wider range of services than does local government elsewhere in the West, being responsible for everything except defence, health and water. Whilst central government provides a large part of the money to pay for these services, it does little by way of service provision: it has never built a house, taught a pupil or run a bus, for example.

Strange though it may seem in the light of subsequent parts of this chapter, the large part which British local government has come to play in service provision owes much to the reforms of local government associated with previous Conservative governments. For example, the current Minister for education, Sir Keith Joseph, piloted the legislation which brought the GLC into existence in 1963. Twenty years on, he is a supporter of that body's proposed abolition. And it was Mr Heath's government in 1972 which created the system of large local authorities which we know today: authorities created very much in the name of functional efficiency which was one of the early hallmarks of that administration. And it is Mr Heath, Mrs Thatcher's defeated opponent for the party leadership in 1975, who backed much of the opposition to the proposed abolition of the GLC and the introduction of rate-capping.

Despite this oddity, however, it was the Labour government of 1974–9 which started the process of retrenchment and cutback in local government expenditure and which, in a variety of ways, sowed the seeds for the subsequent conflict between centre and locality. Faced in 1976 with an economic and financial crisis of enormous properties, the Labour government was forced to call in the IMF for assistance, and the price imposed by the latter was severe cuts in both the planned and actual levels of public expenditure in Britain. Given the share of public expenditure which British local government takes, it was inevitable that the expenditure cuts would fall most heavily on local authorities, a policy which was reinforced by the introduction of artificially low cash limits on public expenditure increases, which ensured that the actual 'increases' were well below the level of inflation.

Until June 1979, when the General Election intervened, the Labour government's policy worked. Public expenditure was held in check: local government's share of it fell and was on target. For example, in 1974–5, local government expenditure accounted for 15.9 per cent of GDP and 32.2. per cent of all public sector expenditure. By 1978–9, it had fallen to 12.8 per cent of GDP and 28.3 per cent of public-sector expenditure, a significant drop. In terms of targets, local government was 0.3 per cent overspent in 1975–6, and only 1.8 per cent in 1978–9, after four successive years of reducing expenditure. It was this situation which the Conservatives inherited after the June election. As a specific issue local government and its future had not featured strongly in the Conservative manifesto and its campaign during the election. Admittedly in 1974 Mrs Thatcher had committed the party to abolishing the rates (unwisely as subsequent events have shown), but no such explicit commitment was made in 1979, nor was anything said about reforming the structure of local government. The process that brought the new Conservative government into conflict with the localities was much more indirect, and in practice much of what the government has done in policy terms has been as much a consequence of its policies and priorities in other directions as it has been a direct policy commitment to doing something about local government in general.

In the first place, the new government's commitment to reductions in public expenditure, as required by its adherence to monetarist philosophy, brought it directly into conflict with local government. Given other priorities as well, such as the commitment to increase defence expenditures, and the fact that central government actually directly spends very little itself on Welfare State services, a commitment to reduce public expenditure in effect meant reducing expenditure on those services by and large controlled by local government. Of all the main services such as education, housing, transport and health, only the latter is not within the responsibility of local authorities. Inevitably, therefore, a policy of public expenditure reductions meant reducing local government expenditure.

But the new Conservative government also had other objectives which ensured that local authorities would find themselves under pressure on fronts other than the expenditure one alone. The Conservatives' concern to reduce the *scope* of government, as part of its social market philosophy, as well as its enthusiasm for the operation of market forces and is commitment to the privatisation of much of the state sector, all meant that services provided by local government could expect to be reviewed and revised. Mrs Thatcher's belief in the Victorian virtues of self-help and self-reliance also ensured a personal commitment on the part of the Prime Minister. If 'rolling back the Welfare State' meant an inevitable reduction in the status and importance of local government, then such a consequence was seen as a small price to pay if other, more important, central objectives would be achieved.

In seeking to achieve these objectives the new government found itself with a number of willing allies from the ranks of the main government departments. Ministers and their supporters seeking one set of objectives based on their political ideology and programme found partners amongst many of the civil servants in the main spending departments, but overwhelmingly they had the support of the Treasury, which had been seeking to reassert its control over local government spending over since it had soared ahead during the early expansionist years of the Heath government almost a decade earlier. In other words, as has been argued elsewhere,[2] there were other forces at work within the centre which also sought greater control over local government, particularly in the Treasury, but also in some of the service departments. During the late mid-1970s in areas like planning, housing and transport, and to a lesser extent in health and social services, the functional departments had introduced a series of policy planning systems, which, established under the guise of increasing local autonomy, had in practice increased central control over what local authorities did in these areas through use of central powers of approval for plans and of appropriate financial incentives to see that central government policy priorities were followed.[3] With the introduction of the Consultative Council over Local Government Finance in 1975, the Treasury had reestablished some degree of control over local government expenditure planning and had succeeded in divorcing the local authority associations, the representatives of local government at the centre, from their members.[4] The election of the Conservative government in 1979 thus forged what has been called 'an unholy alliance' between politicians and bureaucrats at the centre, concerned once and for all to reduce local government back to its former status of 'low politics'.[5]

In practice, this change of status has proved difficult to achieve, not least of all because of other changes, some in local government, some in the economy, which have made the government's target of reducing public expenditure difficult, if not impossible. As far as the economy is concerned, some of the government's policies aggravated rather than improved the situation. This effect was particularly noticeable in the early 1980s, when Britain was faced with the twin evils of rising unemployment and double-digit inflation, from which some critics have argued that it is doubtful whether she will ever recover, even though recently inflation has fallen and employment levels improved slightly. But the effect of rising unemployment has been to increase the contribution made to public expenditure by social security payments to the unemployed. These, together with planned increases in defence and polie expenditures, have helped to maintain public expenditure at high levels, with the result that the Conservatives have been less successful in reducing public expenditure overall than their Labour predecessors. But it has also meant that those reductions that have occurred in public expenditure have fallen most heavily on those services provided by local government. The result has been constant pressure on local government since June 1979 on all fronts, climaxing in 1984 with the government's legislation to introduce rate capping and to abolish the GLC and the Metropolitan Counties.

It is in this context of constant pressure to reduce local government expenditure that local government has had to operate, and it is in order to achieve this objective that central government has devised a range of different strategies. Faced with legislation designed to give each authority an expenditure target (itself changed frequently), together with sanctions for overspending, and then with legislation designed to limit the amount of income they can raise from their own souces (i.e. the rates, or local property tax), local authorities have had to operate in an environment whose key feature has been uncertainty, and one which not only Labour but also many Conservative-controlled authorities have felt to be a hostile one. As a result, local budgetary and service policy decisions have become increasingly difficult to make, and some Labour controlled authorities, particularly the GLC and some other London boroughs, together with cities such as Sheffield, Liverpool and Newcastle, have adopted policies which bring them into direct confrontation with the government.

Nevertheless, it is also correct to say that many Conservative-controlled authorities have followed government policy guidelines, and that these authorities constitute by far and away the large majority of all local authorities in Britain. Such a result is to be expected: most local authorities of a partisan nature are Conservative, those controlled by Independents are not generally heavy-spending authorities, and local authorities have traditionally accepted the idea that they should follow the broad guidelines laid down by government economic and service policies. What has been increasingly resented by authorities of all political hues has been central government's increasing involvement in the details of policy which traditionally have been left to the discretion of individual authorities to decide for themselves.

Such intervention is not solely the prerogative of the present Conservative government: most of the bureaucratically inspired planning systems, from the 1968 land use planning legislation through to the 1978 housing investment programmes, were introduced by Labour governments. Such changes were introduced with the symbolic claim of increasing local autonomy: detailed control followed later, as these planning systems became routine bid-allocation processes, under which local authorities sought support for particular proposals, and the centre approved (and allocated funds for) those proposals which fitted its own predispositions. For example, allocations for and approval of housing investment programmes (HIPs) have frequently been linked either to the selling of public housing or to the levels of rent for such housing. Since many of these planning systems apply to policy areas involving capital expenditure, they have become easy targets for cutbacks and control as the centre has sought to reduce local government expenditure. All commentators agree that central government control over local authority *capital* expenditure has been and is (and probably always will be) total.

Even though the process of *detailed* control and intervention began with Labour governments, undoubtedly the increase in hostility between centre and locality dates from the 1979 election of a new Conservative government, one attached to new and radical ideas generally known as the New Conservatism, and led by a skilful and determined leader. Given the immediate priority of reducing public expenditure, as well as previous commitments to reform local government finance, local spending became an immediate target.

At this point, the government and, perhaps more specifically, its advisers from the Treasury, made what might be regarded with hindsight as a major tactical error. Rather than simply reducing the *overall* level of support given by the centre towards local *current* expenditure, a tactic employed by the former Labour government with little opposition from local government, the government decided to introduce a new grant system which would effectively allow it to control the expenditure of each and every local authority, a change achieved with the introduction of the Local Government, Land and Planning Act 1980. This change, with the associated expenditure targets and sanctions (withdrawal of grant) that accompany it, aroused tremendous opposition amongst local authorities, many of whom still do not accept it. Yet the need for change in the grant system was not unsupported, even from within local government itself, for the old system was largely incomprehensible to anybody outside the actual grant negotiators themselves and it was particularly felt to favour high spending authorities: the more such authorities spent the more they were likely to receive higher levels of grant.[6]

The government accepted the proposal for a new grant system because it believed it would bring down local government expenditure, something which in 1979 they saw as a top priority in their attempts to reduce public expenditure overall. Yet the new system was far from foolproof, and, in its initial stages, lacked sufficient strength to contain local expenditures.

First, for example, the Government gave local authorities expenditure targets on its assessment of their expenditure needs — the grant related expenditure assessment or GREA as it is known. Faced with the fear that previously underspending local authorities (i.e. those spending below GREA) would now increase their spending *up* to their GREA targets, whilst at the same time knowing that some of the Labour-controlled overspending authorities would not *reduce* their expenditure to target levels, the Department of the Environment was obliged to give local authorities another expenditure target, based on the 1979 total volume of expenditure. The government feared that a combination of underspending local authorities spending up to GREA and overspending authorities refusing to reduce expenditure would result in an increase in the overall level of local government expenditure, which was precisely the opposite of what was intended. Faced with new spending targets half way through the financial year, local authorities faced even more confusion, uncertain as they were as to which target was the most appropriate for them to pursue.

Overspending authorities reluctant to reduce expenditure settled for a variety of strategies, most of which provoked central government into retaliatory action. Some authorities drew heavily on their reserves, others resorted to other strategies known generally as 'creative accountancy': creating special accounts, capitalising expenditure ansd so on. Other authorities chose to raise the rates, by levying a supplementary rate.

Making the financial targets more severe and turning its attention to the income side of the income-expenditure equation became the next moves adopted by the government. The latter move was designed to stop authorities from raising local taxes, which would lead to expenditure reductions automatically, since British local authorities cannot run defecits from one financial year to the next. British local authorities have only one independent source of income, property taxes, but they have had the power to levy such taxes for almost 400 years. Mrs Thatcher's government decided to limit this power, first by abolishing local authorities' power to have a second bite at the local tax cherry by levying supplementary rates (which the government did in 1982 by legislation) and second, by taking powers through further legislation to limit the level at which individual authorities can set rates each year.

This latter proposal, introduced in legislation in the 1983–4 session, is best seen as a measure adopted by the Conservatives not only to force further expenditure reductions by (particularly) high spending authorities (nearly all Labour controlled), but it is also designed to encourage local authorities to minimise increases in taxation levels, for fear of the sanctions which might otherwise be imposed. The legislation produced widespread opposition, particularly amongst the local authority associations, and included many stongly controlled Conservative authorities, who saw this 'rate-capping' legislation as an unwarranted (and unconstitutional) intrusion on their traditional right to set their own levels of taxation. Yet the central government could (and did) justify its proposals as being in the interest of protecting local taxpayers,' particularly the 'disenfranchised' taxpayers, namely business and commerical companies whose owners were not resident in the authority. Such ratepayers have no 'democratic' voice (vote) in local politics, though their influence on local authority decision making has been considerable on more than one occasion.[7]

Whatever the merits of this argument, the government found itself with the largest backbench revolt since 1945 on its hands, including a former Conservative Prime Minister and several former

Thatcher government Ministers amongst its ranks, and, as a result of the opposition both inside and outside Parliament, the Minister concerned with seeing the legislation through Parliament was forced to make concessions (albeit limited) to his general powers to set local tax levels.

The overall result of both the rate-capping legislation and the use of expenditure targets has been to give central government — in theory at least — virtually total control over the level of current income and expenditure of every local authority in the country, control equal to that which the centre exerts over local authorities' capital expenditure. But it is a control which the centre will find difficult to exercise in practice, especially if individual authorities decide on a policy of confrontation with the government.

The most drastic of these confrontations to date has been occasioned by Liverpool's refusal to accept expenditure cuts and to increase local taxes, and by the Labour council's determination to fix an illegal deficit budget. The City had been particularly hard hit by reductions in central government grants and by the fact that previous non-Labour administrations had cushioned local tax increases by using financial reserves to balance their budgets. Yet the City has one of the higest rates of unemployment, some of the worst housing and derelict areas in the country, together with all the associated social problems such as high rates of crime and drug addiction. The Minister responsible threatened to send in independent commissioners to run the City's services and to introduce the necessary cuts in both services and jobs. The game of threat and counterthreat continued long after the budget should have been set. The Labour party increased its majority on the Council after the May 1984 elections: the Minister, through his own and regional officials, sought to compromise, whilst still waiting to see whether the authority would fix an appropriate, balanced budget. In the end, both sides effected a compromise. The government, by agreeing to increase some of its special grants to the city, found another £6 million: the Labour council agreed to an increase in rates, but to a much lower level than that which the original expenditure reductions expected by the government would have meant. Both sides claimed victory in the dispute, but honour was saved, especially for the local authority. The dispute had lasted six months: such a confrontation, if repeated on anything like the same scale with more than a few authorities, would make a nonsense of the idea that the centre could actually control the income and expenditure of each and every locality. If Scottish experience is any guide,[8] arguments about rate levels, targets and so on would embroil the centre in a level of detail from which it would be difficult to escape. Given that all the Labour authorities threatened with sanctions in the 1984-5 financial year have refused to use the appeals machinery established under the rate-capping legislation, one can foresee a number of 'little local difficulties' arising in the future.

Having said that, there were and are other things dear to the Prime Minister's heart and which also form part of the dominant ideology within the current Conservative government. Some also directly affect local government. So far discussion has centred upon financial issues, because reducing public expenditure has been a primary goal of the Government. But Mrs Thatcher and her colleagues have also been very concerned with reducing the scope of government activity generally, and with reducing the extent to which people look to the state to provide goods and services. The government has had objectives of privatisation and of contracting services out to the private sector, of reducing the range of goods and services the state provides, and of increasing people's capacity for, and belief in the virtues of, self-help. For Conservatives, this stress on social market forces and on individualism is the ultimate form of decentralisation, the achievement of which first requires a centralisation of power to the government in Whitehall.

Local government, because it undertakes so much of the provision of State services in Britain, has also been very much at the centre of this debate, finding itself again frequently in conflict with central government. Labour authorities concerned with preserving and extending services, with protecting and creating jobs, have a perception of the role of government almost diametrically opposed to that of Mrs Thatcher and her colleagues. Such authorities view services such as education, housing and social services as part of an essential process of redistribution to and protection of the less fortunate members of our society. By contrast, many Conservative authorities and certainly the government would adopt a minimalist view of such services, seeing welfare services as an umbrella designed to provide minimal protection. Inevitably political conflict is the result. Labour-controlled authorities such as the GLC, Liverpool, Sheffield and South Yorkshire, some of the London boroughs, the North-east authorities and some of those in the West Midlands and Greater Manchester and a small number of shire counties find themselves both completely opposed to the present government's policies and increasingly powerless to do anything about it. As a result they adopt the politics of confrontation rather than conciliation, and find a central government currently prepared to engage in such a conflict.

Municipal housing provides a good example of this situation, as well as demonstrating the asymmetrical nature of the power relationship betwen centre and locality in Britain. Since 1945, public housing has largely replaced private housing as the main source of rented accommodation, but as time has passed, both main political parties accepted that owner-occupation was a major objective for most people. On its election in 1979, the Conservative government saw the opportunity of furthering its commitment to owner-occupation, principally by the simple legal device of giving all public housing tenants the right to buy their accommodation, thus effectively prohibiting local authorities from not selling their housing stock, something many Labour-controlled authorities chose not to do whilst they had long lists of applicants waiting for housing. Many such authorities had long viewed the provision of council housing as a major means by which they could improve the lot of their working-class supporters. Selling their housing stock was something which came hard to them. Despite their attempts at delaying sales and not encouraging tenants to apply to buy their houses, local authorities have had to sell large parts of their housing stock, (especially the newer, better quality accommodation) especially in the light of the courts' decision in the Norwich case, and the generous discounts the government allows tenants on the purchasing price.

Forced to sell council houses, Labour authorities have also found their building and improvement programmes have been restricted through controls over capital expenditure. The result has been almost a complete halt to new council house building and an erratic record on improvement, the result of alternating stop-go policies depending on the central government's financial position. Towards the end of financial year 1982–3, for example, authorities were encouraged to spend money on capital projects which could be finished within that financial year. The following year their capital expenditure programmes were cut yet again. Furthermore, authorities have been obliged to increase the rents paid by their tenants, as the central government has limited the extent to which local authority housing accounts can be subsidised out of general local authority income.

Of course, it is metropolitan, inner city Labour authorities which are most affected by such a strategy, though there is evidence that Scottish local authorities (where over half the housing stock used to be under municipal control) have been similarly hit.[9] These authorities, with a large number of council houses, also have a high proportion of their housing stock in need of improvement. A similar problem has faced the Northern Ireland Housing Executive where, since housing conditions in Northern Ireland are amongst the worst in Britain, the Executive has been obliged to sell off its housing stock in order to raise the funds needed for new housing and improvement projects. Only after a great deal of political persuasion was the government persuaded to allow the new building programme to be introduced, and then only at the expense of further expenditure cuts in the health and education sectors in the province.

By contrast, however, many small rural Conservative shire districts in England have been prepared to sell off their small housing stocks to existing tenants. Funds so raised have been used to offset cuts imposed by the centre on expenditure generally, a creative accounting device also used by a number of Labour-controlled authorities. Nevertheless, it is clear that most Conservative authorities, many with only limited housing stock, would support the centre's policies, just as they would accept and implement other strategies designed either to privatise or contract out services. In practice, the complete privatisation of public services under local control has proved extremely difficult without the complete removal of functions from local authorities. The result has been that contracting out, that is having the service provided by the private sector but paid for by the local authority concerned, has become the more usual practice adopted. Thus, for example, many Conservative authorities have sought to contract out such services as refuse collection, school meals and cleaning, or else have persuaded their own workers to provide the service at lower cost, either by accepting redundancy or reductions in pay. The city of Birmingham was the jewel in the Conservatives' municipal crown, having extensively privatised or contracted out services such as school meals and cleaning, and persuaded its workforce to bid for the refuse collection contract at a much lower cost than before. The success of these changes may be considered doubtful in the light of the fact that the electors chose to return Labour to power in the city in the May 1984 elections.

Transport provided another early example of the kind of conflict between Mrs Thatcher's government and Labour-controlled authorities which has become so familiar since 1979. The problem arose early in 1981 over the Labour-controlled GLC's attempts at reducing fares on London's buses and Underground. In effect, the policy involved using local taxpayers' money to subsidise fares. The policy did not meet with the approval of the government, who did nothing to discourage an outer London Conservative controlled borough, Bromley, from contesting the legality of the GLC's policy in the Courts. The cause went to the House of Lords, whose Law Lords decided to raise fares again only months after they had been reduced. However, similar cases in other metropolitan areas, whose fare-fixing powers had a different legal basis from those applying in London, were divided in favour of the metropolitan county authorities, who were thus able to maintain their cheap fares. Subsequently, the GLC were also able to reduce fares again, finding a different legal basis on which to do it.

Cheap, subsidised transport, however, remains an issue between central government and local authorities. Under legislation passed in 1983, the Minister took powers which allowed him to determine the exact level of subsidies transport authorities could give to fares, whilst in the case of London a further piece of legislation in 1984 removed London's transport from the control of the GLC and placed it in the hands of a non-elected body; leglislation proposed for 1985 will bring about the complete deregulation of public transport and allow private bus companies to compete alongside publicly owned buses in London and elsewhere, again part of the implementation by the government of its policies designed to encourage a return to the virtues of market forces.

But apart from the rate-capping legislation, the one issue which has provoked continuous opposition both inside and outside Parliament is that concerned with the abolition of the Greater London Council and the metropolitan counties. Introduced first by the government as a White Paper, *Streamlining the Cities*, (1983) the proposal meets the government's election promise to abolish an 'unnecessary' tier of local government; the metropolitan area-wide county councils, as from 1986. The proposal involves the transfer of a number of the functions currently undertaken by those authorities to the district councils, and the creation of non-elected bodies (joint boards) to run such area-wide services as transport, police, fire and some aspects of planning. However, to achieve this change on time, the government also decided it needed to abolish the local elections for these areas which were due to take place in 1985. It was this particular proposal which provoked the second backbench revolt because it would have effectively changed the political control of the GLC from Labour to Conservative without an election, but the legislation eventually passed through the House of Commons unmodified. Again the proposals were justified in terms of efficiency and ratepayers' money, both themes close to the heart of the present Prime Minister, who, as early as 1974 had pledged the Conservative party to abolish the local property tax, something no government is ever likely to do completely.

However, in the light of the backbench revolt in the Commons, followed by a defeat when the bill came to the House of Lords, the government was obliged to withdraw its proposal to abolish the 1985 elections. Instead it chose to prolong the term of office of existing members until the abolition of the councils in 1986. The legislation which will perform this task, and transfer the various functions undertaken by those councils due for abolition to be transferred to the lower tier authorities and to the special purpose bodies proposed is due to wend its way through Parliament in the 1984–5 session. Not only will the legislation arouse further opposition when it is introduced (a large number of interest groups commented most unfavourably on the original proposals), but the campaign launched by the GLC and the other Metropolitan Councils will continue, a campaign which has already been described as the largest lobbying campaign ever undertaken in this country. Meanwhile, about the only achievement of the debate so far has been to transform the image of the current GLC leader, Ken Livingstone, from something like Left-wing revolutionary ogre to that of public martyr. Something of this was caught in the recent GLC by-elections, which, as part of the campaign against abolition, came about following the resignation of Mr Livingstone and some of his colleagues. The Conservatives boycotted the by-elections, and campaigned to persuade people *not* to vote; the Alliance parties fought all four seats but won none, whilst only Mr Livingstone of the Labour canditates successfully increased his majority.

In this matter, as in so much of what the Conservative government has done about local government since 1979, one senses a kind of inconsistency, ill-defined intention, lack of directness and clear purpose in government's policy towards local government. It is other priorities and other objectives which come first, and, as an indirect consequence have implications for what local authorities do and how they do it. Much of what Mrs Thatcher and her colleagues have sought to achieve in terms of these priorities and objectives would have the support of Conservative councillors and MPs, party supporters and sympathisers and of many Conservative voters. But the overall impact on the world of local governement which such policies have had is something which those involved in local government often find difficult to accept, regardless of their political persuasion.

Occasionally Conservative-and Labour-controlled authorities have come together in opposition to the central government's proposals. This alliance has been noticeable in the planning area, for example, where, despite attempts by development interests to remove many planning controls and to weaken the planning system, much of it has remained intact. A good example is the opposition which was aroused against the government's attempts at weakening Green Belt policy, part of its efforts at deregulating land use, from just such a coalition of Labour urban and Conservative suburban and rural authorities, as well as a number of other well organised interests, such as the Town and Country Planning Association and the Council for the Preservation of Rural England.

Mention of such interests also leads to a final element in Conservative policy which involves local government and which is also central to Mrs Thatcher's view of it, namely her strong anti-corporatist feelings. She has a strong dislike of anything remotely smacks of corporatism, of the close involvement of strongly organised vested interests able to influence (and subordinate) government into 'featherbedding' them. Undoubtedly she sees local government as just another of these groups, similar to such other interests as nationalised industries, the health service and the trade unions, all of which are to be weakened so that their ability to influence government is reduced. Government, and particularly Conservative government, must be seen to govern, to be firm and decisive, as well as superior. Anything which stops this happening must be opposed, and if a conflictual style of government results, so be it. The outcome is a very different style of British politics over the previous three decades, regardless of which party was in power.

It is this denial of a special status for local government as a democratic institution, part of the fabric of the British way of life, with its own traditions and values, elections, responsible and accountable politicians and dedicated, professional public servants, which so infuriates those who seek to defend local democracy and local government from the government's attacks, and who fear what they see as an increasingly dangerous centralisation of power in Britain. Academics, constitutional lawyers, councillors and paid officials came together in opposition to proposals for rate-capping and abolition of the Metropolitan Counties. In so doing they were joined by such unlikely partners as Edward Heath, the former Conservative Prime Minister, and Ken Livingstone, the Left-wing Labour leader of the GLC. Such an opposition coalition may not have been what Mrs Thatcher and her colleagues intended when they set out along their new Conservative path in 1979; nevertheless, such is the Prime Minister's and her party's position in power, it is unlikely that the present government will be dissuaded from continuing along that path. As a result, local government will find it has a new, reduced role to play in the democratic life of the country and in the provision of State services in the latter part of the twentieth century. Whether such a change is for the good or ill of Britain remains to be seen: what is clear is that local government will never be the same again as a result of its exposure to the Conservative government under Mrs Thatcher.

Notes

1. See J. O'Connor, *The Fiscal Crisis of the State* (St Martins Press, New York, 1973); for a discussion see K. Newton *et al.*, *Balancing the Books* (Sage, London, 1981) and L.J. Sharpe (ed.), *The Local Fiscal Crisis in Western European States* (Sage, London, 1981).

2. M. Goldsmith and K. Newton, 'Central-Local Government Relations: the Irresistible Rise of Centralised Power' in H. Berrington (ed.), *Change in British Politics* (Frank Cass, London, 1984), pp. 216–33.

3. A. Midwinter, M. Keating and P. Taylor, 'The Politics of Scottish Housing Plans', *Policy and Politics*, vol. 11, no. 2 (1984), pp. 145–66.

4. See R.A.W. Rhodes, B. Hardy and K. Pudney, *Corporate Bias in Central-Local Relations*, Discussion Paper no. 1 (Essex University, Colchester, 1980).

5. The phrase is Jim Bulpitt's, see his *Territory and Power in the United Kingdom* (Manchester University Press, Manchester, 1983).

6. The easiest discussion of this topic is to be found in T. Burgess and T. Travers, *Ten Billion Pounds* (Grant MacIntyre, London, 1980).

7. See, for example, P. Saunders, *Urban Politics: A Sociological Interpretation* (Hutchinson, London, 2nd revised edn, 1982).

8. A. Midwinter, M. Keating and P. Taylor, 'Excessive and Unreasonable: the Politics of the Scottish Hit List', *Political Studies*, vol. 31, no. 3 (September 1983), pp. 394–417.

9. See A. Midwinter, M. Keating and P. Taylor, 'The Politics of Scottish Housing Plans'.

SECTION FOUR: FOREIGN POLICY AND DEFENCE

10 MRS THATCHER'S EUROPEAN COMMUNITY POLICY

Ali El-Agraa

The *Conservative Manifesto for Europe 1979* (CME 1979) states quite categorically that the Conservative government would be committed to the proposition that Britain's future lies unequivocally within the European Community.[1] It goes on to say that *We want not only a better deal for Britain but a better, stronger Europe for all Europeans.*' It follows on by declaring that the Conservatives want Britain to recover her influence in the world by demonstrating commitment to the EC's true ideals and purposes. They will do this in four main ways: by promoting an outward-looking Community; by encouraging a common-sense approach; by pressing for reform; and by making the European Parliament more effective.[2]

The rest of the CME 1979 is about specific objectives: reform of the CAP (a devaluation of the Green pound before 1984 and a price freeze for products in surplus);[3] creating a Common Fisheries Policy (CEP) which distributes catches fairly and which conserves resources;[4] supporting an Energy Policy which reduces the EC's dependence on imports and promotes cooperation particularly for costly projects;[5] supporting and joining the EMS;[6] and reforming the EC Budget by reducing expenditure on the CAP and controlling expenditure overall.[7]

The CME 1979 has a lot to say about a number of other European issues, for example: enlargement is encouraged;[8] foreign policy must be co-ordinated within the EC;[9] links with the Third World must be enhanced;[10] and competition and harmonisation must be fostered.[11] However, in one chapter it is not possible to discuss everything without being superficial. Hence, I have given special emphasis to those aspects of Mrs Thatcher's European policies which are of the utmost importance and urgency. Before examining her record to date it should be pointed out that the policies in the CME 1979 are fully endorsed in two major speeches delivered by Sir Geoffrey Howe after he assumed the role of Foreign Secretary: the first was given at Chatham House (London) on 4 November 1983; and the second was delivered to the Royal Institute for International Affairs (Brussels) on 20 February 1984. It is vital to mention these simply to avoid the unnecessary discussion regarding whether or not a manifesto is an agenda for action.

The EC Budget and the CAP

Mrs Thatcher has a public image which portrays an obsession with the EC Budget and the CAP. Hence, before assessing her performance in the EC as a whole, it is important to find out whether or not such obsession is justified.

The Budget

The General Budget of the EC is one of two elements of EC fiscal policy, the other being the question of tax structure and harmonisation. Very widely interpreted, fiscal policy comprises a whole corpus of public finance issues: the relative size of the public sector, taxation and expenditure, and the allocation of public sector responsibilities between different tiers of government. Hence fiscal policy is concerned with a far wider area than that commonly associated with it, namely, the aggregate management of the economy in terms of controlling inflation and employment levels.

Experts in the field of public finance have identified a number of problems associated with these fiscal policy issues. For instance, the relative size of the public sector raises questions regarding the definition and measurement of government revenue and expenditure, and the attempts at understanding and explaining revenue and expenditure have produced more than one theoretical model. The division of public sector responsibilities raises the delicate question of which fiscal aspects should be dealt with at the central government level and which aspects should be tackled at the local level. Finally, the area of taxation and expenditure criteria has resulted in general agreement about the basic criteria of allocation, equity, stabilisation and administration. However, a number of very tricky problems are involved in a consideration of these criteria. In discussing the efficiency of resource allocation, the choice between work and leisure, for example, or between private and public goods, is an important and controversial one. With regard to the equity of distribution, there is the problem of what is meant by equity: is it personal, class or regional equity? In a discussion of the stabilisation of the economy, there exists the perennial problem of controlling unemployment and inflation and the trade-off between them. A consideration of administration must take into account the problem of efficiency versus practicality. Finally, there is the obvious conflict between the four criteria in that the achievement of one aim is usually at the expense of another; for example, what is most efficient in terms of collection may prove less equitable than what is considered to be socially desirable.

The above relates to a discussion of the problems of fiscal policy in very broad national terms. When considering the EC fiscal policy, there are certain elements of the international dimension that need spelling out and there are also some inter-regional (intra-EC) elements that have to be introduced. Very briefly, internationally, it has always been recognised that taxes (and equivalent instruments) have similar effects to tariffs on the international flow of goods and services — non-tariff distortions of international trade. Other elements have also been recognised as operating similar distortions on the international flow of factors of production. In the particular context of the EC, it should be remembered that its formation, at least from the economic viewpoint, was meant to facilitate the free and unimpeded flow of goods, services and factors (and other elements) between the member nations. Since tariffs are not the only distorting factor in this respect, the proper establishment of intra-EC free trade necessitates the removal of all non-tariff distortions that have an equivalent effect. Hence, the removal of tariffs may give the impression of establishing free trade inside the EC, but this is by no means automatically guaranteed, since the existence of sales taxes, excise duties, corporation taxes, income taxes, etc., may impede this freedom. The moral is that not only tariffs, but all equivalent distortions, must be eliminated or harmonised.

The above clearly indicates why there are at least two elements to fiscal policy: the instruments available to the government for fiscal policy purposes (the total tax structure) and the overall impact of the joint manoeuvring of the instruments (the role played by the budget). In this chapter we shall confine discussion to the EC Budget.[12]

The revenue sources for the EC Budget are basically two: all tariff revenues collected on imports coming into the EC from outside the EC, be it manufacturing or agricultural extra-area imports; and up to 1 per cent of the VAT calculation base. The tariff revenues are usually quoted as two sources, one for manufactured products and the other for agricultural levies but, in the strict context of the EC Budget, this distinction has no practical or theoretical significance.

These sources of revenues are termed 'own resources'[13] of the EC in that they automatically accrue to the EC authorities and that it is the EC decisions which determine them: the EC specifies the common external tariff rates, the agricultural levies and the tranche of VAT base, up to 1 per cent, that should be collected. In other words, decisions at the EC level determine these revenues for EC purposes.

Table 10.1 gives these sources of EC Budget revenue for 1982 and 1983. In terms of the classification presented here, the first four items represent the tariff revenues on imports and VAT, as mentioned above. The remaining two items are too insignificant to warrant separate consideration. Note that if more than 1 per cent of the VAT base yield is required as an increase in 'own resources', further legislation to be ratified by all the number nations would become necessary, hence the popular debate on increasing financial resources for the EC.

On the expenditure side, the EC Budget provides for two broad categories. Firstly, there are the administrative expenses (staff salaries, information, etc.) of the institutions of the EC: the Commission, the Council, the European Parliament, the Court of Justice, the European Coal and Steel Community (ECSC), the European Social Fund (ESF) and the European Regional Development Fund (ERDF); and secondly, the operational expenditures of the Commission such as Fonds Européen d'Orientation et de Garantie Agricole (FEOGA) intervention and guidance expenses, ERDF support grants, Food Aid, etc. The EC Budget also provides for a miscellaneous collection of minor expenditures.

Table 10.2: General Budget of the EC 1973–83

Year	Total (ECUm)	FEOGA Guarantee (%)
1973	4,641	77.4
1974	5,037	67.3
1975	6,214	69.6
1976	7,993	71.8
1977	8,483	76.8
1978	12,363	70.2
1979	13,716	69.3
1980	16,233	73.0
1981	18,438	65.9
1982	21,984	62.1
1983	21,901	64.2

Sources: *Bulletin of The European Communities*, vol. 15, no. 5 (1982) and *Fifteenth Report of the Activities of The European Communities* (1981).

Table 10.1: Revenues of the EC Budget, 1982 and 1983

Revenue	1982		1983		Change
	ECUm	(%)	ECUm	(%)	(%)
Agricultural Levies	1,899.1	8.6	1,558.5	7.1	− 17.93
Sugar and Isoglucose Levies	786.0	3.6	1,013.2	4.6	+ 28.91
Customs Duties	6,939.0	31.6	7,574.5	34.6	+ 9.16
VAT	11,998.3	54.6	11,384.5	52.0	− 5.12
Financial Contributions	197.5	0.9	180.4	0.8	− 8.66
Miscellaneous Revenue	164.5	0.7	190.5	0.9	+ 15.81
Total	21,984.4	100.0	21,901.6	100.0	− 0.38

Source: *Bulletin of the European Communities*, vol. 15, no. 5 (1982)

In 1983, the EC Budget amounted to about 22 billion European Currency Units (ECUs) which is roughly equivalent to £15 billion at current rates — see Table 10.2. Of this total, 62 per cent[14] was expenditure on the 'guarantee' section of FEOGA. Hence, the total size of the EC Budget is of the same order of magnitude as that of a large UK Department such as Health and Social Security or Education and Science.

The EC Budget expenditure is divided into two categories: compulsory and non-compulsory. The former is the expenditure emanating essentially from commitments in the Treaties (such as FEOGA price support and certain types of foreign aid to Third World countries) while the latter arises from the operational areas of the EC Budget (such as some of the expenditures of the ERDF and the ESF). Hence, compulsory expenditures have a priority claim which is why the EC Budget is necessarily 'functional', i.e. the EC has been endowed with revenues to discharge certain specific functions arising from the well-defined activities it was required to undertake either in the original Treaty or as subsequently agreed by the Council.[15]

Table 10.3 gives gross contributions, gross receipts and net receipts broken down by member nation. It should be clear from the table that the UK and Germany provide the largest share of gross contributions with regard to all three categories of EC Budget revenue; the levies and tariffs categories are easily explained in terms of the two countries' large extra-EC trade. The table also shows Germany and the UK to have been the only net losers with regard to net receipts; this has been the main reason for the UK budgetary battles with the EC, particularly since the UK has been the second largest net loser when its position in the league of GDP has been third from bottom. This problem of high UK contributions arises simply because a large percentage of the EC Budget expenditure goes on agriculture although the 'size' of the agricultural sector is not strictly related to GDP (Denmark with a large agricultural sector has the highest *per capita* income in the EC). Moreover VAT contributions, which are to a large extent related to GDP, only make up about half of the total EC Budget revenues.

Finally, although the EC Budget is meant to be balanced, it is not strictly true that gross contributions and expenditures sum to zero; there has been 'a small but significant increase in cash balances held by the Community which exercises a small deflationary effect on the system as a whole'.[16]

Table 10.3: EC General Budget: National Receipts and Payments

	Gross Contributions 1980 (% Share)	Gross Contributions by Source, 1980 (5)			Gross receipts, 1980 (% Share)	Net Receipts (£m)		
		Agricultural Levies	Industrial Tariffs	VAT		1979	1980	1981
Belgium-Luxembourg	6.1	11	7	5	11.9	+ 394	+ 250	+ 351
Denmark	2.4	2	2	3	4.4	+ 246	+ 174	+ 157
France	20.0	13	15	24	20.0	− 50	+ 41	+ 102
West Germany	30.1	20	30	31	23.5	− 924	− 1177	− 1260
Ireland	0.9	0.5	1	1	3.8	+ 352	+ 372	+ 340
Italy	11.5	20.5	9	14	16.8	+ 345	+ 329	+ 215
Netherlands	8.4	15	9	6	10.5	+ 186	+ 215	+ 81
United Kingdom	20.5	19	27	16	8.7	− 549	− 203*	− 56*

*These figures allow for refunds to the UK in 1980 and 1981.
Sources: W. Wallace (ed), *Britain in Europe* (Heinemann, London, 1980) and EC Commission, various publications.

The Common Agricultural Policy

The objectives of the CAP are clearly defined in Article 39 of the Treaty of Rome. They are:

1. 'to increase agricultural productivity by promoting technical progress and by ensuring the rational development of agricultural production and the optimum utilisation of all factors of production, in particular labour';
2. to ensure thereby 'a fair standard of living for the agricultural community, in particular by increasing the individual earnings of persons engaged in agriculture';
3. 'to stabilise markets';
4. 'to provide certainty of supplies';
5. 'to ensure supplies to consumers at reasonable prices'.

The final objectives of the CAP were established after the Stresa Conference in 1958 which was convened in accordance with the Treaty. The additional objectives were in the spirit of the Treaty:

1. to increase farm incomes not only by a system of transfers from the non-farm population through a price support policy, but also by the encouragement of rural industrialisation to give alternative opportunities to farm labour;
2. to contribute to overall economic growth by allowing specialisation within the Community and eliminating artificial market distortions;
3. to preserve the family farm and to ensure that structural and price policies go hand in hand.

It can be seen, therefore, that the CAP was not concerned simply with the implementation of common prices and market supports; it also included a commitment to encourage the structural improvement of farming. However, the EC expenditure on the structural aspects of the CAP remains very small indeed (less than 6 per cent of total CAP expenditure).

Before tackling these objectives, it is important to have some general background information. The economic significance of agriculture in the economies of the member states can be demonstrated in terms of its share in the total labour force and in GNP. The most significant observations that can be made are:

1. at the time of the signing of the Treaty many people in the original six member states were dependent on farming as their main source of income. Indeed, 25 per cent of the total labour force was employed in agriculture — the equivalent percentage for the UK was less than five;
2. the agricultural labour force was worse off than most people in the rest of the EC;
3. a rapid fall in both the agricultural labour force and in the share of agriculture in GNP occurred between 1955 and 1981.

It is also important to have some information about the area and size distribution of agricultural holdings. The most significant factor to note is that in the original Six, around 1967, approximately two-thirds of farm holdings were between 1 and 10 hectares in size. At about the same time, the equivalent figure for the UK was about one-third.

A final piece of important background information that one needs to bear in mind is that, except for Italy and the UK, the EC farming system is an owner-occupier system rather than one of tenant farming. This is important because if an agricultural policy supports farm products it does not follow that it supports farmers, since farmers may be workers rather than owners of land: all the benefits will accrue to land-owners not to farm workers.

As has been seen, the agricultural sector has been declining in relative importance and those who have remained on the land receive incomes well below the national average. Governments have, therefore, always found it necessary to practise some sort of control over the market for agricultural commodities through price supports, subsidies to farmers, import levies, import quotas, etc. Hence, it should not come as a surprise to learn that most advanced countries have been adopting some sort of 'agricultural policy'.

From the foregoing one is in a position to attempt a specification of the necessary elements in an agricultural policy and to point out the difficulties associated with such a policy. In most advanced mixed economies where living standards have been rising, an agricultural policy must:

1. as a minimum requirement, avoid impeding the natural process of transferring resources from the agricultural sector to the non-agricultural sector of the economy, and if necessary promote this process;

2. aim at protecting the incomes of those who remain occupied in the agricultural sector;
3. aim at some kind of price stability, since agriculture forms the basis of living costs and wages and is therefore the basis of industrial costs;
4. make provision for an adequate agricultural sector since security of food supplies may be deemed essential for a nation;
5. ensure the maintenance of some population in rural areas.

Unfortunately, these objectives are, to a large extent, mutually contradictory. Any policy which aims at providing adequate environmental conditions, secure food supplies and agricultural incomes equal to the national average interferes with the economy's natural development. The provision of stable farm incomes, let alone rising farm incomes, is not compatible with the provision of stable agricultural prices.

The CAP scheme incorporates aspects of several of the types of policy which were in existence before its inception and is a relatively complex package of procedures which apply differently to different products. However, the major features of the system can be outlined using the example of the pricing of cereals.

First a 'target price' is set which reflects the price which the market is intended to reach in the area where cereal is in shortest supply, Duisburg in the Ruhr valley. The target price is not a producer price since it includes the costs of transport and storage. The target price is variable in that it is allowed to increase on a monthly basis from August to July in order to allow for storage costs throughout the year.

The 'threshold price' is then calculated in such a way that, when transport costs incurred within the EC are added, cereals collected at Rotterdam should sell at Duisburg at a price equal to, or slightly higher than, the target price. An import levy is then imposed to prevent import prices falling short of the threshold price. The import levy is calculated on a daily basis and is equal to the margin between the lowest priced consignment entering the EC on the day — allowing for transport costs to one major port (Rotterdam) — and the threshold price. This levy is then charged on all imports allowed into the EC on that day.

If target prices result in an excess supply of the product in the EC, the threshold price and import levy become ineffective in terms of the objective of a constant annual target price and support buying becomes necessary. A 'basic intervention price' is then introduced for this purpose. This is fixed for Duisburg at about 7 or 8 per cent below the target price. Similar prices are then calculated for several locations within the EC on the basis of costs of transport to Duisburg. National intervention agencies are then compelled to buy whatever is offered to them (provided it conforms to standard) at the relevant intervention price. The intervention price is therefore a minimum guaranteed price.

Moreover, an export subsidy or restitution is paid to EC exporters. This is determined by the officials and is influenced by several factors (world prices, amount of excess supply, expected trends) and is generally calculated as the difference between the EC intervention price and the world price.

Agricultural prices are fixed within the CAP in terms of European Currency Units (ECUs),[17] which are linked in value to the currencies which form the European Monetary System (EMS). In order to translate prices from ECUs into the various national currencies each country uses a 'Green exchange rate'. In principle, these Green rates give member countries scope for varying their *internal* agricultural prices independently of the prices agreed for the EC as a whole at their annual review. However, the policy of devaluing or revaluing the Green pound (or the Green franc, etc.) is only available with the agreement of other members and, even then, only within certain limits.

A further aspect of the problems caused by exchange rates can best be illustrated with an example. In August 1969 the French franc was devalued by 11.11 per cent. This move, by itself, would have benefited French farmers within the CAP since agricultural prices expressed in francs would rise. This in turn would obviously stimulate French farmers to produce more and so further aggravate the problems of excess supply. In trying to avoid this aggravation, the CAP could not respond by lowering price levels measured in units of account since this would have discriminated against farmers outside France. Therefore a more complicated policy was adopted. CAP intervention prices payable in France were reduced by the full 11.11 per cent, eliminating the internal benefits to the French farmers; but this would generate different prices in different parts of the EC, so a system of border taxes and subsidies was also introduced. France was required to subsidise imports from the rest of the EC and levy taxes on its own exports to the EC countries so as to compensate for the trading effects of the original devaluation.

The term 'Monetary Compensatory Amounts' (MCAs) was coined to describe this system of border taxes and subsidies. Since 1969, the MCA system has become very complicated as the exchange rates of the member countries have varied. The EC has recently announced its intention to discontinue the MCA system but it is likely to be with us for some considerable time yet since such decisions have been taken before without being implemented.

CAP Claims on the Budget

From the above it should be apparent that the CAP mechanism favours those countries which are more than self-sufficient since they can sell surplus production to the EC at a guaranteed price. Moreover, since a country which produces surpluses does not import, it contributes nothing to the EC's 'own resources' in terms of levies collected on imports from outside the EC. This is the crucial link between the EC Budget and the CAP: the CAP claims about two-thirds of the EC Budget expenditure but also provides about 13 per cent of the EC Budget revenues. Therefore, a country like Britain which is not only less than self-sufficient but also imports from both the rest of the EC and the rest of the world, suffers relative to its EC partners in two respects:

1. It does not receive as much financial support for agricultural production from the EC Budget as do those countries which produce surpluses.
2. It contributes to the EC Budget revenues from levies collected on agricultural imports from outside the EC. Hence, Mrs Thatcher is absolutely correct in her insistence that any reform of the BC Budget, and in particular any increase in the EC Budget revenues (like raising the 1 per cent limit on VAT base) must be considered simultaneously with reform of the CAP: to increase the EC Budget revenues without controlling expenditure on the CAP would be detrimental for British interests.

Monetary Integration

The question of monetary integration is a very tricky and sensitive one. The aspirations of the EC are for complete monetary integration and the Werner Report[18] suggested its achievement, by stages, in 1980. When the Six became Nine in 1973 and the world monetary system was in complete disarray, it was inevitable that the 1980 date should be scrapped.[19] However, in 1978 the Bremen Conference affirmed its commitment to achieving European Monetary Union (EMU) in the near future by adopting the EMS.[20]

Before assessing Mrs Thatcher's record, it is important to define what is meant by monetary integration in the EC. Monetary integration has two essential components: an exchange rate union and capital market integration. An exchange rate union is established when member countries have what is *de facto* one currency. The actual existence of one currency is not necessary, however, because if member countries have permanently fixed exchange rates amongst themselves, the result is effectively the same even though the member currencies may vary in unison relative to non-member currencies.

Capital market integration is concerned with convertibility. Convertibility refers to the permanent absence of all exchange controls for both current and capital transactions including interest and dividend payments (and the harmonisation of all relevant taxes and measures affecting the capital market) within the union. It is of course absolutely necessary to have complete convertibility for trade transactions, otherwise an important requirement of the customs union aspect of the EC is threatened, namely the promotion of free trade between members of the union. Convertibility for capital transactions is related to free factor mobility and is therefore an important aspect of capital market integration which is necessary for the common market element of the Community.

Monetary union, therefore, takes place when an exchange rate union is accompanied by capital market integration. However, it has now been recognised that, in practice, the definition should include:

1. an explicit harmonisation of monetary policies;
2. a common pool of foreign exchange reserves;
3. a single central bank.[21]

True monetary integration has many advantages — all the advantages of having one European currency and one authority to manage it: the promotion of trade and investment; economy in the use of foreign exchange reserves; a commitment on the part of those member nations in temporary surplus to help those with temporary deficits; a common policy towards structural regional imbalance, to name a few. These advantages[22] outweigh any conceivable disadvantages such as the extra deflation/inflation which is induced by forgoing the rate of exchange as a policy instrument.[23]

However, the process of actually achieving these aspirations is an extremely difficult one[24] and some commentators would therefore advocate that it should be postponed for as long as possible. The EMS is arguably a step in the right direction but it is not complete monetary integration since it relates to areas of monetary stability, rather than complete fixity of exchange rates, the common pooling of foreign exchange reserves, the creation of a Community central bank and the coordination of monetary and economic policies. That is why most economists would agree that, 'however indispensable to full economic integration, monetary union could prove disastrous by itself if it was not accompanied by the political and other conditions inseparable from full integration and collective economic management'.[25]

Mrs Thatcher's Record

It would be futile to discuss the achievements or lack of progress of each summit meeting for Britain. What I intend to do here is to consider the latest situation (April 1984) in comparison with the targets the Conservatives set themselves in their CME 1979.

1. Britain remains outside the EMS in spite of the Conservatives' strong attack on the previous Labour government for not joining it. Mrs Thatcher will no doubt justify this contradictory position by emphasising that the economic performances of the members of the EC have not yet converged[26] and that an appropriate exchange rate for sterling is yet to come. Neither justification should be acceptable since it could be argued that membership of the EMS will in itself force the member nations to converge in economic performance[27] and that it would be difficult to establish what is an appropriate exchange rate for sterling prior to membership of the EMS now that sterling is a petrocurrency. Hence, it would seem reasonable to state that Mrs Thatcher's policy has been one of 'wait and see' though she professed to be fully committed in 1979.

2. As for the CAP, for the first time since its introduction, the farm ministers of the EC countries have agreed on 31 March 1984 not to pay dairy farmers open-ended subsidies for producing surplus

quantities of milk. The package which was agreed on that date reduces the Community's common farm prices by 0.5 per cent and relies on a system of 'quotas' to restrict milk production from 103 million tonnes in 1983 to 99.2 million and 98.4 million in 1984 and 1985 respectively; thereafter it will be pegged for a further three years. Ireland, whose dairy production is equivalent to 9 per cent of its GNP, has been awarded a special dispensation, in that its 'quota' has actually been increased (see Table 10.4); Greece is of course undergoing transition, hence treatment better than Ireland's is accorded to her. Moreover, the quotas which already apply to sugar beet have been extended to other surplus products such as cereals, oilseeds and processed tomatoes. Also, in order to reduce wine production, new vine plantings have been banned until 1990. Finally, various production and consumption subsidies to livestock, butter, fruit and vegetables have been reduced, and the MCAs will be phased out over four years.

Table 10.4: EC Changes in Milk Production, 1984 (%)

	Milk Quota
Belgium	− 3.0
Denmark	− 5.7
France	− 2.0
West Germany	− 6.7
Greece	+ 7.2
Ireland	+ 4.6
Italy	Nil
Luxembourg	+ 3.5
Netherlands	− 6.2
United Kingdom	− 6.5

Source: Commission of the European Communities, 1984.

These changes will affect countries like West Germany, the Netherlands and the UK by the full impact of the proposed price cuts since they have positive MCAs. Countries with weak currencies will find that the proposed price cuts actually result in price rises ranging from 1.5 per cent for Denmark to 17.6 per cent for Greece — see Table 10.5. 'The outcome of the MCA changes is to turn the apparent 0.5 per cent cut in ECUs into an average rise of 3.2% in national currencies, which are the ones farmers get paid in'.[28] Note that in all EC countries farmers will experience a fall in their real earnings when the forecasts for the 1984 inflation rates are taken into account: British farmers will suffer the largest fall (5.9 per cent) and

Table 10.5: Price Changes for the 1984–5 Farm Year

	% Change in ECUs	% Change in National Currency	1984 Inflation Forecast
Belgium	− 0.6	+ 2.7	5.8
Denmark	− 0.7	+ 1.5	4.9
France	− 0.6	+ 5.0	7.1
West Germany	− 0.6	− 0.6	2.8
Greece	+ 0.4	+ 17.6	19.8
Ireland	− 0.6	+ 2.7	7.8
Italy	− 0.4	+ 6.4	11.0
Luxembourg	− 0.5	+ 2.8	7.4
Netherlands	− 0.5	− 0.5	2.0
United Kingdom	− 0.6	− 0.6	5.3

Source: Commission of the European Communities.

the French farmers the smallest (2.1 per cent).

It may come as a surprise to learn that the agreed package does not reduce costs but actually raises them in 1984 and 1985. The package will cost 900 million ECUs in 1984 and 1.4 billion ECUs in 1985. However, in the long run costs will of course be reduced. Mrs Thatcher can therefore claim that the agreed package is consistent with the objectives stated in CME 1979.

3. With regard to the Community Budget, Mrs Thatcher has indeed managed to reduce our net contribution substantially (see Table 10.6; note that 2 billion ECUs are equivalent to about £1.2 billion). Moreover, the discussions in progress (April 1984) clearly indicate that Mrs Thatcher wants Britain's net contribution to be reduced by 75 per cent to about 500 million ECUs. She was, however, offered a rebate of 1 billion ECUs for 1984, and was prepared to accept that, but wanted a rebate of 1.5 billion ECUS for 1985 and 1986. It would seem that, before the summit closed in failure, Mrs Thatcher was ready to accept rebates of 1.25 billion ECUs and the rest of the EC was willing to offer rebates of up to 1 billion ECUs. Hence, an initial gap of 1 billion ECUs was reduced to a mere 0.25 billion ECUs. Expressed in sterling, the EC was offering a rebate of £450 million while Mrs Thatcher was asking for £600 million. Moreover, it was agreed in the summit that after 1986 a lasting corrective mechanism would be introduced.

Table 10.6: UK Net Contribution before Compensation, Compensation and Net Contribution after Compensation, 1980-3 (ECU million)

	Net Contribution before Compensation	Compensation	Net Contribution after Compensation
1980	1,512	1,175	337
1981	1.419	1,410	9
1982	2,036	1,079	957
1983	about 1,900	750	about 1,150

Source: Kindly supplied by Commissioner Christopher Tugendhat.

It should be added, however, that these concessions by the rest of the EC were conditional on the agreed 1984–5 agricultural package and an increase in the Community Budget revenues by raising the VAT tranche to 1.4 per cent in 1986 and 1.6 per cent in 1988. The June 1984 settlement was along these lines: Britain will get back 66 per cent of the difference between her VAT contribution and the EC Budget expenditure in the UK; the VAT tranche is to be raised to 1.4 per cent; there will be a much stricter control of expenditures, particularly with regard to the CAP; and the whole package will be reviewed in 1987–8 when a further percentage increase in the VAT tranche will be due for negotiation.

Mrs Thatcher will, therefore, be perfectly in order to claim success here. However, one should be sceptical about the nature of this success since the agreed package does not include the introduction of an income-tax type of EC Budget.[29] The point is that countries with higher *per capita* GDP seem to have a higher percentage of their GDP spent on investment, hence a VAT contribution is essentially regressive — VAT is based on consumption expenditure.

4. A Common Fisheries Policy has been agreed which covers four aspects. First, the policy has a 'system' for the conservation of sea resources within the Community. Secondly, the policy has a common organisation of the market. Thirdly, the policy includes 'structural' measures. Finally, the policy asks for fisheries agreements with non-member countries and for formal consultations between Community nations so that they should act in concert in the context of international agreements.

With regard to the conservation of resources, the Council has adopted a Regulation establishing a Community system which provides for measures to curtail fishing activities, sets rules for utilising resources and makes special provisions for coastal fishing. Hence both access and total allowable catches are aspects of crucial importance here.

The market organisation covers fresh, frozen and preserved products and its main objective is to apply common marketing standards and to facilitate trading between the member nations of the Community. More precisely, however, it should be stated that the objectives of the marketing aspect are to guarantee an adequate income to the producers, to enhance rational marketing, to alter supply in accordance with market requirements, to ensure that consumer prices are reasonable, as well as to promote common marketing standards.[30]

The structural measures can be described more precisely by stating their aims. Their main objectives are: to ensure that the resources of the sea are rationally utilised; to ensure that the fishermen of the different nations of the Community are treated on an equal basis; and to conserve resources or reduce over-capitalisation.[31] With regard to these aspects, the Council agreed on 25 January 1983 to activate, within six months, special EC measures which are designed to 'adjust capacity and improve productivity of fishing and aquaculture'. These measures consist largely of proposals put forward by the Commission between 1977 and 1980 and include: 'aids for laying up, temporarily or permanently, certain fishing vessels so that capacity can be adjusted in the light of conservation needs'; 'aids for exploratory fishing and cooperation with certain non-member countries in the context of joint ventures in order to encourage the redeployment of the Community's fishing capacity'; and 'aids for the construction and modernisation of certain fishing vessels and aquaculture facilities and for the installation of artificial structures to facilitate restocking and develop the fishing industry generally'.[32] These measures are to apply for three years and will qualify for Community financing to the total of 250 million ECUs: 76 million ECUs for capacity adjustment; 18 million ECUs for redeployment; and 156 million ECUs for encouraging investment.

Finally, with regard to agreements with non-member countries, framework fisheries agreements have been signed with the Faeroes, Guinea, Guinea-Bissau, Norway, Spain, Sweden and the USA. Moreover, talks are in progress with Mauritania and will be resumed with some other African countries. The Commission has also been authorised to negotiate fisheries agreements with the Caribbean countries of Antigua, Dominica, St Lucia and Surinam. Also, multilateral agreements have been concluded with a view to the Community's participation in international agreements covering the North-east and North-west Atlantic, the Antarctic and salmon in the North Atlantic, and talks are in progress with regard to the Community's participation in international agreements on tuna and whaling and to joining the organisations which control fishing in the Baltic, and the Central and South-east Atlantic.

Although the agreement on the Common Fisheries Policy has been much applauded, a great deal of caution should be exercised. First, the use of such words as 'rational' and 'fair' immediately reminds one of the problems of the CAP where similar terminology came to mean self-sufficiency and an income to the farmers much closer to, if not in excess of, the national average. Secondly, there is the apparent conflict between the structural aspects and market organisation since the structure seeks conservation while the market organisation encourages larger catches by giving price supports which are directly related to the size of the catch. Thirdly, it is inevitable that total allowable catches will be negotiated annually, hence a ripe atmosphere will be generated for tense bargaining over quota allocations; this reminds one of the classic case where it is desirable for oligopolists to pursue a policy of joint profit max-imisation but where the outcome is for each oligopolist to try and maximise his share of the profit. Fourthly, as Cunningham and Young[33] rightly state, even if the structural measures can be achieved,

> almost complete reliance is placed on management methods which might be termed 'biological' in that, while they generally improve the condition of the fish stock itself, they will not result in any long-term improvement in the economic health of the fishery. Typical of such biological techniques are net-mesh size restrictions, closed seasons, closed areas and limitations on the use of certain efficient methods of capture.

Finally, unless the accession treaties to be signed by Spain and Portugal cover all aspects of Community membership, there is the potential problem regarding total allowable catches and quotas when these countries become members — the Spanish fleet used Community waters before 1977.

It is of course too early to make firm predictions about the appropriateness or otherwise of the Fisheries Policy. However, the points mentioned above do indicate that there are potential problems which the Community Commission must keep constantly in mind if the situation is not to be potentially explosive. Having stated all that, one must conclude by sharing in the applause for the *reaching* of agreement after negotiations which took six years of hard bargaining and mackerel wars with Denmark. Hence, Mrs Thatcher may be justified in claiming progress here, but it must be emphasised that the quota allocations have been detrimental to the UK: historically, Britain accounted for 60% of the Community total and its quota under the Fisheries Policy is only 36% (having been prepared to settle for 45%).

5. One could of course carry on assessing every possible aspect of Community policy but we have covered the major points at issue, particularly since success in political cooperation has just begun (a common stance during the Falkland's crisis and a common approach to the Middle East) and the third EC-ACP conference is about to start—hence progress in relations with the Third World would also seem to be satisfactory. This leaves one aspect: the ability of Mrs Thatcher to persuade our Community partners to adopt strictly monetarist policies. This is a subject which will need a book in its own right, but I have demonstrated elsewhere[23] that the rest of Europe has been more liberal in terms of government expenditure than has Britain.

Conclusion

The obvious conclusion is that Mrs Thatcher's balance sheet of performance in the EC, if taken merely in terms of the items involved, is very impressive indeed: apart from a clear debit item in respect of membership of the EMS, she can claim credit on practically all the other aspects. However, this success is subject to a number of reservations. First, the EMS is a very crucial aspect both in terms of its importance for exchange-rate stability and for further progress in European integration. Hence, by remaining outside it, Britain is undermining both these important considerations. Secondly, the items on the table regarding the reform of the EC Budget fall short of a proper system of contributions according to ability to pay. Hence, Mrs Thatcher should not be content until a system of providing revenues via a progressive income tax structure is introduced. Thirdly, the agreed reforms to the CAP do not have an overall coherence about them. Success here can only come about by an alignment of Community agricultural prices to world prices and by introducing a system of direct subsidies to achieve the admirable objectives of the CAP, rather than a system of price supports and occasional quota allocations. Moreover, the reforms say nothing about structural aspects. Finally, but not exhaustively, the Community still remains without a common approach to the unemployment problem. A Community Budget without this dimension would seem to be far from successful.

At the outset reference was made to Mrs Thatcher's European Community aspirations. These have proved elusive. We have been given such vague statements as: 'we are in the Community and we are staying in. In believe that it is for the good both of Britain and of the larger world that the free nations of Europe are able to work together';[35] 'The European Community is the world's largest trading group . . . withdrawal . . . would be a fateful step towards isolation, at which only the Soviet Union and her allies would rejoice';[36] 'We are . . . very fully integrated into the Community, and we are keen to develop it further. More needs to be done on regional and social policies . . . we do not yet have major common policies in the industrial field; more can . . . be done to build . . . an energy strategy; the internal market is still far from complete . . . we need to exploit more fully the economies of scale . . . if we are to compete effectively with the United States and Japan. We in Britain are determined to see the Community develop in these and other directions';[37] 'This Government believes in the European Community. We want it to work better. We have ideas . . . as *communautaire* as anyone else's. We want to restore a sense of confidence and purpose. To do so, we must help steer the ship . . . into the sea beyond, with a clear idea of where we want to take it'.[38] It would seem that those clear ideas are yet to come.

However, there is a prevalent feeling that Mrs Thatcher's approach to the discussion at the European summit conferences, most particularly those recently dealing with the British net contribution, raising the ceiling on the VAT tranche and the fixing of agricultural prices, has been unhelpful since a spirit of positive compromise would seem to have been missing. Moreover, the lack of such spirit has been interpreted as a lack of a 'European' attitude on the part of Mrs Thatcher. However, once it is realised that the UK net contributions for 1984 and 1985 will become the basis of future projections and that the present structure of the EC Budget is not one of paying according to ability, one should immediately recognise that utterances about an uncompromising position are not only of no particular significance but actually seriously distract from the real issue of a long-due proper reform of an essentially misconceived budgetary structure. In short, Mrs Thatcher's strong stance here, if seen in the appropriate light, should surely be deemed to be more 'European' than the simple nicety of fudging such an important issue. But that is not to say that a public display of antagonism is justified; after all those dealing with these important and sensitive issues are supposed to be both politicians and diplomats.

Notes

1. *Conservative Manifesto for Europe 1979*, p, 5.
2. Ibid., p. 8.
3. Ibid., p. 13.
4. Ibid., p. 14
5. Ibid., pp. 14–15.
6. Ibid., p. 16.
7. Ibid., p. 19
8. Ibid., p. 10
9. Ibid.
10. Ibid.
11. Ibid., p. 17.
12. For a discussion of other aspects, refer to A.M. El-Agraa (ed.), *The Economics of the European Community* (Philip Allan, Oxford, 1980, and 2nd edn. 1984); and El-Agraa (ed.) *Britain Within the European Community: the Way Forward* (Macmillan, London, 1983).
13. The principle of 'own resources' was adopted after the Council decision of 21 April 1970; it replaced in 1980 the previous system which has entirely based on national contributions.
14. Except for 1982, this was the smallest ever percentage.
15. See T. Rybczynski, 'Fiscal Policy under EMU' in M.T. Sumner and G. Zis (eds.), *Europan Monetary Union* (Macmillan, London, 1982).
16. See W. Godley, 'The United Kingdom and the Community Budget' in W. Wallace (ed.), *Britain in Europe* (Heinemann, London, 1980), p. 76.
17. Previously these were fixed in units of account.
18. See 'Report to the Council and Commission on the Realisation by Stages of Economic and Monetary Union in the Community' (the 'Werner Report'), *Bulletin of the European Communities*, 11, supplement (1970).
19. See *Report of the Study Group 'Economic and Monetary Union 1980'* (the Marjolin Report') (Commission of the European Communities, Brussels, 1975).
20. However, it is arguable whether or not the EMS is a step in the right direction towards EMU.
21. Due to space limitations, one cannot go into the reasons for the inclusion of these elements, but see W.M. Corden, 'Monetary Integration', *Essays in International Finance*, 93 (April 1972); Corden, *Inflation, Exchange Rates and the World Economy* (Oxford University Press, Oxford, 1977); A.M. El-Agraa, 'Has

Membership of the European Community Been a Disaster for Britain?', *Applied Economics*, vol. 16 (April 1984); El-Agraa (ed.), *The Economics of the European Community* (1980). One only needs to stress that these elements hint at the advantages of adopting a single currency.

22. See El-Agraa (ed.), *The Economics of the European Community*, Chapter 9 (1980) and Chapter 5 (1984).

23. See Corden, 'Monetary Integration' and Corden, *Inflation*.

24. See Sir Alec Cairncross *et al., Economic Policy for the European Economic Community: the Way Forward* ((Macmillan, London, 1974); El-Agraa (ed.), *The Economics of the European Community* (1980), Chapter 10; Corden, 'Monetary Integration'.

25. Cairncross *et al. Economic Policy*, p. 34.

26. For a technical discussion of the necessary conditions for a successful EMS, see El-Agraa (ed.), *Britain Within the European Community*; Sumner and Zis (eds.), *European Monetary Union*.

27. Lord Eric Roll, 'The Case for the Common Market', *Times Literary Supplement*, 27 January 1984.

28. *The Economist*, 7–13 April 1984.

29. A.M. El-Agraa and A. Majocchi, 'Devising a Proper Fiscal Stance for the European Community', *Rivista di Diritto Finanziario e Scienza della Finanze*, vol. XLII, no. 3 (1983).

30. See S. Cunningham and J.A. Young, 'The EEC Fisheries Policy: Retrospect and Prospect', *National Westminster Bank Quarterly Review* (May 1983).

31. Ibid., p. 3.

32. *Bulletin of the European Communities*, 1 (1983), p. 2.

33. Cunningham and Young, 'The EEC Fisheries Policy', p. 3.

34. El-Agraa (ed.), *The Economics of the European Community* (1984).

35. Mrs Thatcher, quoted in a Foreign Office publication (1983).

36. *The Conservative Manifesto 1983*, p. 44.

37. Francis Pym, Copenhagen, 10 September 1982.

38. Sir Geoffrey Howe, 'The Future of the European Community: Britain's Approach to the Stuttgart Negotiations', speech delivered at Chatham House, London, on 4 November 1983.

11 THE DEFENCE POLICY OF THE CONSERVATIVE GOVERNMENT

Nigel Bowles

Introduction

Mrs Thatcher has changed the agenda of British politics. Much that went unquestioned during the 1960s and 1970s has, since the 1979 General Election, been subject to examination and modification. This has been true of social and educational policy, of the size and shape of the nationalised industries, and, in certain respects, of financial and fiscal policy. The ideological debates between the parties about the purpose and possibilities of government have sharpened; Mrs Thatcher's leadership of the Conservative Party has both symbolised and promoted this change. In no area, even prior to her forming a Conservative administration after the election victory of 1979, has her distinctive reshaping of the agenda of British politics seemingly been more apparent than in defence policy. In 1979 the Conservative's proposals for 'significant increases' in defence spending reflected the tone and content of Conservative opposition to the 1974–9 Labour government's defence policies.[1] That opposition had continued even after the then government pledged in 1977 to plan for a 3 per cent annual real growth in defence spending. By the 1983 election, the Falklands campaign and the acquisition of new nuclear weapons systems made defence an important issue in the campaign. The 'unilateralist' tag did not work to the advantage of the Labour Party.[2]

Prime Ministers typically devote much of their time and political energies to foreign and defence policy and to all matters touching upon national security. Mrs Thatcher cultivated this habit as leader of the opposition where her personal commitment to sizeable increases in defence spending was evident from early in her leadership.[3] She affirmed the policy after Harold Wilson's Labour administration introduced the 1975 Defence Review, clarified it in a major speech at Kensington Town Hall in January 1976, and ensured it a prominent place in the Conservatives' policy statement, *The Right Approach*, published in October of the same year. It was an elemental part of the Conservative's new image and purpose.

'Strength' at home and abroad had appeal across the electoral divide, not just to confirmed Conservative supporters but to marginal supporters from the skilled working-class.[4]

Low pay had long been a cause of discontent within the services; the practice of limiting pay increases in the public sector in pursuit of the policy of restraining public spending had been largely responsible for the heavy exodus of personnel from the armed services during the lifetime of the Labour government. The Conservative opposition had exploited the issue to considerable effect in Parliament and pledged to honour the findings of the Armed Services Pay reviews. Yet the execution of this undertaking caused approximately half of all defence spending to be effectively exempted from the controls of cash limits for the first two years of the government's term. The outflow of service personnel was reduced from nearly 50,000 in 1978–9 to less than 29,000 in 1982–3. The premature release of commissioned officers fell from 1,444 in the earlier period to 843 in the latter. In each case, the decline was a combined function of improved service pay and declining job opportunites elsewhere as the economic recession intensified.[5]

Much more important issues in defence policy during Mrs Thatcher's first administration were the questions of a strategic replacement for the Polaris strategic missile system; the decision by NATO countries in December 1979 to modernise American theatre nuclear forces in Western Europe, and the divisive political consequences of that decision; the Defence Review of 1981, and the Falklands War of the spring of 1982. This chapter is concerned primarily with the overall shape of British defence policy and budgeting under the Conservative administrations of 1979 and 1983. It is therefore necessarily concerned with the fourth of these issues insofar as it had consequences for that overall shape, and with the third for the same reason. The second had fewer consequences for British defence policy as such, although the party political ramifications were immensely important. Britain did not pay for the ground-launched Cruise missiles based in Britain; they were and are specifically American weapons and American property — hence the budgetary advantage, and the political problem.[6] The first issue, that of the strategic replacement, also raised party political questions, though somewhat different in kind; this chapter will address some of its budgetary and policy implications.

This chapter argues that, contrary to the expectations of some and campaign rhetoric of others, the Conservative administrations of

1979 and 1983 adopted policies for defence which broadly continued those of their predecessors. There was no rapid expansion of the defence budget such as was successfully implemented in the United States from 1981 onwards (the Conservative government's claimed pursuit of the expansion of the defence budget by 3 per cent per annum was a commitment inherited from the previous Labour administration). The chapter notes that the first fundamental reassessment and redefinition of Britain's defence requirements under John Nott's guidance in June 1981 was politically undermined by the Falklands War, but concludes that a redefinition of still greater scope will be forced on a British government well before the end of the decade by inexorable budgetary constraints.

Rhetoric and Reality

As with much else in British public policy from 1945 to 1979, rhetorical exchange about defence policy in Parliament and on the hustings concealed broad underlying consensus or, at least, a retrospective acceptance by one administration of its predecessor's actions. Disagreement (much of it sharp) there most certainly was and not only over defence but its (often separated) spouse, foreign policy. The process of accommodation to the withdrawal from empire, to a bipolar world where the superpowers' stocks of nuclear weapons vastly outstripped those of second-ranking powers such as Britain, was painful.

The full implications of Britain's much-diminished influence and authority could not be safely drawn by politicians until the 1970s, and to a certain extent not even then: the fact of global foreign policy interests and the illusion of a global capacity to buttress those interests by military means survived the post-war division of Europe, Suez, the failure of Blue Streak, French rejection of Britain's application to join the EEC, and the final withdrawal from the Gulf and the Far East. In certain respects, the illusion took on a further lease of life with the extraordinary events in the South Atlantic in the spring of 1982. The recapture of Port Stanley fostered anew the chimera that British power was still of worldwide significance. Such a perspective did not merely have short-term electoral or political utility; it influenced the minds and actions of policymakers.

In 1984, the process of adjusting Britain's vital national interests, of aligning them with her economic strength, and of marrying each with her defence policy, is incomplete. The past exerts its pull. Yet the squeeze of continuing weak British economic performance (by comparison with most of her NATO allies and with the aspirations of the British government and people) on a wide range of defence commitments grows tighter by the year. It is certain that in the probable absence of a marked rise in the rate of growth of GNP over the rest of the decade and beyond, this process will continue.

The Continental Commitment

A brief note on the post-war historical context of British defence policy is key to this debate. It lies in the decision taken in 1954 by Churchill's last administration to maintain a large standing army and tactical air force in West Germany under the terms of the Brussels Treaty. This is a substantial continental commitment, and quite at variance with traditional British practice, albeit one made in distinctively new strategic and political circumstances. In retrospect, the decision to commit British forces to Germany (in 1983, they numbered 56,761 Army and 10,207 Royal Air Force personnel exclusive of the detachment based in West Berlin)[7] is customarily explained by reference to NATO's defence efforts against the massive conventional military power of the Soviet Union and the forces of her Warsaw Treaty Organisation (WTO) allies to the east.[8] The political and military intentions of the Soviet Union towards Western Europe and NATO are the subject of continual debate, but there can be no doubting the awesome military capabilities of the Eastern bloc forces. As such, the deployment of British troops in Europe may well be appropriate.

This was, however, by no means the sole or even the primary justification for the decision to deploy in 1954. Robert Schumann feared then that without a British decision to create a British Army of the Rhine (BAOR), and a tactical air force, under the command of the Supreme Allied Commander in Europe (SACEUR), French fears of a German military threat would intensify, with the possible consequent collapse of the Western alliance. The problem for British policy-makers in 1954 was Germany, or, more specifically, French fears of German revanchism.

By the mid-1950s, Germany had already more than recovered her industrial power. The problem, as Denis Healey saw it in the debate on the Brussels Treaty in the House of Commons on 17 November 1954, was of '. . . fitting into the framework an ex-enemy country which had recovered her economic strength.'[9] Healey's view (overwhelmingly that of the shadow cabinet)[10] echoed the dominant view on the Conservative benches. The collapse of the European Defence Community left Churchill's administration with little choice other than to provide a military guarantee to the French and thereby, in effect, to the structure and character of the North Atlantic Alliance. Eden, then Foreign Secretary, had written to the Prime Minister on 27 September:

> . . . the hard fact is that it is impossible to organise an effective defence system in Western Europe, which in turn is essential for the security of the United Kingdom, without a major British contribution. This situation will persist for many years to come. By recognising this fact and giving the new commitment, we may succeed in bringing in the Germans and the French together, and keeping the Americans in Europe. If we do not, the Conference may fail and the Atlantic alliance fall to pieces.[11]

Thus the need to hold the Western Alliance together in the face of Soviet expansionism, French fears of German military revival, and the absence of a general post-war political settlement in Europe brought about the decisive break with past British policy. 55,000 men and the Second Tactical Air Force were deployed to Germany. The agreement was made, of course, at a time of conscription. Maintaining the British Army of the Rhine and RAF Germany with professionals drawn from a very much smaller total force is today a more burdensome proposition. Until 1954, the occupation costs had fallen on Germany; now, the British taxpayer met the bill. Although the terms under which Britain committed her forces contained an escape clause allowing her to remove a portion of them in the case of exceptional need elsewhere, or in the event of the drain on the balance of payments becoming especially severe, the Conservative government in practice committed a substantial proportion of Britain's standing army to a continental role with a consequent reduction in the freedom of policy manoeuvre for future British governments.

In 1957, Duncan Sandys attempted in his defence review to reduce the strength of BAOR as part of his proposed rundown of conventional, and reliance upon nuclear, forces, but BAOR remained.[12]

The subsequent drain on the balance of payments proved considerable; indeed, the high foreign exchange costs were a constant preoccupation of later governments. As pressure on sterling's fixed exchange rate of $2.80 increased during the tenure of the Labour governments of 1964–70, the Treasury repeatedly raised the question of BAOR and RAF Germany — by cutting the cost of foreign forces abroad, sterling's position could be eased. (Indeed, this was the rationale for much of Britain's retreat from world-wide military responsibilities in the 1960s and 1970s.) But in Germany, the Brussels Treaty provisions of 1944 locked governments into relative immobilism; despite occasional rumblings from backbenchers in the House of Commons and threats from Chancellors of the Exchequer and their officials, the clause enabling Britain to reduce her BAOR strength in periods of exceptional balance of payments difficulties was not invoked. The fear of American withdrawal from Western Europe, and of the possible unravelling of the post-war settlement, served to buttress the British deployment.

The adjustments, cancellations and withdrawals elsewhere which gradually resulted in the Brussels Treaty commitment becoming the centrepiece of British defence policy were pursued by governments of different political colours; the final withdrawal from the Gulf was undertaken by a Conservative government in 1971 in pursuance of the previous Labour government's 1968 Defence Review.[13] Similarly, the decision of Harold Wilson's administration to abandon plans for a new generation of aircraft carriers was not reversed by Mr Heath's administration. By the mid-1970s, the process of shrinkage back into the Eastern Atlantic naval, and European air and ground roles was all but complete and, the puff of Parliamentary debates aside, enjoyed broad cross-party support. By the end of the decade, only Belize, Cyprus, Hong Kong and the Falklands still drew on British 'out-of-area' resources to any appreciable extent.

The Strategic Deterrent

Just one major defence role remained outside this European/Eastern Atlantic framework: the Polaris strategic nuclear system. The Labour Party had pledged when in opposition to abolish the force but, when elected, chose to retain it, contenting itself with the cancellation of the fifth boat. The later 1976 Labour administration under James Callaghan was engaged in preliminary, highly secret, studies of the options available for the replacement of the ageing Polaris system when the 1979 General Election intervened.[14]

After forming her administration in May of that year, Mrs Thatcher established a formal Cabinet committee (MISC 7) to examine several major questions of nuclear policy, among them British policy towards the modernisation of theatre nuclear forces in Europe, and Polaris replacement. Together with a parallel official committee, the options available for the second of these were examined in the light of the generally accepted view that Polaris would reach the end of its useful life during the 1990s. This view, widely shared but rarely critically examined, emphasised the finite life of the submarine hulls and other components which, with the decommissioning of the American Polaris force, would become more costly and difficult to maintain and refit.[15] The warheads, of British design and manufacture, had themselves been the subject of a hugely expensive modernisation programme codenamed 'Chevaline', initiated by the Conservative administration of Edward Heath, and continued by the following Labour governments under Harold Wilson and James Callaghan — though without Parliamentary debate or public acknowledgment of the programme's existence and worth. Reference was limited to the promise made in the Labour Government's 1975 Defence Review that the effectiveness of the system would be maintained. Subsequently, as Bill Rodgers later recalled, he was 'instructed', whilst Minister of State at MOD '. . . to say that the Government was 'updating' Polaris, although not going in for "a new generation" of nuclear weapons'.[16] The Chevaline 'updating' consisted of a programme to enhance the missile's chances of overcoming the Soviet Union's 'Galosh' anti-ballistic missile system around Moscow, by incorporating a sophisticated array of decoy 'chaff' and penetration aids. As MISC 7 went about its business of consultation within Whitehall on Polaris's successor, the then Defence Secretary, Francis Pym, echoed the assurance given by the previous Labour government, promising to continue with improvements to Polaris until a strategic replacement could be agreed upon.[17]

Agreement was quickly forthcoming. It was clearly signalled in the Commons debate in January 1980 when Mr Pym revealed the existence of the 'Chevaline' programme;[18] confirmation that the government had opted to buy American Trident missiles for installation in purpose-built British submarines came in a statement by him shortly before the House rose for the summer recess in 1980.[19] The alternative options of a more radical upgrading of Polaris, possibly by including parts of American Poseidon or Trident 1 (C4) missiles, or of cruise missiles launched from submarines, were rejected.

MISC 7 also supported a policy of the radical modernisation of theatre nuclear forces in Europe. One of the main consequences of this was that, as decided by the NATO foreign ministers meeting in December 1979, Britain would accept the installation of 106 cruise missiles on her soil with deployment beginning in late 1983. This, together with the decision to proceed with the purchase of *Trident* from the United States, fractured the often fragile consensus on nuclear policy between the Labour and Conservative parties. It also split the Labour Party within itself and among its supporters. The two decisions raised powerful moral questions, highly complex and interrelated issues of strategic theory, and difficult calculations of political judgment. Trident 1 (C4) missiles have a capability of delivering warheads very much farther than Polaris: 4,000 as compared with 2,500 nautical miles.[20] Although assigned to NATO, and fully integrated with American targeting plans, the system is said to comprise an 'independent' deterrent; and as a member of NATO, sheltering under the American strategic guarantee, the security afforded Britain (or NATO) by any strategic weapons system is marginal at best.

An increment to British security of such marginality is bought at high cost; this is the kernel of Britain's nuclear deterrent dilemma. The original estimate for the purchase of Trident with Mark I (C4) missiles was 'around four and-a-half to five billions pounds' at 1980 prices.[21] Thus the purchase of Trident involves not only moral questions of great moment, and complex theoretical issues on which different judgments may be made, but fundamental policy choices hinging on opportunity cost. Such opportunity cost has increased still further since the July 1980 announcement with the government's decision in April 1982 to opt for the more advanced Mark II D5 missile variant, giving a range of 6,000 nautical miles, a greater launchweight and the benefit of compatibility with US Navy missiles although, unsurprisingly, at a higher price.[22] This, added to general cost inflation (always significantly higher in defence budgeting than for the rest of the economy) and the declining value of sterling against the dollar, caused cost estimates to rise rapidly. The government noted in the 1984 Defence White Paper that 'There has been no change in the estimated cost of the Trident programme given in last year's *Statement* other than for inflation and exchange rate variations.'[23] If a Minister of Agriculture were to observe that the cost of agricultural goods had not risen in the past year except for inflation and exchange-rate variations, she/he would properly be subjected to derisive laughter if not political humiliation. Such is the curious world of defence economics. As it is, the language of the 1984 *Statement* hides an increase of £1.2 billion within twelve months, or £100 million per calendar month. The 1984 estimate of a total cost of £8.7 billion is certain to fall well short of the final cost. It is already falling short at the time of writing (August 1984) due largely to the continuing decline in sterling's value against the dollar. Because 45 per cent of the total cost is spent in the United States, Trident's price-tag is highly sensitive to exchange rate fluctuations: a fall of 1 cent in the value of the pound against the dollar causes, according to the calculation of the House of Commons Select Committee on Defence (HCSCD), a £25 million increase in the cost of the programme.[24] Thus, assuming a long-run tendency for sterling to continue its decline against the dollar, the cost of the programme will increase well beyond the probable current cost of approximately £10 billion.

The estimate published in the 1984 *Statement* is that the cost of Trident will be '3% of the total defence budget over the period of its procurement, and 6% of the equipment budget'.[25] Again, the phrasing conceals more than it reveals. The purchase of expensive items of capital equipment invariably involves a 'bunching' of outlays; the cost is not evenly spread across the period from the decision to buy to the moment of final assembly. This is true of defence capital expenditure in general, and of exceptionally costly items of new defence capital expenditure in particular. 6 per cent represents a 'smoothed' average percentage impact on the budget; the programme's share of the equipment budget will, by David Greenwood's calculation, be between 12% and 18% between 1988-9 and 1992-3. Greenwood has further estimated that, assuming a final cost of £10 billion, the capital cost of the project will vary between £375 million and £1,250 million in any one financial year.[26] The budgetary and financial planning problems are thereby commensurately enhanced; the opportunity cost calculation is considerably sharpened. During 1984, there were indications that Conservative backbench reservations about the cost of the project were growing, especially as news emerged of the tiny scale of British manufacturing participation in the missile.

This chapter has not addressed itself to questions of arms control. Yet the implications for arms control of the purchase of Trident should be noted, if only in passing. Trident is not a replacement for Polaris but a substantial qualitative and quantitative advance upon it. It is probable that each boat will have sixteen missile tubes; each missile can carry a maximum of 14 warheads. The simple arithmetic demonstrates the considerable increase in the number of deliverable warheads compared to Polaris. In addition, unlike Polaris (even with Chevaline), Trident will be a MIRVed system. *The Economist* of 18 September 1982 estimated that the new system would have 624 Soviet targets within range. It is scarcely a weapons system '. . . of the minimum size necessary to provide a credible and effective deterrent' as the government claims, even though it is improbable that the maximum payload will be employed on each missile. It is possible that the British government's coolness towards negotiations on a Comprehensive Test Ban Treaty from 1979 onwards arose in part from its desire to undertake such tests on the new system as the Ministry of Defence judged necessary. Although not a violation of the letter of the non-proliferation treaty, it is an infringement of its spirit. It is also likely to pose problems in future arms control negotiations: the Soviet Union is unlikely to assume that the British Trident system carries less than its maximum possible warhead payload.

The Way Forward

The Conservative government's policy of reducing public expenditure came into public conflict with the rising defence budget just 18 months after the 1979 election. Speeches by government ministers changed tack during 1980 to emphasise, as their Conservative and Labour predecessors had on comparable occasions since 1945, the importance of matching British defence efforts to the financial resources available, rather than to the scale of the threats presented to British security interests.[27] The latter has made for appealing opposition speeches; the former has more frequently been the stuff of government policy, formulated as ever under fiscal and financial duress. The recession brought the government's dilemma into sharper focus as 1980 progressed: one of the prime causes for the MoD's exceeding its cash limits in that year was the urgency with which the Ministry's cash-starved contractors and suppliers presented their invoices.

The Treasury responded to the MoD's apparent profligacy by requiring a cut of £500 million in the defence budget. Francis Pym, citing the commitments made by the (previous) government to expand British defence spending by at least 3 per cent per annum in real terms, threatened on two separate occasions to resign in protest. In November 1980, the Chancellor announced a cut of £200 million in the MoD's cash limit for each of the three following financial years;[28] Pym's defence of his department had had some effect but the squeeze was none the less severe. To save fuel, aircraft were grounded for much longer than was operationally desirable, and many ships kept in port. Chichester and Wilkinson later claimed that the reductions in fuel allowances for the Royal Navy were so great that ships in the operational fleet could spend only three days at sea between Christmas Day 1980 and Easter Day 1981.[29]

In the nature of Cabinet politics, however, Pym paid for his resistance to the Treasury's demands which had the support (surprisingly, perhaps) of the Prime Minister. He was sidetracked into the position of Leader of the House of Commons, and succeeded early in 1981 by John Nott who moved quickly to initiate a major defence review. Authors of previous reviews had had the comparative luxury of preserving the thrust of the defence effort in the Eastern Atlantic and Western Europe by withdrawing from remoter commitments. With the withdrawal from Malta in 1979, that option effectively no longer existed. Nott knew in the spring of 1981 that difficult choices would now have to be made between strategic priorities at the centre of Britain's defence and foreign policies.

Trident, Nott affirmed, was exempted from the review; the government adhered to the view that the strategic deterrent should be maintained and replaced. The British pledge to maintain large ground and air forces in Germany under the provisions of the Brussels Treaty was similarly confirmed. Nott held, in evidence to the House of Commons Select Committee on Defence (HCSCD) in May 1981, that '. . . to pull out of the central front . . . would do great damage to NATO and that we must not do'.[30]

As with budgetary politics in general, so with defence budgets: the key problem for those who would reduce them is that much of a budget is effectively uncontrollable. Early in the Conservative government's first term, the uncontrollable items had been increased by the underwriting of the Armed Services Pay Reviews; now, they were increased by the exclusion of the strategic replacement and the continental commitment from consideration. It was therefore inevitable that the cuts would fall disproportionately heavily on one or two defence roles.

Nott none the less insisted that it was imperative to redefine Britain's strategic priorities, '. . . to see if we can concentrate our efforts rather more sensibly within the existing roles we perform'.[31] Gone were the confident assertions of the party when in opposition that increased defence spending was vital to meet the range of threats presented to British security; public spending targets constraints were now the controlling factor. Nott accurately, if ruefully, reminded the House of Commons Select Committee on Defence in 1981 that Britain's geographical position and political obligations required her to perform more roles than any other European member of NATO. The government's determination to reduce public spending obliged him to assess how those roles might be fulfilled more cheaply.[32]

Nott recommended that Britain's naval forces in the Eastern Atlantic should bear the brunt of the cuts. He secured Cabinet approval for his proposals in *The Way Forward*, which implied a 25% reduction in operational surface ships — from 56 to 42.[33] One of the three new carriers was to be sold; the two amphibious assault ships would be scrapped and not replaced; mid-life modernisation for frigates and destroyers would cease and, as a significant footnote, the Antarctic patrol ship *Endurance* would be withdrawn from the South Atlantic where it had been deployed with the intention of demonstrating Britain's defence guarantee to the Falkland Islands and dependencies.[34] The government noted that the Royal Navy's role was largely one of anti-submarine warfare in the Eastern Atlantic and could now be performed with greater despatch by relatively invulnerable submarines rather than surface ships which were increasingly open to devastating attack from cheap anti-ship missiles. The White Paper noted that a reduced surface fleet would require less extensive dockyard facilities; Chatham was to close, and employment at Portsmouth would be reduced.[35]

The reaction from the naval lobby was intense. Keith Speed, the Navy Minister, publicly disavowed the government's policy in a speech on 15 May 1981, having had an increasingly acrimonious set of discussions with John Nott in the preceding months as the implications for the Royal Navy of the Secretary of State's review became clear. Three days later, the Prime Minister dismissed him from the government. Speed's dismissal both symbolised and enhanced disquiet within the Navy. Some critics of Nott's plans, including Speed, pointed to the hole torn in the Navy's budget by funding Trident from it, and not from a separate strategic budget. Whilst there had been little public opposition to Trident from the Conservative benches, a number of backbench MPs expressed disquiet about the impact its acquisition would have on the Navy's conventional forces. Parliamentary critics from both sides of the House emphasised the inherent flexibility of surface naval power to forestall conflict, to signal political will, to project power, and to protect a merchant fleet of 3,000 ships in the NATO area.[36] At the same time, some pointed to the strategic and tactical rigidity of the continental commitment under the Brussels Treaty. (BAOR and RAF Germany emerged unscathed from the *Review* except for a restructuring of one British Crops in West Germany from a four-to a three-division format, composed of nine brigades.)[37]

Defenders of the naval surface role had difficulty in demonstrating its importance and efficacy. The need for home air defence, for example, was clearly and popularly recognised, not least because the Battle of Britain wrote it so firmly into the popular consciousness; that for a surface naval fleet rather less so because of the subtlety and indirection of its peacetime role. The surface role, the government concluded, was marginal to the central task of defending Britain and Western Europe in what most planners outside the Royal Navy confidently assumed would be an intense, but short, war in Europe. One senior naval officer commented wryly after the announcement of the cuts: 'What we need now is a small colonial war requiring a lot of ships.'[38]

The Falklands

Within a year, the government found themselves embroiled in precisely this: the Argentinian seizure of the Falkland Islands and South Georgia brought forth a large British naval response. A task force, with two aircraft carriers at its heart, and a civilian fleet requisitioned from Britain's diminishing merchant navy which eventually amounted to some 45 ships, was assembled and despatched to the South Atlantic with no clear battle plan, but the general objective of the prosecution of a small, and wholly unexpected, colonial war; the senior officer's wish of a matter of months before had been granted.

Some comment upon the Falklands conflict and the lessons to be drawn from it claimed that had the government's 1981 plans to reduce the strength of the surface fleet been implemented by the spring of 1982, the Falklands could not have been retaken. This is not certain; fewer of the ships deployed to the South Atlantic were scheduled for withdrawal than has sometimes been supposed. Indeed, the military lessons to be drawn from the conflict are in many respects ambiguous. The lethality of modern submarines was demonstrated by the devastating attack on the Argentinian cruiser *General Belgrano*; yet the circumstances of the attack raised powerful moral questions and its outcome represented a substantial political defeat for the British government; the Commander of HMS *Conqueror* had no option other than those of attack or of remaining unseen beneath the surface. (It should also be noted that *Conqueror*'s Commander chose to use the venerable Mark 8 torpedoes against *Belgrano* rather than one of the wire-guided Mark 24 'Tigerfish' torpedoes because of widespread doubts about the modern weapon's reliability.)[39] Much, too, was made of the apparent invincibility of the 'Exocet' anti-ship missiles used by the Argentinians. Yet 'Exocet' sank only one Royal Navy ship, HMS *Sheffield*; it is even possible that the warhead failed to explode on this occasion, the burning of the ship being caused by ignited missile propellant.[40] Even careful critics emphasised that the widespread use of aluminium which melts at just 700°C — less than half the temperature of steel — in the superstructures of Royal Navy ships contributed to the total loss of ships that could otherwise have been saved.[41] But aluminium is not employed in this way in all naval vessels, and not at all in Type 42 destroyers, a class which includes HMS *Sheffield* and *Coventry*, both of which were lost by fire.[42]

There were, none the less, certain important lessons; most ships had been under-armed, or inappropriately armed; ship damage and fire-control was inadequate; deploying a task force without sophisticated Airborne Early Warning (AEW) cover was a policy fraught with risk, but inescapable in the regrettable absence of large conventional aircraft carriers. Still more important were the old virtues of the decisiveness of 'training, stamina, leadership . . . and . . . military professionalism'.[43]

But the Falklands did more than cause detailed, if important, modifications to be made by the services to equipment, logistical design and military practice. Its major consequence was that the British government found itself obliged to garrison the Falklands, negotiations over the future of the islands now being politically impossible. Thus to Trident, BAOR and RAF Germany, the Falklands were now added as a sanctified commitment. Hitherto, Mrs Thatcher's administration, like her immediate predecessors', had searched for a solution by agreement to the problems of this remote outpost of empire; quick release from the political commitment to defend the Falklands was now impossible. Further, the emasculation of the Royal Navy's surface fleet along the lines of *The Way Forward* was, in the immediate future, impossible. Moreover, such questions as were prompted in observers' minds by the apparent vulnerability of surface ships during the campaign (thereby confirming in rough outline some of the thinking behind John Nott's reassessment of naval operations in the Eastern Atlantic) were now dismissed from the political agenda. The government decided to retain the third aircraft carrier and an amphibious capability. Symbolically, too, HMS *Endurance* was reprieved.[44] In the 1984 *Statement*, Michael Heseltine (who had succeeded John Nott as Defence Secretary before the 1983 election) announced that an operational fleet of 50 ships would be retained.[45] Although elements of Nott's 1981 plan remained, its central purpose, that of re-examining the nature of Britain's defence roles, had, in effect, been shelved.

Conclusion

Yet it is certain that the shelving can only be temporary. The factors which caused Mrs Thatcher to restrain the high rate of growth in defence spending after the first 18 months of her administration remain, the recovery in economic activity notwithstanding. The government announced in 1984 that the commitment to increase Britain's defence spending by 3 per cent per annum in real terms would cease in 1986.[46] Britain continues to perform more defence roles than any of her European NATO allies, and does so from a weaker economic base than most. A review of a fundamental kind cannot long be delayed; it was probable before the escalation of the cost of Trident and the acquisition of the Falklands garrison. These two events have made it inevitable; in pursuit of a rational defence policy, neither should be excluded from the scope of the review.

John Nott's 1981 review had the virtue of intellectual coherence, and yet, by removing Trident and the continental commitment from consideration, narrowed its focus. It is clear that for the marginal addition it brings to Britain's security and safety, Trident's price and opportunity cost is excessive. It will occupy valuable building space in Britain's sole submarine yard at Vicker's and so deprive the Royal Navy for some years of the opportunity to add to its Fleet and conventionally-powered submarine force; its share of the equipment budget will be considerably larger than the government suggests, and it has damaging implications for arms control policy precisely because it is not the 'minimum deterrent' that its defenders claim.

Similarly, there may be more scope for a reordering of defence tasks among the European members of NATO which would allow Britain to modify and reduce its Brussels Treaty continental commitment whilst making its political commitment to the political integrity of NATO unmistakably clear. A reduction in BAOR, for example, coupled with a stated willingness to shoulder a rather more substantial naval role in NATO's defences as part of a policy of functional specialisation within the alliance, could enhance Britain's long-term contribution to the Alliance rather than weaken it. At the very least, such possibilities should be explored. The new simplified system of advice from senior service chiefs may well ease the path of a Secretary of State in such an exploration.[47] The alternative prospect is for a continued erosion of defence capabilities across the board — except for the purchase of a new, large and excessively sophisticated strategic system. It is the argument of this chapter that such a policy, although it follows in a long post-war bipartisan tradition, is no policy at all, but an aspiration which there is no prospect of affording. Policy-making requires choices to be made between several options, more of which are desirable than can be afforded. In order to develop a defence policy consonant with Britain's foreign-policy interests and economic circumstances, such choices will have to be made. The items which were left off Mr Nott's agenda in 1981, together with the matter of the new Falklands garrison (a political solution for which will gradually become both possible and necessary) must therefore be put back on the next review's agenda for fresh and imaginative political and military consideration.

Notes

1. *Conservative Manifesto for Scotland 1979*, p. 32.

2. D. Butler and D. Kavanagh, *The British General Election of 1983*, (Macmillan, London, 1984), p. 282.

3. As Prime Minister, after the Falklands conflict, Mrs Thatcher attempted to strengthen her control over foreign and defence policies by adding specialist advisers to her personal staff.

4. *The Economist*, 18 June 1983, p. 34.

5. *Statement on the Defence Estimates, 1984*, Cmnd. 9227-II, Table 4-14.

6. The government claimed in 1981 that Theatre Nuclear Force (TNF) modernisation would cost £5 billion as a whole, to be met 'entirely by the US'. Base construction costs of £16 million were to be met out of the NATO infrastructure budget to which the UK contributed. (*Statement on the Defence Estimates, 1981*, Cmnd. 8212-I, para. 218).

7. *Statement 1984*, vol. II, Table 4-10.

8. Ibid., vol. I, para. 102.

9. Hansard, 553 HC Official Report (5th series), col. 509 (17 November 1954).

10. P.M. Williams, *Hugh Gaitskell* (Jonathan Cape, London, 1980), pp. 331-2.

11. A. Eden, *Full Circle* (Cassell, London, 1960), p. 166.

12. *Defence: Outline of Future Policy*, Cmnd. 124 (1957).

13. *Statement on the Defence Estimates, 1968*, Cmnd. 3540.

14. L. Freedman, *Britain and Nuclear Weapons* (Macmillan, London, 1980), pp. 54-5.

15. Nailor and Alford took the view in 1980 that 'Polaris A3 will remain an adequate missile even if new platforms have to be built to carry it' ('The Future of Britain's Deterrent Force', *Adelphi Papers*, no. 156, p. 36). Others hold the view that recent advances in refitting and refurbishing techniques could prolong the life of Polaris submarine hulls into the twenty-first century.

16. W. Rodgers, *The Politics of Change* (Secker and Warburg, London, 1981), p. 150.

17. *The Guardian*, 27 October 1979.

18. Hansard, 977 HC Official Report (5th series), cols. 672-85 (24 January 1980).

19. Hansard, 988 HC Official Report (5th series), cols. 1235-6 (15 July 1980).

20. *Jane's Fighting Ships* (London, 1982-3), p. 545.

21. *Defence Open Government Document* (DOGD) 80/23, para. 23.

22. *Statement on the Defence Estimates 1982*, Cmnd 8529-I.

23. *Statement 1984*, vol. 1, para. 405.

24. *HCSCD*, HC 436.

25. *Statement 1984*, vol. 1, para. 405.

26. D. Greenwood, *The Trident Programme*, Aberdeen Studies in Defence Economics, Centre for Defence Economics, Aberdeen, 1982) pp. 30-1.

27. Compare 'There is no military strength whether for Britain or for our alliances except on the basis of economic strength; and it is on this basis that we best assure the security of this country'. with 'It is of crucial importance that we should overcome our deep-seated economic problems to permit sustainable growth in defence spending over the longer term'. The first speaker was Harold Wilson in January 1968; the second, Lord Strathcona, then Minister of State at the Ministry of Defence, twelve years later. (Hansard, 756 HC Official Report (5th series), col 1580 (16 January 1968); Hansard 415 HL Official Report (5th series), col 413 (3 December 1980).

28. *Statement 1981*, Cmnd. 8212-I, para. 607.

29. M. Chichester and J. Wilkinson, *The Uncertain Ally*, (Gower, Aldershot 1982), p. 66.

30. Evidence to HCSCD, 2nd report, HC 302, para. 293.

31. Ibid., para. 291.

32. Ibid.

33. *The Way Forward*, Cmnd. 8288.

34. *Hansard*, 9 HC Official Report (5th series), col 488 (28 July 1981).

35. *Hansard*, 12 HC Official Report (5th series), cols 67–8 (10 November 1981).

36. See, for instance, the speech by Mr A.E.P. Duffy on 7 July 1981, *Hansard*, 8 HC Official Report (6th series), col. 336.

37. See the subsequent discussion in *Statement 1984*, para. 416.

38. *The Times*, 18 June 1981.

39. M. Hastings and S. Jenkins, *The Battle For The Falklands* (Michael Joseph, London, 1983), p. 149.

40. Ibid., p. 153 and L. Freedman, 'The War of the Falkland Islands', *Foreign Affairs* (Autumn 1982), p. 204.

41. B. George and M. Coughlin, 'British Defence Policy after the Falklands', *Survival*, vol. XXIV, no. 5 (Sept/Oct 1982), p. 203.

42. *The Falklands Campaign: The Lessons*, Cmnd 8758, para. 220.

43. Freedman, 'The War of the Falkland Islands', p. 207.

44. *The Lessons*, para. 310.

45. *Statement 1984*, para. 436.

46. Ibid., paras. 203–4.

47. Ibid., Chapter 2.

12 CONCLUSION: BRITISH POLITICS AND THE FAILURE OF OPPOSITION

D.S. Bell

This book was not intended to have an explicit conclusion but one does emerge despite the divergent standpoints of the various analysts, who have closely followed the results of policies in their particular fields of expertise. This conclusion is that Mrs Thatcher's government has stuck to a conviction approach, that there has been some startling mismanagement, and that the outcome of monetarist policies has been disappointing. Such a summary points up a contrast between the mid-1970s when many influential converts were made to monetarism and conviction politics, and the mid-1980s when the climate amongst opinion makers was less receptive to such ideological fervour.

Yet at the same time as the pundits began to hedge their judgments about the policies of the Thatcher government, the voters in the 1983 elections gave a resounding *satisfecit* to the Conservatives. The difference between popular electoral success and the generally hostile commentators may not be as great as it seems, or might be an effect of the electoral system, but it might also be a result of the failure to provide a strong, convincing, opposition. It is possible to imagine other forms of electoral system which, given what is known about people's voting intentions, would have produced as much less spectacular Conservative victory in June 1983. But the apparent 'failure' of the electoral system should not be exaggerated, since no electoral system yet devised will give completely consistent and unparadoxical results and, although the electoral system magnified the extent of the Conservative majority, the Tories were still the largest party with 44 per cent of the vote to Labour's 28 per cent and the Liberal-SDP Alliance's 26 per cent. The Conservative lead of 16 per cent over the next party was an impressive one, even if unequally distributed across the country.

Politically speaking, the situation is not the result of a capricious electoral system but of the inability of anti-Conservative forces to combine to make headway against a failing government. Before the Falklands crisis even the Conservative Party was becoming restless and scepticism about the government's deflationary monetarism had made both the government and Mrs Thatcher unpopular. The war to regain the Falkland Islands was used by the government in domestic politics to reduce opposition to Thatcherism within the Conservative Party as well as to show up the ineffectual nature of opponents outside the Conservative Party. The opportunity presented by the Falklands war was effectively exploited by the government, but the ensuing victory for Thatcherism was more a matter of luck than good judgment. What the Falklands crisis created was not so much solidarity with the government as a realisation that the opposition was so divided and incohesive as to be unfit to form an alternative government.

Thus, at a time when unemployment continued to increase, in which industries continued to lose markets and when the recovery has been but fitful, the commentator's interrogation had to be turned from the economic success of the Thatcher government (which, as Chapter 2 shows, is by no means unqualified) to the reasons for the deficiency of opposition. It is sometimes said that the decline of Labour is part of a long-term secular trend, but parties have changed, risen and fallen before — there is nothing deterministic about politics. The factors which explain the decline of the Labour Party are in the party itself, it is therefore in the political arena that the explanation is to be found.

Labour's problems are, like those of the British economy, so numerous that it is difficult to know where to start. If the ephemeral and contingent nature of leadership incompetence is placed on one side (although the contrast between the popularity ratings of Foot and Kinnock should not be underestimated) the fact remains that Labour, with the advantage of being the second party in parliament and having the status of the official opposition, has not capitalised on its strengths. As Edward Heath, Earl Stockton, Sir Ian Gilmour and others have shown there is a case against the government's handling of the economy waiting to be made; but so far Labour has not made sufficient impact on public opinion. It is possible to fault the presentation of the Labour Party's case but the flaw runs deeper than personalities: Labour is still divided and has neither solved its internal disputes nor evolved a credible policy. Divisions in the Labour Party have been emphasised in its continuing inability to resolve the problem of infiltration by Militant. Militant, the Trotskyite 'enterist' organisation, has an uncertain place in a democratic party and its aims and principles are probably incompatible with those of Labour. Yet the Labour Party lacks the necessary determination to root out this organisation — something which would require drastic surgery. Labour's paralysis is not a matter of lack of willpower; such paralysis exists because, although the leadership has a majority on the National Executive, the balance is too precarious to enable it to take action. The departure to the SDP of what used to be called the Labour Right has deprived the leadership of the support which would be needed to expel Militant as an organisation. The atrophy of Labour's own organisation means that only small numbers of activists are needed to make a substantial impact (hence Militant's success) but it is a measure of Labour's decline that the numbers are just not mobilised.

Neil Kinnock's tactics during the miners' strike were hampered by the same divisions within the party: he was forced to tread the line between appealing to the centre electorate (which Labour needs to do to win power) and conceding to rank-and-file pressures (which would end any possibility of Labour taking power). It is not surprising, given the intensity of conflicting pressures, that Labour's balancing act proved ultimately unconvincing and Kinnock's high standing in the polls dropped during 1984. Labour's cause is recuperable but it would require determined action (to open out the selection of candidates to all party members, for example) which would in turn mean long, open and divisive battles within the party (but majorities for change seem, in any case, to be absent).

But there is a futher aspect of Labour's difficulties: its policy. Where a credible policy matters most — in economics — the concept of an alternative remains hazy and Labour is bedevilled by a serious deficiency: the lack of an incomes policy. Labour advocates reflation and public spending on capital projects, all of which is eminently sensible, but the government's supporters are able to deride the financial indiscipline which this implies and to equate reflation with inflation. Because Labour cannot propose a convincing incomes policy and because powerful costituencies in the Labour Party (and in British society) remain hostile to incomes policy, the Labour alternative remains *Hamlet* without the Prince of Denmark. Unfortunately incomes policies are linked by the public (probably wrongly) with industrial disruption and economic decline. The association of incomes policies with Britain's economic failures of the 1970s will have to be tackled for any advocacy to be really convincing. Selling the idea of incomes policy to a wary public is taxing enough but it could be done; however, unless the missing element is supplied Labour's plans for reflation will remain an easy target. Yet if an incomes policy is desirable, the Labour Party, with its extensive union contacts, remains the best vehicle for the purpose. A pessimist might remark that this is only another way of saying that an incomes policy, after the experience of the 1960s and 1970s, is no longer politically feasible.

The Alliance faces obstacles of an equally disabling kind: there are difficulties stemming from the fact that it is an alliance as well as from the nature of its components. The Liberals and the SDP need to maintain their united front and intensify their joint activity; they cannot afford the luxury of internal divisions. As to the Liberal Party, it has for a long time suffered from its position as an also-ran on the margins of serious politics and, in consequence, is not ideally placed to become a party of government. The Liberal Party is a patchwork of decentralised, divergent and often conflicting interests. Vitality has been a characteristic of Liberal politics, but this intensity is one facet of a form of activist conviction politics which is difficult to administer and which is not necessarily amenable either to coalition politics or (more essentially) to the compromises of government. Liberalism, until recently, depended for its success on local politics and the organisational use of activist resources at by-elections: this created the network of independent local strongholds which are based on individual and divergent strengths rather than on the central party. Were the Liberals to win 100-150 constituencies at the next election the force of local and activist politics would be diluted, but centrifugal pressures remain a weakness in the meantime.

For the Social Democratic Party the problems are of a slightly different order: the SDP has lost the experienced group of former Labour MPs which, during the 1979–83 parliament, gave the Alliance its strength in the House of Commons and its credibility as an alternative government. The Alliance on longer has the benefit of this SDP contingent and finds it difficult in what is, as far as the House of Commons is concerned, still a two-party system. Mounting a challenge to a government which has all the advantages which come from the possession of power and backing from the civil service demands experience and strength in depth, so it is not surprising that the small SDP has struggled to make an impact since 1983. Meanwhile the 'Gang of Four' has become the 'Gang of One': the SDP is now Dr Owen's party and Roy Jenkins has been eclipsed. There are not enough SDP MPs and there is a danger in over-dependence on one individual; the task of parliamentary opposition has more often than not fallen on Dr Owen and the Liberals have struggled in this domain. Telling points have been made against the government by the SDP leader but the freshness and range of attack which is provided by a strong team has not been evident.

Although it is often stated that SDP has no policies the SDP's real difficulty lies elsewhere: namely in its inability to get its many and detailed policies taken seriously. As with the Labour Party this criticism applies especially to incomes policy, something the Alliance has always advocated as the alternative to monetarist-style deflation. Alliance politicians will have to address the problem of how to obtain trade union cooperation without the institutional advantages which the Labour Party has. It could also be noted that the 'winter of discontent', which caused such hardship in the last months of the Labour government, resulted from political misjudgments and from a lack of understanding of those very unions of which Healey and Callaghan claimed to have a special understanding. Running an incomes policy requires nice political judgment; something which, in the last resort, neither Callaghan, nor Healey, nor, for that matter, Heath, showed. Whether the Alliance has the political insight (or the political machinery) to run an incomes policy is an open question. As a partial counter to this last point, it could be argued that the electorate, and the rank and file in businesses in particular, have seen the alternative (3–4 million unemployed, declining social services) and seen that it does not work, so that the task of persuasion would be that much easier next time round. However, the unions have not shown that they appreciate this point, nor would they be willing to support a new version of an incomes policy in a run-up to the election merely to help the Alliance.

There is one other provenance from which opposition to Thatcherism has come: that is from within the Conservative Party itself. The normally pragmatic and non-ideological Conservative Party has its own opposition to monetarism known, in Mrs Thatcher's homely phrase, as the 'wets'. The 'wets' are, however, a heterogeneous, leaderless group, which ranges from the ironic intellectualism of Sir Ian Gilmour through the rather austere, eirenic Mr Pym to the maverick Mr Heath. It is surprising that some of the most pertinent criticisms have come from the Conservative benches and from the House of Lords: Tory 'wets' have made an academic and polemical case against the government which has been as witty and as articulate as that of the opposition parties (to the extent that it must be asked why some of them remain in a Conservative Party which is so resolutely set on another direction). Yet Mrs Thatcher has picked off the 'wets' one by one, and the Cabinet after the 1983 elections was composed of Ministers who shared Mrs Thatcher's convictions or, with few exceptions, were prepared to go along with deflationary policy. Where power is exercised in the British system of government, the Thatcherites have been moved into position and the 'wets' have been removed — the task of remaking society is, it seems, not for faint hearts.

At least, for the Alliance, the position is clear-cut in one way: they have to make a breakthrough in by-elections during the mid-term of parliament in order to present themselves as the real opposition to the government. In the 1979 general election Labour was the dominant anti-Conservative force: those who wanted to vote against the Conservatives had strong pressures on them to vote for the Labour Party as the best placed opponent. By 1983 the Labour Party was no longer in that dominant position among non-Conservative parties and, in addition, it had lost the support of many traditional Labour voters. In that situation the Alliance was an attractive force but, although it was able to challenge Labour, it was not able to displace it as the principal anti-Conservative party. The re-establishment by Neil Kinnock of Labour credibility and the subsequent seesaw between the two main non-Conservative forces since 1983 has not made the voters' choice any simpler. If the Alliance did make its essential advance and then did sustain its position as the second party in the polls, the position could change very rapidly: non-Conservative voters would switch to the Alliance in order to vote the Thatcher government out of office. It is unlikely that there is anything in British political culture or in the nature of British working-class institutions which can keep a vote attached to a losing Labour Party. The Nationalists and Liberals have shown, by their victories in the past, that the big cities and housing estates are not immune to a strong challenge from outside parties. At British elections voters wanting to oust the sitting government have to combine to do so and the most credible opposition party will inherit this anti-Government vote — provided the position is clear enough. If the Labour Party is to retain its 'natural' working-class constituency it will have to work hard to do so but the task which the Alliance faces to detaching that vote is equally daunting.

At the end of 1984 that the government had a huge parliamentary majority and faced very weak opposition. This situation has not resulted from the failure of British institutions as such, but is a consequence of the combination of moves by other actors in the political system who did not intend to keep the Conservatives in power. It is not the *immobilisme* of Fourth Republic France, in which there were majorities to block measures but none to take action, nor the debilitating conservatism of Italy where a major party is permanently excluded from government; the British problem shows none of these features, rather it is a result of a split in the opposition to the Conservative Party and the capture of the Conservative Party by a determined 'convinced' group. Until the issue between the Alliance and Labour Party is settled an effective opposition is unlikely to appear. Moreover, the Government has so far resisted enormous pressures to change: in other words the emergence of a credible opposition may not be a matter of just one more election; it could require two.

SELECT BIBLIOGRAPHY

Abel-Smith, B. and P. Townsend, *The Poor and the Poorest* Occasional Papers in Social Administration (G. Bell & Sons, London, 1965).

Andrews, M. and S. Nickell, 'Unemployment in the United Kingdom since the War' *Review of Economic Studies*, vol. XLIX (1982), pp. 731–59.

Bain, G.S. (ed.), *Industrial Relations in Britain* (Blackwell, Oxford, 1983).

Bosanquet, Nick, *After the New Right* (Heinemann, London, 1983).

Dilmot, A.W., J.A. Kay and C.N. Morris, *The Reform of Social Security* (Institute for Fiscal Studies, 1984).

Dunn, S. and J. Gennard *The Closed Shop in British industry* (Macmillan, London, 1984).

Hendry, D. and D. Erricsson, 'Assertion without Empirical Basis: an Empirical Appraisal of Friedman and Schwarz,' Bank of England Academic Consultants Panel Paper 22 (1983), pp. 45–101.

Lewis, R. and B. Simpson, *Striking a Balance* (M. Robertson, Oxford, 1981).

Kay, J., *The Economy and the 1982 Budget* (Blackwell, Oxford, 1982).

Keegan, W., *Mrs Thatcher's Economic Experiment* (Allen Lane, London, 1984).

Klein, Rudolf, *The Politics of the National Health Service* (Longman, London, 1983).

PSI, *The Reform of Supplementary Benefit* (PSI, London, 1984).

Pond, C., 'Back to the Sweatshop', *New Society* 62 (1049–50) (1982), pp. 508–9.

Riddell, P., *The Thatcher Government* (M. Robertson, Oxford, 1983).

Russel, T., *The Tory Party* (Penguin, Harmondsworth, 1978).

The Scarman Report, (Penguin, Harmondsworth, 1982).

NOTES ON CONTRIBUTORS

John Alderson, formerly Chief Constable of Devon and Cornwall, is visiting professor in Police Studies at the University of Strathclyde. His publications include: *Policing Freedom* (1979) and *Law and Disorder* (1984).

Dr David S. Bell is a lecturer in Politics at Leeds University.

Dr Nigel Bowles is a lecturer in Politics at Edinburgh University. His main interests include American and British government. He is currently preparing a book for publication by Oxford University Press entitled *White House and Capitol Hill*.

Dr Doreen E. Collins is Senior Fellow in the Department of Social Policy and Health Studies, Leeds University.

Dr David Deaton is Research Fellow at the Industrial Relations Research Unit, University of Warwick. His research interests include unemployment and the analysis of large-scale industrial relations. He is the co-author of *Labour Hoarding in British Industry* (1982).

A.M. El-Agraa is Senior Lecturer in Economics at Leeds University and in 1984–5 was the Visiting Chair in Charge of International Economics and Middle Eastern Studies at the Graduate School of International Relations, International University of Japan. His main research interest is in international economics, particularly international economic integration. His recent books include: *The Economics of the European Community* (editor), 1980; *The Theory of Customs Unions* (with A.J. Jones), 1981; *International Economic Integration* (editor), 1982; *The Theory of International Trade*, 1982; *Britain within the European Community; the Way Forward* (editor), 1983; and *Trade, Theory and Policy: Some Topical Issues*, 1984.

Robert Elmore is Staff Tutor in Public and Social Administration at the Department for External Studies, Oxford University.

Mike Goldsmith is Professor of Government and Politics (and Director of the North West Public Sector Research Centre) at Salford University. He has been Research Coordinator, SSRC Research Initiatives on Central-Local Government Relations, since 1979. He is author of *Politics, Planning and the City* (1981); Co-author of *Public Participation and Planning in Practice* (1980) and *Public Participation in Local Services* (1982). He has done research on public participation and planning for DOE, 1974–7 and his particular interests, outside of central-local government relations, are in planning and housing research, and in public policy generally.

Peter Gosden is Professor of the History of Education in the University of Leeds and is particularly interested in the development of educational policy and administration. His books include *Education in the Second World War* (1976), *The Development of Educational Administration* (1966), *The Evaluation of a Profession* (1972) and *The Education System since 1944* (1983).

Peter Holmes has been a lecturer in economics at the University of Sussex since 1974. He studied at Cambridge (BA & PhD) and at Harvard Universities. He has published various books and articles on economic policy issues including *French Planning in Theory and Practice* (1983, with Saul Estrin) and has acted as an adviser to the House of Lords European Affairs Committee and the EEC Commission. He has been a visitor at the Universities of British Columbia and Grenoble.

Steven Winyard has been a lecturer in Social Policy at the University of Leeds, since 1978. He previously worked as a research officer with the Low Pay Unit with which he continues to have a close involvement: in 1983 he was employed as co-ordinator of a regional low pay campaign, funded by West Midlands County Council. He is currently working as a consultant to the Merseyside 'Fight Low Pay' campaign.

INDEX

Page numbers in italics refer to tables.